DOGS ON THE COUCH

Dogs on the Couch

Behavior Therapy for Training and Caring for Your Dog

Dr. Larry Lachman and
Frank Mickadeit

THE OVERLOOK PRESS
WOODSTOCK & NEW YORK

*The names and certain identifying details of some of the dogs
and their owners have been changed.*

First paperback edition published in the United States in 2002 by
The Overlook Press, Peter Mayer Publishers, Inc.
Woodstock & New York

WOODSTOCK:
One Overlook Drive
Woodstock, NY 12498
www.overlookpress.com
[for individual orders, bulk and special sales, contact our Woodstock office]

NEW YORK:
141 Wooster Street
New York, NY 10012

Library of Congress Cataloging-in-Publication Data

Lachman, Larry.
Dogs on the couch : behavior therapy for training and caring
for your dog / Larry Lachman, Frank Mickadeit.
p. cm.
Includes index.
1. Dogs—Behavior therapy. 2. Dogs—Training. 3. Dogs—Psychology. 4. Dog
owners—Psychology. 5. Family psychotherapy. I. Mickadeit, Frank. II. Title.
SF433,K335 1999 636,7.088'7—dc21 98-48067

All photographs by Jebb Harris, unless otherwise noted
Book design and type formatting by Bernard Schleifer
Manufactured in the United States of America
1 3 5 7 9 8 6 4 2
ISBN 0-87951-922-3 (hc)
ISBN 1-58567-250-5 (pb)

CONTENTS

ACKNOWLEDGMENTS

No ideas, including my own, arise from a vacuum. Although I am solely responsible for the ideas and techniques outlined in this book, there have been many outstanding psychologists and animal behaviorists, and many great friends, who have had a profound impact on me and my way of thinking about behavior.

In the human-behavior arena I'd like to acknowledge: Dr. Alfred Aldler, Dr. Carl Rogers (who I met with in 1978), Dr. Elisabeth Kübler Ross (who I met in 1981), Dr. Gerald Jampolsky (who I met in 1981), Dr. Murray Bowen (who I spoke with in 1982), Dr. Fritz Perls, Dr. Salvador Minuchin, Dr. Milton Erickson, Virginia Satir, Dr. Aaron Beck, Dr. Albert Ellis, and the two great pioneers in behaviorism, Dr. Joseph Wolpe and Dr. B. F. Skinner. In addition, I'd like to acknowledge the influences of Dr. William Glasser, Jay Haley, Dr. Edward T. Hall, Dr. Leo Buscaglia, Dr. Matthew McKay, and therapists or psychologists who I have either worked with or been inspired by: Dr. Aghop Der-Karabetian, Dr. Lisa Hoshmand, Don Wasson MFCC, Donna Mognett MFCC, Dr. Maggie Klassen, Dr. James Carter, Dr. Stephen Alkus, Lola Gilliland MFCC, Dr. Stuart Bloom, Mary Franz MFCC, Gary Zager MFCC, Kimberly Akamine MFCC, Dr. Maggie Dekker, Dr. Roselyn Colombo, and Dr. Stuart Kirschbaum.

In the animal-behavior arena I'd like to acknowledge the influences of: William Campbell, Dr. Ian Dunbar, Dr. Daniel Tortora, Dr. Stanley Coren, Karen Pryor, Dr. Bruce Fogle, Dr. Roger Mugford, and Dr. Jane Goodall. Also, my colleagues: Lori Agon of Mannered Mutts, Diana Guerrero of Ark Animals, and Julie Strauss of Teacher's Pet.

To those friends who believed in this project from its inception without waiver: James Brull, Nashoma Carlson, Eric Cilley, Joe Cello, Dr. Steve Feig, Bill Hewitt, Stephen Lim, Sue Mulcahy, and Don Richardson.

Finally, I must recognize our publisher, Peter Mayer; our agent, Barbara Braun; the photographer, Jebb Harris; and my parents, Leon and Joan, for believing in *Dogs on the Couch* and for helping to make it happen. Thank you.

— LARRY LACHMAN

INTRODUCTION

"Buster and I 'failed' the obedience class. The instructor asked me to hang Buster in mid-air when he jumped and to jerk his head down with my leg to get him to lie down. I just couldn't bring myself to do it. There has to be a better and gentler way to do this. I called our veterinarian and he recommended we come to you. Can you help us?"

"Do you recommend getting a purebred or mutt? Should we get a dog from a breeder or a shelter? Do you recommend a puppy or an older dog?"

"My husband and children have been begging me to get a dog for two years now. I've always said no because I'm afraid of dogs. When I was five, a neighbor's dog bit me. Ever since them, I've been really scared and nervous around dogs. But my kids really want one. Can you help me?"

The need for positive, effective, and safe techniques to train and to cure the behavioral problems of our dogs is a growing necessity because of their burgeoning population, the ineffectiveness of traditional training techniques, and an annual increase in the number of dog bites reported in the United States each year. Veterinarians tell us that the great majority (ninety percent, some say) of the dogs brought into their offices to be put to sleep are brought in solely because of behavior problems. Problems include barking, jumping, urinating in the house, and not getting along with a family member—or another dog or cat. Well-meaning pet owners, not knowing what to do, or after having attempted outmoded, harsh training techniques which only made the problem worse, throw up their hands. A revolutionary change in how we approach dog misbehavior is desperately called for. *Dogs on the Couch* provides such a change.

In *Dogs on the Couch*, Larry Lachman shares his twenty-two years of behavior therapy experience; twelve of which have been successfully applied to treating dog and cat behavior problems. The behavioral-therapy tools we describe are the same ones Larry has used to successfully treat abused children, violent adolescents, depressed adults, fighting couples, and chronically or terminally ill medical patients.

Dogs on the Couch is the first book to use the tools of family-systems therapy and behavior therapy to analyze and treat the variety of dog-behavior problems that are often not correctable by traditional dog training methods.

What Is Family Systems Therapy?

One of the main themes of this book is recognizing the need to treat the *entire* family system when trying to either prevent or change a dog-behavior problem in a loving and safe way. It is not enough to merely focus on the dog—no matter which techniques you use. The humans in the family must change the way they relate to their dog in order for the dog's behavior to completely change. The structure and emotional boundaries of the family must be modified to effect a complete "cure" in the problem dog's behavior. This is called structural family therapy.

Structural family therapy is defined as the "theory and techniques that approach the individual in his social context." This therapy, first outlined by family therapist Dr. Salvador Minuchin, is based on changing the organization of the family. Once the structure of the family group is transformed, the positions of members in that group are transformed too. As a result, the individual family member's (or, in this case, the dog's) perspective changes.

Applying Family Systems Therapy to Dogs

In my treating of dog-behavior problems, I have found that problems as minor as ignoring the owner's commands or as serious as dominance aggression are rampant in families in which the emotional boundaries between the family and dog are are not well enough defined. The relationships between humans and dog are too enmeshed. Problems can also occur when the emotional boundaries between pet and owner are too rigid. Such problems can range from the dog always following the owner around the home to serious behavior problems such as fear aggression or separation anxiety. The goal of the animal behaviorist, like the human family therapist, is to create change in the family system by restructuring the humans' emotional boundaries with the dog and eliminating dysfunctional relationships and the problem behavior.

The tools used to restructure dysfunctional relationships and create a more loving atmosphere include: marking emotional and physical boundaries by making them explicit; assigning tasks to alter dysfunctional transaction patterns; and supporting, educating and guiding the family in learning new ways of relating to its dog.

In applying a family systems model to dog behavior, Larry bases his four main behavioral principles on this axiom: Any behavior that has been learned can be un-learned and re-learned. The four basic principles are positive reinforcement, negative reinforcement, extinction, and punishment.

Positive reinforcement involves adding something pleasant to someone's environment that will increase the likelihood that the person—or animal—will repeat a specific behavior. For instance, if you heap praise on your child every time he or she picks up toys, your child will soon learn that picking up toys can be desirable.

Negative reinforcement means removing something negative or painful from someone's environment to elicit a desired response. For example, "I will remove this gun from your head when you sign this confession." If you don't release the tension on your dog's choke-chain collar until the animal stops pulling, then that's negative reinforcement.

Extinction occurs when a behavior that had been positively rewarded is no longer reinforced. This can create problems: If a baseball coach consistently praised a certain player at bat for holding the bat in a certain manner and then one day he abruptly stopped, the player might stop holding the bat correctly. If we stop giving the student the "A" in school, or the employee the bonus at work, or the dog the food treat—if the strokes and the attention stop coming—the desired behavior might disappear. However, using extinction to remove rewards for dog misbehavior can be an effective therapy tool.

The fourth principle, **punishment**, is adding something painful or distasteful to someone's environment to make him stop a specific behavior, like washing a child's mouth out with soap for cursing or hanging a dog by its leash for not heeling.

In writing this book, our intent is fourfold: 1) give families the tools they need to select the dog that's right for them, and then help them enjoy training and caring for their dog to the fullest extent possible; 2) stop unnecessary mistreatment of dogs who are misbehaving or who are being abused in obedience classes; 3) lower the absurdly high number of dogs euthanized in the United States each year—three to six million, according to *Veterinary Medicine* magazine—often solely because of minor and easily correctable behavior problems; 4) reduce the high number of dog bites. (If you are an American, there's a one in fifty chance you will be bitten by a dog this year.)

Here are some of the questions tackled in *Dogs on the Couch*, questions not found in the run-of-the-mill dog-training manuals: How can you match your personality temperament with the right breed of dog? Why are traditional training methods harmful to your dog? What's the best way to go about adopting a dog from an animal shelter? How does one best deal with a terminally ill pet? How do you explain a pet's death to children? What is cynophobia (the fear of dogs) and how can you help a family member get over it? How do you safely and effectively deal with an aggressive dog? How do you introduce your dog to your cat? Why does obedience training have no effect on behavior problems? Are psychiatric medications effective in curing dog behavior problems or is their use merely a passing fad?

The way we treat our pets is truly a reflection of how we treat each other. In learning how to develop a committed, safe, and trusting relationship with your dog, you are apt to learn a lot about yourself, too.

LARRY LACHMAN AND FRANK MICKADEIT
Orange County, California
November 1998

FOREWORD

By Eric Van Nice, D.V.M.
Olympiad Animal Hospital
Mission Viejo, California

Pet behavior complaints are some of the most frequent and frustrating problems presented to veterinarians. Let me share with you three examples from just the past few days in our animal hospital:

In the first case, a thoughtful husband surprised his wife by bringing home a four-month-old puppy. Unfortunately, the cute new pup was a frightened Rottweiler, which immediately terrified the couple's two-year-old and five-year-old daughters by growling and snapping at them. Fearing for their safety, we suggested that another breed might be more appropriate for this family. The pet store, however, refused to consider a refund or exchange, and suggested that they work it out with a good trainer.

In the second case, a gentleman and his wife brought in a nice, healthy Persian cat because it had been urinating on the carpet. Examination of the cat and a urine analysis revealed no underlying medical excuse, so we inquired about other cats in and around the house and suggested some changes in the number of litter boxes, their style, locations in the house, and the type of filler. The owners said that they were frustrated and had already tried everything—they never picked up their cat.

In the last case, a nice older lady called for advice about her German shepherd's lick sores on its front legs. We informed her that these unsightly skin lesions are often signs of underlying behavioral problems, and she revealed a recent stressful history of moving to a newer, smaller house and yard. She proudly told us that she and the dog had been working closely with the best German shepherd trainer in the world, but he had not been able to stop the dog's wide variety of behavior problems, including its aggression toward people and other dogs. She inquired about putting her dog on Prozac, so we made an appointment to check the lick sores and consider some more conventional treatment options first.

When the lady arrived at our animal hospital, she and the dog were engaged in a contest of pulling, lunging, vocalizing, and yanking hard on a big spiked choke chain. The dog was winning. I believed that by themselves Prozac and lick-sore lotion would be doomed to failure, but a new beginning with a more gentle approach to behavior training would most likely give this owner and pet a much happier life together.

It's not necessary to repeat or belabor the grim statistics. They are covered elsewhere. But we all know well that there are far too many children bitten by dogs and far too many pets abandoned and destroyed because they were mismatched to a particular family situation, barked too much, were too destructive, or just couldn't be housebroken.

The shame is, we are punishing and destroying these pets for exhibiting their normal, natural behavioral patterns rather than educating ourselves and other pet owners. We need to understand what makes our pets behave the way they do, so we might set them up in appropriate situations, encourage desirable behaviors, and eliminate undesirable behaviors.

This is Larry Lachman's approach. My staff and I have worked with him in all of these situations and many more, including the training of our own pets and the concurrent education of our families. We learn how our pets learn, and then put them in situations in which they can only succeed. We reward their small successes with praise and attention, and gradually watch their small successes blossom into good new habits— rather than wait for them to fail without guidance and then yell, rub their noses in it, or hang them by a choke chain.

Of course, even the most enlightened approach is doomed to failure without the diligent participation of a motivated human family. This is often the biggest frustration of veterinarians and trainers working with the pet-owning public. Here also, Larry has the advantage of many years of education and experience with the motivations, social behaviors, and learning patterns of the human species.

So read on and experience a more gentle approach to making your pets more enjoyable members of your household. You will feel better about the results and the process of understanding and working with animals than you ever did with those "alpha-dog" dominance moves or that choke chain. Then share your experiences with others. Working together to educate pet owners everywhere, we can help stop the tragedy of disposing all of those pets that never get a fair chance to fit into someone's family.

PART ONE:
CRISIS INTERVENTION
AND SHORT-TERM
THERAPY

1

PUPPY NIPPING AND CHEWING

"My husband and I originally got the puppy for our two young children. It's now become an absolute nightmare. The kids are afraid of the puppy. The dog continues to chase after them and bites them on their hands and legs. If you can't help us, we're getting rid of the dog."

"We just adopted a young dog from the animal shelter. She's so sweet but she continues to play-bite and it hurts. My mother, who is sixty-five, lives with us and she's had to go to the doctor twice now because the dog keeps nipping at her hands and she ends up with infections."

"I can't even put my dog's collar and leash on without getting mauled. It's embarrassing. He won't let me check his ears or even brush him. This isn't what I expected with this dog. I'm ready to give him back to the breeder."

FROM LARRY'S CASE FILES:
"Mason" the Rottweiler-Piranha Mix

FILE # 93-000444
DOG'S NAME: Mason
BREED: Rottweiler mix
AGE: 5 months
PROBLEM: Puppy nipping

In 1993, I went out on an in-home consult regarding a five-month old Rottie mix named Mason who was chewing up the place like a piranha with fur. In taking a behavioral history—my standard procedure—I learned from Mason's owners that he was jumping on them and nipping at their hands, feet, and clothing. Mason was especially interested in nibbling on the three young children in the home. Mason had been purchased from a family who had a litter of puppies. Mason's new owners never met the dog's parents, and there was no information about his behavior compared to his littermates. Was he overactive, underactive, or the same compared to his siblings?

I also learned that Mason had not been fully integrated into his new family, as they continued to relegate him to sleeping in a crate in the kitchen rather than in the same room with a human family member. The owners also had inadvertently reinforced Mason's nipping by giving him clothing to chew on, such as socks and shoes. In addition, the kids would engage Mason in chase-me games that would induce him to jump on them. Hence, the jumping was also reinforced through play.

Mason did appear somewhat hyperactive to me when I observed his behavior with the family members. The kids, anticipating being nipped, would suddenly pull away and raise their hands frantically above their heads, thereby inducing the very jumping and nipping they wanted to avoid. Also, the family was engaged in excessive petting of Mason around his face and played tug-of-war games with him. Both activities reward and increase nipping and biting.

Finally, Mason was teething, and therefore required appropriate chew objects to reduce the irritation and pain. I reviewed with the family the anti-nipping program outlined below.

Chewing and Nipping

Dogs chew by nature, just as they bark. Dogs are closer to the ground than we are and use their head, nose, and mouth more than we do. They are genetically programmed to sniff, lick, bark, and chew. Your young puppy is practicing what is hardwired into its brain: preparing to hunt and take down that caribou in your neighborhood in order to survive.

In addition, your puppy will also be chewing a lot due to teething and simply because it is naturally orally fixated at this age. In fact, this oral fixation parallels human development, at least that development as outlined by Freud.

Freud taught that human personality development depends on changes in the distribution of sexual energy, or libido, in regions of the body he called "erogenous" zones. At different ages, or stages of development, the libido is concentrated at different erogenous zone points. Failure to progress smoothly through a particular stage may lead to "fixation": a tendency to continue to engage in behavior associated with that stage. Freud characterized the first year of infancy as being the "oral" stage of development because the infant gains pleasure from oral activities, such as biting, sucking, and chewing. If the infant is not adequately weaned from the oral stage, that child as an adult might be "orally fixated" and demonstrate a host of oral–oriented problem behaviors—verbal cruelty, ingestion of mood-altering substances, etc.—to feel better.

Well, your puppy, especially in its first six months, is naturally orally fixated and will chew and nip, which becomes a problem when a dog munches on items the owner does not want the dog to chew. Dogs typically chew excessively when they are teething, and when they suffer feelings of anxiety after being isolated too long from their pack—which is you, their human family. This nervous kind of chewing is not altogether unlike people chewing their fingernails out of anxiety. When dogs try to relieve their anxiety through chewing, they typically select items or areas of the home that most smell like their owners: television remote controls, hats, shoes, sunglasses, couch cushions, and so on. Why? Because the familiar scent of their owners helps relieve their overall anxiety levels. The worst kind of response to such behavior is physical punishment. The dog will only become more nervous, more anxious, and the problem will grow worse.

The nipping behavior-treatment program consists of a lot of things owners should *not* do:

- Do not pet your puppy around its face or head for six months. Pet instead on the chest or back. Petting and handling around the face or head brings out Pac-man–like oral activity and you are unknowingly reinforcing it through the continued petting!
- Do not play tug-of-war games. This teaches your dog to bite, chew, and become aggressive. And the dog will look at you as being lower than it is in the family power structure or hierarchy.

A dog might see a tug-of-war game as more than a game; it is a physical contest between the dog and you, not unlike the physical contests its wolf cousins face in the wild. The dog will not want to give in. You might realize that you will not be able to win without hurting the dog, so you may give in and release the object. But to the dog it has won and it will feel and act dominant over you. Even if the dog doesn't win, it will feel it has the right to challenge you. Down the road, this can lead to jumping, humping, ignoring commands, aggressive growling or biting, even all-out attacks. Tug-of-war may be fun when your dog is forty pounds and playing, but when it is 140 pounds and growling and won't let you out the door to go to work, you have a big problem.

- Do not give your dog clothing items to chew. This teaches it to chew on such items, whether there is a human in them or not.
- Do not punish your puppy by clamping its mouth shut or hitting it on the muzzle. This will also bring out excessive nipping, biting, and aggression.
- Do not reward any type of oral contact your dog has with you.

Frequently, puppy nipping begins with a single lick, then many licks, then little nips, then taking your arm in its mouth, then full-on biting. Nip the nipping in the bud by not looking at, talking to, or petting your dog if it engages in any of these oral, or mouth-centered, activities.

How to Discipline the Dog in the Act of Nipping

Dogs, particularly young dogs and small dogs, often try to nip and tug at pant legs and skirt hems. You should correct this problem as soon as it appears. Use the "S-R-R" method: Startle, Redirect, and Reward.

When you catch the dog *in the act* of nipping, startle it. Shake a soda can with some pennies inside. Squirt it in the face with a blast of water from a squirt bottle or large syringe. Or give a loud admonishment, like "Out!" Then wait five minutes and redirect it to an appropriate replacement behavior, in this case a safe chew toy. Reinforce that behavior with reward and praise. The dog quickly learns that chewing or biting you is off limits and that it should chew on its bones.

The S-R-R method is a key technique to remember. This will be used to correct many problem behaviors. Don't forget: The dog must be caught and corrected while *in the act* of the misbehavior. Otherwise, the behavior-modification techniques are pointless and actually harmful—the dog won't know why it is being corrected, and so it might actually "correct" some desired behavior. This will be discussed in more detail later.

Boredom-Induced Chewing

If the dog seems to be chewing out of boredom—if it has nothing to do or chew on and it goes from object to object looking for something—you need to take a look at its daily activity level and how much time it gets to be with its pack. Of course, your dog should be sleeping inside with you each night, and when you're home you should have the dog inside with you so it can have your companionship and interaction.

Puppy Teething and Appropriate Chew Items

Dogs typically teethe from four to six months of age. During that time, they'll try to chew anything that they can get their paws on in order to relieve the pain in their gums. After that, the teething-induced chewing frenzies usually fade away.

During the teething phase, you should gently take away any inappropriate items the puppy tries to chew and redirect the dog to appropriate chewing objects. Among the best are the Gimborn Natural Sterilized Bones. (If your pet supply store doesn't stock them, contact Gimborn US, 4280 Northeast Expressway, Atlanta, GA, 30340, phone: 1-800-755-7056.) Get the seven-inch-long plain versions. These are real bones treated not to splinter and have a one-half-inch to one-inch-diameter cavity running through them. To maintain the dog's interest in the sterilized bones, cram the cavities with cheese, beef jerky, or peanut butter (*but make sure you flick off with a knife any protruding sharp material inside the bone before you stuff it with treats*). Or, you can pre-boil them in chicken broth so they retain the taste and scent of the broth. Provide your teething piranha with three of these every time you leave it alone and one during the evening and it will gladly turn its teething-induced chewing away from bland objects such as wood molding or flooring.

You also can provide your dog with hard rubber toys, Nylabone hard plastic bones, or Kong chew toys. As a matter of safety, make sure to stay away from rawhide bones and chew sticks, thin plastic squeak toys, and cow and horse hooves. Dogs have a tendency to chew the rawhide into a taffy-like consistency and then try to swallow it whole. The material can become lodged in the digestive tract or airway, causing the dog to choke. Why take that chance? The plastic squeak toys frequently have small inner parts that the dog might try to swallow, and some are coated with a paint that will make the dog sick.

You can also give the puppy a teething towel. Take an old towel, put two or three knots in it so it won't resemble a normal towel, wet it and put it in the freezer for an hour or so before giving it to your puppy. This cold and crunchy treat will help numb the pain in the gums.

The Bottom Line

Most dogs with nipping problems are too enmeshed with their owners. If the dog licks, nudges, or nips on their owner's hand, the owner pets the dog, thereby reinforcing the behavior. The dogs with nipping problems tend to be:

- Young
- Petted excessively around the face or head
- Allowed to play tug-of-war
- Given clothing objects to chew on
- Disciplined by corporal punishment around the face or head
- Lacking sufficient appropriate chew objects
- Lacking sufficient aerobic exercise
- Isolated from the family, their "pack"
- Given attention when they act up
- Overly enmeshed with one or more members of the family

Your dog requires daily exercise and should have chew toys such as the ones already described. Taking these steps should satisfy the dog's need to release energy through chewing. It should also adequately address your dog's need for social contact, in addition to warding off boredom. If, however, the chewing is related to full-blown separation anxiety, a true behavior disorder, a more comprehensive intervention plan is required. This is discussed in Chapter 8, which is about separation anxiety.

Case Study Postscript

After four to six weeks of implementing the anti-nipping therapy program, Mason's owners reported that his nipping had dropped about eighty percent, and was well on the way to ceasing altogether.

2

Housebreaking and How to Make Your Home Safe for Your Dog

"He seems to be getting the idea of pooping outside, but he's still urinating in the house when we're gone."

"We've tried everything. We've been taking her out every few minutes. We've been putting newspaper down. We've been sticking her nose in it. Nothing seems to work."

"She was fine for years. Then all of a sudden, she started piddling in the house again."

From Larry's Case Files: "Sage" the Soiling Keeshond

FILE # 95-00049
DOG'S NAME: Sage
BREED: Keeshond
AGE: 5 years
PROBLEM: House-soiling

In 1995, I went on a consult regarding a five-year-old female Keeshond that was urinating in the house. Sage had been adopted from a pet-adoption center by her adult female owner and had been in her new home several months. The dog had no history of major illness nor of any previous surgery, except for being spayed. She was not on medication. She initially barked at visitors but would eventually warm to them. There were many positive signs in the dog-owner relationship: Her new owner would discipline her by using a firm "no," and would reward her with verbal praise. Her owner could take a bone and toy away from Sage without provoking any guarding or growling response. She also could pet and interact with

Sage while the dog ate out of her food bowl with no problem.

However, Sage was having house-soiling accidents during the night. If caught—which was seldom—her owner would punish her by banishing Sage to the backyard.

Part of the problem, I discovered, was that Sage was associating her target toilet area with punishment. Punishing her and putting her outside was creating a negative association in Sage's mind with the yard. She no longer wanted to urinate out there.

There were other factors: Her owner was giving Sage too much freedom at night. And Sage was experiencing a reward for soiling in the house because her bladder instantly felt better and her owner could rarely catch her in the act.

Our program for Sage consisted of: planning when to take Sage out and how long she should stay out; determining what the owner should do when Sage was outside; defining exactly where Sage was supposed to go; regulating the dog's food and water; changing the association Sage had about urinating in the house; tightening up supervision to prevent Sage from roaming around the house and urinating at will; and correctly situating Sage at night.

Sage's case is typical of puppies and dogs new to a home. But, barring any underlying medical problems, it should not be hard to have your dog completely housebroken in no time.

***

Housebreaking

It is a myth that a puppy can be housebroken in a few days. Even the standard dog trainer's claim that it can be accomplished in a week or so needs some qualification.

Most people obtain their puppies when they're around eight to ten weeks old. Not until they are twelve to fifteen weeks old are puppies physiologically capable of being thoroughly housebroken. Yes, in a few days or a week a puppy can be taught to not soil its immediate den—the place it sleeps. But to have a puppy roam free around the home and be completely accident-free takes time.

House-soiling problems usually arise because of a lack of supervision. The pup or house-soiling dog is allowed free range to do its urinating and defecating. Each time the dog does so and is not corrected, it's like someone going to Las Vegas and winning: random rewards maintain the behavior. Being able to empty the bladder and feel the pain go away is rewarding for the dog. The more times a dog is allowed to relieve itself in an off-limits area, the more it will think that's where it's supposed to go.

Adequate supervision means watching the dog carefully. You can loosely tie the dog's leash around your waist so that wherever you go you have a follower, or you can loosely tether it to something in a room where you can continually supervise it. If you do tether it, say, to the leg of a coffee table, be sure to give it enough leash so it can sit up and turn around without choking. And *only* tether a dog when you will be there to watch it, so it won't panic and possibly choke.

Another option is to gate off the dog in the kitchen or laundry room with access to a pet door. This prevents the dog from roaming free and is the way to go if you are going to be gone during the day. More on doggy doors later.

A second common trouble area is not adequately regulating the puppy's intake of water and food and providing food sources that may cause the puppy to relieve itself more than it should.

Until a puppy is completely housebroken—and that means eight weeks of no accidents—it should be on a rigid feeding schedule. This is the opposite of free feeding—leaving food down all day for the dog to snack on as it wishes. While free feeding does regulate, in a more balanced way, the dog's weight gain, it also causes an unhousebroken puppy to defecate more frequently. This makes it difficult for the owner to impose a regulated schedule of bathroom outings so that the dog can develop a sense of routine.

A good regimen is to feed the pup two to three times per day. (The younger the puppy, the more likely it will be three times a day. As the puppy becomes five or six months of age, the feeding is usually reduced to twice a day. Check with your veterinarian.) Leave food down in its bowl for twenty minutes. Then remove the food whether it has eaten it or not. This quickly trains the dog to consume its meal at one sitting and allows you to predict when the dog will have to relieve itself. For most dogs it will be within fifteen minutes of eating.

Successful housebreaking also depends on *what* the dog eats. Whether it is dry food or canned, those typically found at regular supermarkets tend to be formulated to promote "high poop" and "low absorption." Dogs ingesting these foods—which are often high in fat—will probably defecate more frequently and their stools will be looser. Since they aren't getting everything they need in their diet, as most of the nutrients of their food are passed in their feces, they are more inclined to engage in copraphagia: stool eating, which makes it most unpleasant when one of these dogs comes up and gives you a big kiss!

These foods also frequently contain additives and ingredients that can dry out your dog's coat or skin, or indirectly suppress its immune system, making it more vulnerable to illness. Furthermore, the ingredients in canned-meat food tends to duplicate existing nutrients in the dry food. The digestive system will not process redundant supplies of protein and the body will eliminate it in overly soft stools—not what you want.

Unless your dog has a health problem requiring a special diet, buy one of the quality dry foods available at large feed or pet supply stores. Some of the ones that seem to work best and are available at such stores are Iams, Nutromax, Nature's Recipe, and Science Diet. These are formulated to promote fewer feces and greater absorption of nutrients and do not contain excessive chemical additives.

Some veterinarians do not put much credence in nutrition and its beneficial effects on health and behavior. The more modern school of thought, however, is that the quality of the food does affect a dog's physical and psychological well-being and overall activity level. For example, a dog with dry skin or skin allergies tends to improve if switched to lamb-and-rice-based dry food. Hyperactivity also may be corrected by a change of diet. But there's no reason to wait for some malady to arise to treat your dog to a quality diet; start doing so during housebreaking.

Supervision and food regulation are the basics of housebreaking. Beyond that, there is a step-by-step plan I'll take you through. Within four to eight weeks, your puppy should be completely housebroken and trustworthy in your home. Remember, it takes approximately six weeks to break "bad" or undesirable behaviors and three to four weeks to instill good ones. The process recognizes the dog's developing physiology and psychology and the fastidious grooming and denning habits inherited from its wolf ancestors.

What Not To Do

Housebreaking is usually the first thing you will attempt to teach your puppy and is one of the most important first experiences it will have in your home. Your dog's relationship to your family will be substantially affected by your potty-training attempts. This is where a lot of people blow it.

They blow it by using ineffective, heavy-handed punishment techniques. Physical punishment—rubbing its nose in its mess, or worse—will bring out either excessive fearfulness or aggression in your dog, both of which can lead to biting. Also, the excessive fearfulness can lead to submissive urination problems—whenever the dog sees the person who abused it, it pees—which only adds another type of urination problem to the initial housebreaking problems.

Such punishment is usually pointless anyway. The puppy or older dog will not know why you are punishing it if you are punishing it after the fact. It doesn't have the brain matter to make the connection. Dogs are very Zen-like and very present-oriented. If you punish it after the accident, even a few minutes after, the dog will not know why you're punishing it and will most likely think you are punishing it for something entirely unrelated to the house-soiling. And if you do catch the dog in the act and punish it immediately in a harsh way, it will only become more sneaky about its misbehavior. It will begin to do its business inside the house but out of your sight. So using the classic rub-their-noses-in-it is not only cruel, but is completely ineffective.

What You Should Do

The key to just about all successful behavior corrections is catching the dog *in the act* of misbehaving. That's one of the reasons you don't give the dog free, unsupervised reign of the house before it's housebroken.

The most effective way to housebreak your dog is to startle it while urinating or defecating in an inappropriate area. Wait five minutes, then redirect it outside to its designated potty area. Then actively reward the appropriate replacement behavior: the dog going to the bathroom where you want it to. This is the most efficient way to change dog behavior, dolphin behavior, and even mother-in-law behavior. *Startle, wait five, Redirect, Reward.* S-R-R. You'll see this again and again as a method for tackling other behavioral problems.

So, when the puppy starts to go in the wrong place, loudly say "No!" or "Off!" or "Out!" and startle it with a device that will not harm it. There are several methods: rattle a can of pennies or toss one near it (do not hit the dog); blast it in the face with water squirted out of a workout water bottle or 60cc syringe; standing at least six feet away, hold an air horn behind your back (so your body is between it and the dog) and give it a quick blast; depress an ultrasound device from the same distance. Remember, the key to startling the dog is to startle it, *not injure it*. In this way, the pup begins to associate a mild phobic sensation with its undesirable behavior.

After about five minutes, redirect the dog to its designated potty area. As the last poop is dropping or as the last drop of urine is dripping, praise the dog, saying "good potty" or "clean dog" or something like that, and give it a piece of doggy beef jerky or other treat as a reward. Do this consistently and the dog will soon figure out what you want it to do.

The following are keys to making the program work:

- Designate one ten-foot-by-ten-foot area where you want your dog to go and consistently take it to that place each time it goes out. If you take your dog to the backyard one day, the front yard another day, and out on the curb another day you are teaching it that everywhere is "poopable," and it will start going anywhere and everywhere.

- Keep a schedule. A dog will most need to go to the bathroom: 1) when it wakes up; 2) after eating; 3) after playing or car rides; 4) and before bed. That amounts to only four or five times a day. If you take your dog out every two minutes, you're conditioning it to go to the bathroom every two minutes.

- Stay out with your puppy for at least fifteen to twenty minutes when you take it out. Young puppies like to pee and poop, roll around, look at the stars, sniff the grass, then pee and poop some more, and roll around . . . and so on. If you make the common mistake of taking the pup out and coming back in at the first sight of a little tinkle, you are setting up the puppy to relieve itself inside within ten or twenty minutes. Make sure you give your pup ample time to do its business. Also, because of its wolf heritage you want to make a point of going out with your dog, as it wants to be with its pack and have companionship. If you shove the dog out the sliding glass door and stay inside to watch television, it will be lonely and more interested in where you are than in doing its business. So, it will hold it and hold it until you let it in . . . and then let loose on the carpet.

- Pick up its mess each time. If there is too much poop lying around in the yard your dog will stop doing its business there and will start doing it inside the house in the upstairs closet by your shoes. In addition, young puppies frequently engage in copraphagia if there is too much poop lying around. They do this to actually clean up the mess!

- Change the meaning of accident locations. It is an immutable law of animal behaviorism that, unless they are ill, dogs will not poop or urinate where they eat or sleep. You can use this fact to great advantage during housebreaking. When the dog has an accident in the home, clean up the area with a product like Nature's Miracle, or Outright, and let it dry. Then, twice a day for two to four weeks, feed the dog some doggy treats on the very spot where it had the accident. The dog will start associating the area with eating, instead of peeing or pooping, and will stop using that area for its elimination.

- De-worm your puppy. Most puppies come with uninvited baggage: parasitic worms, usually round worms or tape worms that they acquire during nursing or at birth. If your puppy has parasitic worms, it will have loose stools, under-absorb the nutrient value of its food and lose weight, and possibly develop some severe infections.

- Don't feed your dog before bedtime. This seems obvious, but you'd be surprised what some people do—especially people who come home from work late, have just enough time to pop their own dinner in the microwave, pour some chow in Fido's bowl, and then fall into bed. The rule for unhousebroken dogs is no more food for four hours before bedtime, except for that one treat for going potty during its last twenty-minute toilet session. Three hours prior to bedtime, place a few ice cubes in the puppy's water bowl. This allows the pup to quench its thirst, but the ice cubes melt slowly and produce less fluid to occupy the dog's bladder all night than a whole bowl of water. Right at bedtime, pick up the ice bowl and go for the last potty session. No more water until the morning. (For the rest of the day, of course, the dog must have ample water in a bowl where it can get to it.)

- Let the dog sleep in the same room with you at night. This is stressed in a lot of places in this book because it is applicable to so many problems, and so many positive things result from it. For the purposes of housebreaking, it goes back to that immutable law: Dogs will not soil where they sleep. If their den is confining enough and they're with their pack (or family), they will learn to hold their bowels and bladder all night. And that helps them to develop the soft muscle and bladder control necessary to hold it for similarly long periods during the day.

Confining Your Puppy at Night

There are two common ways of confining a puppy with its family at night to teach it bladder control: 1) You can crate your dog at night; or 2) you can tether it in a manner similar to the method described earlier.

Crating is "hot" in the dog-training world right now. There is a lot of bad information going around about this technique, however, so it merits some in-depth discussion.

Crating Your Dog at Night

The crate is a first step in the housebreaking process, so have it ready before you bring your new dog home. What kind of crate should you have? Dogs seem quite comfortable in the Vari-Kennel fiberglass crate and other crates similar to those that airlines use for shipping animals. They are probably easier to move around and clean than anything you could make. How big should it be? Big enough so that the dog can stand up and turn around in it with ease. You may want to buy a crate that will be large enough for your dog when it is fully grown. If you do, you may have to artificially make it smaller by placing an ice cooler or box in the back so that the pup does not have enough room to pee or poop in the back and sleep in the front. You must introduce your dog to its new nighttime home in a positive and fun way, and not just shove it in through the door at bedtime that first night. Invest some time that afternoon. Take apart the crate—the plastic or fiberglass ones are usually built so that the top comes off by turning a few screws—and toss some food treats and toys in the bottom half.

Let the dog run in and out of it. If the crate is large enough, have family members crawl in and out. Have lines of treats coming from the far reaches of the house leading to a treasure of treats in the crate. Your dog will begin to associate the crate with a very positive feeling. It will not be afraid of it at night when it is secured inside.

At night, put the top half back on the crate and place it in the bedroom where the dog will sleep. Position it so that the dog will be able to look through the mesh door of the crate and see the designated family member sleeping. Place a blanket and bone inside. Toss some treats in the crate to lure the dog inside and close the door. If those procedures are followed, your dog should adapt easily to the crate and will quickly learn to hold its bathroom behavior all night.

If the dog seems anxious or whines, you can reduce its anxiety by giving it a towel or shirt with your body scent to sleep on. You can toss in a favorite bone, too. If it continues to bark or cry for fifteen minutes or more, you can use the S-R-R technique and startle the dog in the act of barking. When the dog has remained quiet for two minutes, reward that behavior with "good quiet," and toss in a couple of small treats. This will teach the puppy that it will receive a paycheck for good (quiet) behavior and a pink slip for bad (barking) behavior.

If your dog is normal and healthy, you can close the bedroom door and take the top and door off the crate when the dog has been dry all night for a couple of weeks. Let the dog continue to sleep in the bottom portion without confinement. Progressively, under supervision, expose your dog to more and more areas until it extends its den behavior to your entire home. Voila! The dog is housebroken.

Some Tips and Warnings on Crates

This method will take longer with dogs purchased from pet shops because they have been conditioned to believe that if they relieve themselves in their cages, it will either fall through a screen or they have to sleep with it. So, strict schedule feeding and bathroom outings are doubly essential for the pet shop dog. Also, make it a practice to give it some treats in the crate so it further associates the crate as being an off-limits bathroom zone.

- For dogs with bladder infections, antibiotics and dietary changes recommended by your veterinarian are required to make housebreaking work.
- The crate should be used at night and for fewer than four hours during the day. Otherwise, the constant confinement will make the dog go nuts.
- Just because the dog is trained to not go to the bathroom in the crate, it does not mean it is ready to be turned loose in the home.
- The dog does not need to be crated for the rest of its life.
- Crates should have wire or steel mesh doors. However, crates that are completely made of wire or steel mesh are not recommended. For one

thing, they are physically less comfortable for dogs. But they are also psychologically less comfortable because they do not give them the sense of a wolf den or cave with its protected, enclosed walls.

An alternative to the crate is the loose-leash tether method, which works on the same principle as the crate does. At bedtime, lay down a blanket for the dog. Loosely tether the dog to the leg of the bed or dresser so it has enough leash to sit up and lie down without choking, but not enough leash to go to the far corner of the bedroom and pee and then return near the bed to sleep. Following the same routine as with the crate, gradually give the dog more and more home space in which to wander at night. Unlike the crate method, however, you must never leave the dog unsupervised while it is tethered.

Doggy Doors

Doggy doors tend to speed up housebreaking because the dog can continue to go out to its designated toilet area even when you are busy elsewhere or not home. Such access to the very same area you escort the dog to after it's eaten and before bedtime allows the dog to adapt more quickly to using it as the sole potty area.

If you have a sliding glass door that opens into a safe, fenced-in yard, you can easily install a special pet door that fits in the tracks and requires no construction. You can find these doors at large pet-supply stores, some warehouse home-improvement stores, and some horse and feed stores. If you don't have a sliding door, build or buy a pet door that can be installed in a solid wood or composite door.

Security is a valid issue, but doggy doors are not a red carpet into your home for burglars. A small dog's door is too small for a human to enter. And if your dog door is big enough for a child to crawl through, your dog is pretty large. Most burglars will not attempt to enter a home with a dog that big. They prefer easy targets. Also, having a dog roaming around your home does not preclude you from having a motion-sensitive security alarm; alarm companies can set them to trigger against human invaders and ignore dogs. (At night, when your dog is in the bedroom with you and when you take your dog away from the home, always secure the doggy door from the inside.) In any case, a doggy door should not compromise security if it is constructed and installed properly and is no larger than the dog that will use it.

Be sure to pick a door with a clear plastic flap. Solid or opaque flaps discourage dogs from going through them which, at the very least, will slow the training process. It is also important to make sure that the door threshold is low enough so that the dog does not have to jump or make a steep climb to get through it or will fall when it reaches the other side. If you have to, create some steps using wood, brick, or masonry block.

Don't install the door and then immediately shove the dog through it. If the dog is introduced to the dog door in a rushed, traumatic fashion, you will be actively training your dog to fear the door. Taking a couple of hours to properly teach your dog to use it is worthwhile.

After installing the door, remove the flap or keep it suspended when you are first teaching the dog to use it. One of the most common causes of trauma for dogs during such training is being slapped from behind by the flap or being startled by it making a sudden noise. This creates a startle-phobic response (as we do with our penny cans and water squirt bottles when we intentionally discipline), and the dog learns to fear the dog door and stops using it.

Start the training by positioning two family members at the doggy door. One is situated on the same side of the door as the dog, the other on the opposite side. Both have handfuls of irresistible treats. (Like all training sessions that use food as an incentive, things will go a lot easier if the dog has not just been fed; having it a little hungry really helps.) The person on the opposite side crouches down so that the dog can plainly see him. He begins verbally encouraging the dog to come through the door and starts dropping food bait on his side so that the dog must pass through the door to get it. The other person keeps the flap suspended and tosses food treats and toys through the dog door while verbally encouraging the dog to go get the treats and toys. *Do not try to push or pull the dog through the doggy door.* That will create a fearful experience for the dog and may traumatize it to the point where it will never use the door.

Once the dog goes through the door the first time, make a game out of it. Toss treats and toys back and forth until your dog jumps or scurries through without hesitation. Now gradually phase in the flap. Slowly and gently show the dog how you can push the flap with your hand to raise it. While pushing the flap forward, toss the treats through the dog door toward the other family member, and allow the dog to pass through back and forth. Then, gently take hold of the dog's paw, and gently show it how to push the dog door flap forward and open. Do this while tossing treats through the door and with the person on the other side coaxing the dog to come. Once the dog is relaxed and using the doggy door with no problem, make sure it always uses it to enter and leave the yard.

Going From One Surface to Another

Changing the surface of the dog's potty area—grass to concrete, newspapers to grass, etc.—can be difficult and requires some special work.

If the transition is from grass to concrete, get some sod and place it on top of the concrete area you want the dog to use and take the dog there. Between each potty session, remove a bit more of the sod until the dog is doing its business on cement alone.

When transferring from newspaper, take a couple of your dog's soiled papers and place them outside in the desired location. But be sure to weigh them down with bricks or rocks so they don't blow into your neighbor's yard. In the same way as with the sod, gradually remove portions of the newspaper until it is all gone.

With such transfers, it may help to engage the dog in high-activity playing and running for at least ten minutes in the general area. The physical stimulation should cause the dog to need to vacate its urine and feces, which will give the dog the opportunity to start using the designated area on its own. Another trick is to apply another dog's urine or urine scent at the newly designated areas. This may cause your dog to start re-marking its territory by urinating in the same place, thus creating and locking in a new habit.

If Your Dog Still Won't Go Outside

A special technique is called for if your dog urinates outside, but holds its feces to defecate when returning inside, or if it will not relieve itself outside at all, no matter how long you keep it at its designated area. We call it the "out-in-out."

Take your dog outside at its regularly designated time. After ten minutes without the desired result, go back inside. Take just two or three steps into your home and then turn around and take the dog right back out. It should be ready to do what it had up to that point reserved for doing inside. When the dog does what you want it to, praise it, reward it with a treat, and remain outside with it for another ten minutes.

Continuing problems with house-soiling after implementing the plan may indicate the need for in-home consultation by an animal behaviorist. Or the problem could be medical and require a check-up by your veterinarian; your dog could have parasitic worms, cystitis (bladder infection), cancer or some other ailment. If that's the case, behavioral techniques will have no effect.

Otherwise, work the program diligently for six to eight weeks and your puppy or older dog will be housebroken and will have taken a significant step toward becoming a fully integrated member of your family.

Making the Yard Safe

If you have a doggy door, or if you plan to let your dog remain outside when you can't supervise or confine it, you must make sure its yard is safe. Here's what to do:

- Make sure your dog has an ample water supply that it cannot knock over. Heavy, large, deep plastic buckets of water placed throughout the yard are a good safeguard. There are also self-filling water bowls available and lick-sticks that attach to hose nozzles or water spigots. The latter, however, should be in addition to a bucket or bowl of water because many times the dog cannot get enough water out of a lick-stick to relieve its thirst.
- Make absolutely sure that no matter what the time of day or position of the sun, your dog has ample shade at all times. If it doesn't, it can develop heat stroke and die.
- Make sure that at least one water bowl is in this permanent shade area.
- Make sure your dog cannot leap the fence to get out and that no other animal can get in and kill or harm your dog (or have your dog harm it). In many areas, coyotes prey on dogs left in backyards, and coyotes are notorious for their ingenuity in defeating fences. Nothing makes a better meal for a coyote than an all-but-defenseless small or medium-sized dog in a backyard. Such attacks are common in areas where suburban sprawl has encroached into foothills and other rural areas.

- If you have a pool or spa, make sure your dog knows by heart how to get out of the shallow end and up the stairs in case it falls in or dives in. This takes training, but it is a must. Use at least two family members. Over a period of weeks, repeatedly entice your dog into the pool with treats and then immediately show it how to get to the proper end of the pool and up the stairs. At first, you will want to gently support the dog from below and steer it toward the correct end. Repeat this over and over until it becomes a game. If you fail to do so and your dog falls in the water when you aren't around, it will probably tire and drown, doggy paddle or not.

- Do not use the yard as the dog's banishment/punishment place or it will be traumatized by having to stay out there. Remember, the only effective type of discipline to be used is the *Startle-wait five-minutes-Redirect-Reward* technique.

- Remove all poisonous plants and any snail or pest bait or toxic fertilizers. Consult with your veterinarian and nursery owner if you're not sure about the toxicity of something. Some of the more common poisonous plants to dogs are: autumn crocus, azalea, bleeding heart, buttercup, castor bean, daffodil, Dutchman's breeches, elderberry, foxglove, golden chain, hyacinth, iris, Jack-in-the-pulpit, larkspur, lily of the valley, mistletoe, narcissus, oleander, poinsettia, rhubarb, and yew.

If your dog ingests any of these plants, immediately call your veterinarian, veterinary emergency clinic, or veterinary poison control center. The ASPCA's National Animal Poison Control Center offers these tips:

- Keep on hand a pet safety kit that includes:
  1. Fresh bottle of hydrogen peroxide three percent (USP)
  2. Can of soft dog or cat food, as appropriate
  3. Turkey baster, bulb syringe, or large medicine syringe
  4. Saline eye solution to flush out eye contaminants
  5. Artificial tear gel to lubricate eyes after flushing
  6. Mild grease-cutting dishwashing liquid in order to bathe an animal after skin contamination
  7. Rubber gloves to prevent you from being exposed while bathing pet

8. Forceps to remove stingers
9. Muzzle to keep the animal from hurting you while it is excited or in pain
10. Pet carrier to help carry the animal to your local veterinarian

- You should not attempt any therapy on your pet without contacting either the ASPCA/NAPCC or your local veterinarian.
- Take thirty to sixty seconds to safely collect and have at hand the material involved. This may be of great benefit to the ASPCA/ NAPCC professionals as they determine exactly what poison or poisons are involved.
- In the event that you need to take your animal to your local veterinarian, be sure to take with you any product container. Also bring any material your pet may have vomited or chewed, collected in a Ziploc bag.
- If your animal is having a seizure, losing consciousness, unconscious, or having difficulty breathing, you should contact your veterinarian immediately.

When you call the ASPCA/NAPCC, be ready to provide:

- Your name, address, and telephone number
- Information concerning the exposure (the amount of agent, the time since exposure, etc.)
- The species, breed, age, sex, weight, and number of animals involved
- The agent your animal(s) has been exposed to, if known
- The problems your animal(s) is experiencing.

To reach the National Animal Poison Control Center, call 1-800-548-2423 or 1-888-4ANIHELP (1-888-426-4435). The cost is $30 per case— no extra charge for follow-up calls. You must use Visa, MasterCard, Discover, or American Express when you call.

Making the Inside of Your Home Safe

If your dog will have unsupervised access to areas of your home when you are away, there are several safety measures you want to consider. This is especially true when your dog is in the teething-chewing-exploring stage.

- Eliminate your dog's access to cleaning agents, pesticides, poisonous plants, and garbage.
- If the dog is still chewing, secure it in a safe zone that is free from electrical wires, drapes, and drapery cords. Uncarpeted areas are preferable.
- Make sure no heavy or sharp objects are looming over your dog or are on table surfaces accessible and vulnerable to your dog knocking them down and being cut or struck. Irons sitting atop wobbly ironing boards are a tragedy waiting to happen.
- When you leave the dog, provide it with sufficient and interesting chew objects (described above) so it can direct its natural chewing desire to these objects and not to your wood molding or wall. Of course, also provide it with its bed, water, and a cool environment. You may also want to leave playing a tape recording of your voice so that the dog is comfortable and soothed while you are gone.

Case Study Postscript

Within a month, her owner reported that Sage no longer had urination accidents in the home. The short-term behavior therapy house-soiling program was successful. Case closed.

3

Digging

"We came home after work and found all of our Malibu lawn lights dug up and strewn across the backyard. My husband wanted to microwave our dog. What can we do?"

"I was absolutely livid when I came home. All of the flowers I had planted over the weekend were dug up by our puppy. He had dirt all over his nose and face. I was so angry, I wanted to get rid of him that day."

FROM LARRY'S CASE FILES:
"Nell" the Landscaping Old English Sheepdog

FILE # 92-000154
DOG'S NAME: Nell
BREED: Old English sheepdog
AGE: 9 months
PROBLEM: Digging

In 1992, I went out on a consult regarding a nine-month-old Old English sheepdog named Nell, who was digging up the backyard—which now looked like the lunar surface.

In taking a social, medical, and behavioral history, I learned that Nell had not had any obedience training nor had she been spayed. Her digging occurred whether the family was home or not and whether she had access into the home or not. Clearly, this was something more than a case of separation anxiety (digging as a result of being separated from the family).

As with other members of this breed, Nell was an extremely active dog who ran her Ricochet Rabbit–like zigzags throughout the house at least twice a day in addition to jumping up on people and digging holes. Part of this activity was due to her breed, part due to her age, part due to her being unspayed, and part due to her not knowing any better. A comprehensive anti-digging program was called for; one in which the whole family would need to be involved.

Following my initial in-home consult, Nell's owner made an appointment to have her fixed. In addition, we enrolled Nell in one of my obedience classes, where she would learn to sit, lie down, come, stay, heel on the leash, and not jump up on people. (See Chapter 4, Non-Violent Obedience Training for the Whole Family, for further information.) We further integrated Nell into her family system, or pack, by having her sleep inside at night in view of the owners. We also implemented the anti-digging behavior modification program outlined below.

In addition to focusing on Nell's behavior, we also had to modify and change her *owners'* behavior. The entire family system needed to change in order for us to completely and efficiently change Nell's behavior. How did we do this?

First, the owners were too emotionally "enmeshed" with Nell and were blurring the boundaries, or pack hierarchy positions, between themselves and the dog. They were doing this by allowing Nell to jump up on people and furniture, by giving her human food hand-outs, and by inadvertently rewarding her hyper behavior by giving her attention when she acted out. Just like with human teenagers and their parents, negative attention is better than no attention; frequently the child or dog learns that by acting-out it will get its parents' or leaders' attention. The "problem" behavior is just reinforced. We needed to create more of an emotional boundary between Nell and her owners. We needed to strengthen the hierarchical pecking order.

First, the owners were instructed not to respond to Nell's demands for attention. This included when she barked, jumped, or was hyper. Second, the owners were instructed to notice Nell when she was quietly sitting, standing, or lying down, and to label that behavior with a gentle "good quiet," and lavish her with treats and petting. The owners were instructed not to wait until she was in trouble to start giving her attention, but to do so when she was behaving. Basic positive reinforcement.

The Five Reasons Dogs Dig

1. Dogs dig cooling holes to seek relief from the heat of the day.
2. They dig to create dens in which to give birth.
3. They dig to root out prey, such as gophers and rabbits.
4. Surprisingly, they sometimes dig because we teach them to. If you allow your dog to watch you landscape or garden, don't be shocked if after you finish the initial planting it "helps" finish the job by re-digging it for you. It's a good way for the dog to earn doggy allowance: help dad and mom out in the yard.
5. Dogs also dig to relieve boredom and anxiety. If you stuck me in your backyard all day with nothing to do, I'd probably dig and rearrange your patio furniture, too. Remember, boredom is defined as, "to tire by dullness."

Common Characteristics

Years of observation have shown that there are some characteristics or situations most digging dogs share:

- The dog is alone too much
- The dog is forced to sleep outside at night
- The dog has insufficient exercise
- The dog is intact; it has not been neutered or spayed
- The dog is young, under two years of age
- The dog frequently is of a breed known for digging (terriers, dachshunds, malamutes, and huskies, to name a few)
- The owners consistently punish the dog after the fact
- The owners use harsh physical punishment that raises the dog's overall tension level, which causes more digging
- The dog is frequently on supermarket junk-food diets, and chews roots and eats mineral products it digs up
- The dog has little or no obedience training
- The dog is overexposed to the sun
- The dog has a very high nervous-system activity level

Stopping the Canine Archeologist

A lot of the solutions are just common sense. If the dog seems to be digging for a cooling hole, provide more shade or access indoors (via a doggy door) during the heat of the day.

If the dog is digging because it is in its second or third heat cycle, situate it in an area without dirt or spay the dog.

If the dog is engaging in predatory behavior, take whatever action is needed to remove the prey from the yard. (There are plenty of environmentally safe and dog-safe naturally-derived products that serve as natural anti-rodent or anti-snail agents.) If the dog is digging out of loneliness and anxiety, increase its time inside the house and its pack interaction. Most dogs calm down and are less anxious once they have access inside the house and can smell their pack's scent. But some dogs are just die-hard diggers.

Redirecting the Die-Hards

Terriers (the name comes from the Italian word "terra," or earth, because these dogs were bred to root out burrowing animals), dachshunds, malamutes, and similar breeds have a natural propensity for digging. With these dogs, you must redirect their natural need to dig to appropriate and designated areas so your whole yard does not end up looking like the moon surface. (Trying to stop them from digging entirely may not be possible and may be cruel. Would you stop a pointer from pointing? If you can't set aside a bit of yard space for a terrier, you might want to consider getting another type of dog.)

It's not hard to make a digger happy, anyway. Get a kiddy sand box (like the one you used to play in when you were a young homosapien biped) and instead of sand, fill it with dirt. Bury some treats and some of your dog's favorite bones and toys in it. Then go out and dig with your dog, *actively rewarding* and reinforcing it for digging there with praise, petting, and food treats.

To keep it out of areas it shouldn't dig in takes some stealth. The Startle-Redirect-wait five-and Reward technique of discipline mentioned earlier should be used.

Let your dog out. Get your airhorn and begin spying on your dog from an open window, keeping the horn aimed out the window but yourself out of view behind curtains or blinds. When the dog approaches within three feet of the off-limits area, hit the horn. With repeated applications, the startled pup will truly believe some greater unseen force is watching over the flower bed or lawn and its digging in the off-limits area will cease. It will seek its own, much quieter, play box.

Nutritional Deficiency Possibilities

On occasion, dogs dig to get at certain minerals in the soil or to chew roots or wood products in the ground. This may be caused by a nutritional deficiency, a poor diet, or by a malabsorption condition in which the dog may be eating the greatest food, but is not absorbing the nutrients properly. The dog passes many of the unabsorbed nutrients out through its stools. If you suspect this may be the case, take your dog to the veterinarian. Many veterinarians recommend such high quality dog foods as NutroMax, Iams, Science Diet, and Nature's Recipe. In addition, a stool sample test and blood test will show if your dog has parasites or an anemic condition. Also, a Kay-Zyme enzyme supplement may help your dog metabolize the nutrients in its food more efficiently.

What Not to Do

Abusive techniques—such as filling holes with the dog's feces or with water and then sticking its head in it—not only make the situation worse, but you could actually drown your dog by doing this. There's also the possibility that the dog may become aggressive, so when you approach it or reach for its collar, it will now growl or bite. Then you have a new and more dangerous problem. This might also cause the dog to start digging up and eating its own feces. At the least, the dog might become so frightened of you that whenever you call the dog it runs and hides or submissively urinates. So:

- Do not punish after the fact
- Do not use pain or corporal punishment
- Do not punish by further isolating the dog out in the yard
- Do not jerk on a choke chain to correct the dog's digging

It is much easier and more humane to teach the dog not to jump up or to be housebroken than it is to keep it isolated in the yard, which contributes to its anxiety, boredom, or "hyperness" and thereby causes the very digging (or nuisance barking and yard escaping) you're trying to cure.

Case Study Postscript

Four weeks after my initial home visit, and following Nell's entrance into my Older Dog Obedience Class, her digging stopped. Her owners further reported that after they had her spayed, she calmed down quite a bit. Case closed.

4

NON-VIOLENT OBEDIENCE TRAINING FOR THE WHOLE FAMILY

"Our neighbor told us we had to put a choke chain on our dog and yank as hard as we could to get her to sit. It seems so cruel. Our puppy is so sweet and trusting, we don't want to ruin her spirit. Isn't there another way?"

"Buster and I 'failed' the obedience class. The instructor asked me to hang Buster in mid-air when he jumped and to jerk his head down with my leg to get him to lie down. I just couldn't bring myself to do it. I called our veterinarian and he recommended we come to you. Can you help us?"

FROM LARRY'S CASE FILES:
"Lucille" the "Reform" School Dropout

FILE # 96-000032
DOG'S NAME: Lucille
BREED: German shepherd
AGE: 4 months
PROBLEM: Dog-trainer-induced fearfulness
and exuberant puppy behavior

In 1996, I went out on a consult regarding a six-month-old German shepherd named Lucille whose owners said she had been abused by a previous dog trainer. Lucille now exhibited fearful and nervous behavior. Her owners had hired a traditional "rock 'em-sock 'em" dog trainer to teach them the basics for their puppy. Like most puppies, Lucille was exuberant, and nipped and jumped. When the trainer walked into the home, Lucille ran up to him enthusiastically. According to the owners, the "trainer" then put a choke chain around her neck and hang her in mid-air to "correct" the jumping and nipping. She squealed, cried and urinated and then ran and hid. In those few seconds, an otherwise trusting, happy puppy was *forever* traumatized. Lucille's owners, aghast at what they saw, demanded the trainer leave. Three weeks later, upon referral from their veterinarian, Lucille's owners called me.

My job was now a lot tougher than it would have been had Lucille not been abused. (See Chapter 17, "How Traditional Training Can Be Harmful to Your Dog," for more details on abusive procedures carried out under the guise of "dog training.") She was now fearful of men, cowered, submissively urinated, and she would duck away when people reached for her head. My first job was to desensitize as much as possible these fearful defensive behaviors Lucille exhibited as a result of her traumatic encounter with Mr. Joe Jerk dog trainer. I outlined a behavior-modification plan, and the owners spent three to four weeks working with it. They reported that Lucille was loosening up and was more like her old self. At that point, we all thought it'd be a good idea for Lucille to enroll in my Puppy Kindergarten Class. This would allow her to be further socialized and learn how to sit, lie down, come, stay, and heel on the leash without being touched or choked. In addition, she'd have the opportunity to play with other dogs in the class. The abusive force-method techniques of "traditional" dog training used on Lucille by the first trainer proved to be totally unnecessary, and had only created behavior problems and fears that were not originally there.

Dog-Training Myths Exposed

> "Therefore to this dog will I,
> tenderly not scornfully,
> render praise and favor."
>
> —ELIZABETH BARRETT BROWNING

Unfortunately, Lucille's story is more common than you might think. Many dog trainers out there still use eighty-year-old military training methods from World War I to train pet dogs without ever questioning the rationale or the appropriateness of those methods. Most force-method trainers subscribe to four myths about dog training:

Myth 1: Only one person should train the dog

Myth 2: The dogs must be more than a year old to learn

Myth 3: You must use a choke chain and pain to train your dog

Myth 4: If you practice at home and in class, your dog will respond
equally well in novel situations and environments

Let's look at these in greater detail.

MYTH 1: ONE DOG, ONE TRAINER

If only one person trains the dog, you create a dog that is responsive to that person and unresponsive to others. Quite often, families come to obedience classes with a dog that listens to one owner, but completely ignores the other members of the family. Questioning reveals that the one who feeds the dog, walks it, reprimands it, and attempts to teach it basic commands is the owner it listens to. The rest of the family is nowhere to be found during this process. Very quickly the dog, like a human teenager, figures out which parent or pack leader is consistent in setting down rules and boundaries, and which parent is not. The dog, like the teen, respects and responds to the consistent limit setter and takes advantage of, or ignores, the inconsistent, non-involved parent. This is why the *whole* family needs to be involved in the dog's training and why use of family therapy techniques is so crucial.

STRUCTURAL FAMILY THERAPY

This analogy of parents, children, dog owners and their dogs can be taken further. Salvador Minuchin, a family therapist, has outlined what he calls Structural Family Therapy, in which he examines the level of involvement and relating that goes on in families between the parents and children and between parent and parent. If the parents are emotionally and physically uninvolved with their children, then the parent-child boundaries in this particular family are too "rigid." On the other hand, if the parent is treating a child like a co-parent, and defers inappropriate authority, or is overly involved with the child emotionally or physically, then the parent-child boundaries are too "enmeshed." The task for Dr. Minuchin, and for family therapists like him, is to reorder extreme boundary situations to help the entire family system operate smoothly.

The same is true of your relationship with the family dog. The dog is affected by everyone in the family and, everyone in the family is affected by the dog. The dog does not live in isolation with one family member. If some family members have boundaries with the dog that are too rigid or distant, the dog will not come to view them as higher members in the pack and will be unresponsive to these family members. If a member of the family is overly enmeshed with the dog, the dog will believe it is equal or higher than this person and it may act dominant and aggressive toward him.

To avoid either of these extremes, *all* family members above the age of seven need to be active in the obedience training of the dog. For children under seven, parents should supervise and guide the child through the command techniques described later in this chapter.

MYTH 2: NO TRAINING UNTIL AGE ONE

The main reason traditional force-method trainers perpetuate the minimum age rule is because they rely on choke chains and physical punishment techniques that can injure or kill a young puppy whose muscles and bones are growing.

Puppies can begin some basic training as young as eight weeks. The key is to recognize the short attention spans of dogs this young and to make the training as game-like and fun as possible. This avoids the risk of injuring or killing the puppy.

PUPPY KINDERGARTEN CLASS

The three main purposes of the Puppy Kindergarten Class I started twelve years ago are: 1) to socialize the puppies while they're in their prime socialization period of twelve weeks through six months of age; 2) to teach some very basic commands (sit, come, lie down, and heel); and 3) to overcome a couple of common problems with puppies, such as chewing and house-soiling. Socialization and basic commands are addressed in this chapter; chewing and house-soiling solutions have already been addressed in Chapters 1 and 2, respectively.

MYTH 3: CHOKE CHAINS AND PAIN

We detail elsewhere why choke chains and other pain-induced learning is unnecessary and potentially harmful. But protesting their use doesn't solve the problem of large, rambunctious puppies that pull hard on the leash or older dogs that drag the owner around like a kite. Fortunately, there are alternative humane anti-pull devices.

FIVE ALTERNATIVES TO THE CHOKE CHAIN

The first two alternative humane anti-pull collars are called the K-9 Pull Control and the 4 Paws Anti-Pull Harness. They are anti-pull body harnesses manufactured by Dog Crazy/Focus in San Diego and 4 Paws Productions Ltd, in Hauppauge, New York. We use it for puppies with mild to moderate pulling problems and older dogs that have no snout. Breeds with "pushed-in" faces like bulldogs, pugs, Pekinese, and so on are very susceptible to breathing problems and need to avoid throat traumas caused by choke chains and some other anti-pull devices. These two may resemble regular harnesses; but they aren't. Two straps come around and in front of the shoulders and connect on top of the dog's back with a pulley system. If the dog starts to lunge ahead, its feet and shoulders are constricted. The dog cannot move or is significantly slowed down. The dog soon learns that the only way to go forward is at a slow, relaxed pace.

The third device we use is the Halti Headcollar, which is made in England. This is for the more dedicated pullers, primarily for older dogs and for those breeds with a fairly well-developed muzzle area. The Halti works very much like a horse's halter, but without any bit for the mouth. It is *not* a muzzle. Unlike the choke chain, you never yank on the leash with the Halti, nor do you ever hear the dog gag. All you do is walk at a steady pace with your hands at your sides and the Halti works by itself. If the dog suddenly pulls ahead, the Halti creates generalized tension around the head without choking the throat. When the dog ceases its tugging, the Halti loosens. As with the first two harnesses, the dog quickly learns what position to be in—the heeling position—to avoid tension.

The fourth alternative, The Gentle Leader, is similar to the Halti and operates on the same principle.

The fifth device, called The Martingale Training Collar, is from Canada and is a collar made of mostly cloth material, with only an inch or so of chain. Owners can use this collar to make a snapping noise with the chain without choking or hurting the dog. We'll revisit heeling later on in this chapter.

MYTH 4: DOGS PERFORM THE SAME ANYWHERE, ANYTIME

Students often complain that their dogs respond to commands poorly when at home (or at the park or at the mall) as compared to their responses in class. This can be overcome once the dog is responding well in familiar territory with few distractions; at that point, the owners need to practice in new areas that are unfamiliar to the dog and that have greater and greater distractions. This creates a dog that will more consistently respond to commands and is why trainers of Seeing Eye dogs take their Labs and shepherds to busy city areas with lots of traffic. The dogs are being prepared to respond to their sight-impaired owners no matter what the setting or distraction level. If you only practice with your dog in your living room or at the obedience class, you are setting you and your dog up for frustration and disappointment when you are placed in new and more distracting environments.

Socialization

Before beginning a training program, you should socialize your dog with people and other safe, vaccinated dogs (see Chapter 18, "Your Dog's Mental Health Needs," for a more in-depth discussion of this). The best time to do this is when your dog is a puppy.

Puppies are in an "approach mode" almost all the time. They are eager to investigate, discover, and explore. A puppy's good experiences during socialization training will make it more likely to be friendly to strange people and dogs as an adult. It is important to protect the puppy from negative experiences with other dogs so it will not develop excessive fears that will be hard to change later.

SOCIALIZING YOUR PUPPY WITH OTHER DOGS

When introducing your puppy to another dog, make sure the other dog is friendly and safe. A friendly dog will have its ears partially back, bow down the front part of its body and wag its tail. If the other dog growls, shows its teeth, or develops a rigid stance with its ears up and tail stiff and high, stay away. Make sure the other dog is properly vaccinated and is under adequate leash control by its owner. It's harder to break up a fight if the dogs are loose.

Introduce the dogs on *neutral* territory rather than on one of the dog's home turf. Let the dogs sniff each other and, if possible, cavort and romp around a bit. Keep the tension on the leashes very loose; dogs that sense tension on the leash may aggressively try to fight the tension and provoke a reaction from the other dog. Don't let the leashes become tangled, however. If that happens, the dogs might panic and become aggressive.

Once a puppy is vaccinated, it is important to introduce it, in fun ways, to a variety of environments and people by going on weekly field trips. This reduces the likelihood of your puppy becoming excessively fearful of people of different sizes, shapes, sexes, colors, and of different settings, such as beaches, mountains, malls, and so on. The more places and people your pup is safely exposed to, the more confident and relaxed it will be when visiting these environments or encountering similar persons down the road.

SOCIALIZING YOUR PUPPY WITH PEOPLE

When your pup meets new people, instruct the person to not stare directly into your puppy's eyes (which it may see as a challenge and threat), to not reach for its head, and to not talk loudly to it. Instead, the stranger should crouch down at an angle from your puppy, avoiding direct eye contact, and extend a hand containing a puppy treat. Allow the puppy to make the first approach. If all goes well, increase the interaction to more direct handling, such as allowing the person to pet the dog gently on its chest.

When you take your puppy to new terrain, bring along a favorite toy or ball and some scrumptious snacks so it is introduced to potentially threatening and unknown places while having fun or eating. The puppy will then make a positive association with these places.

What You'll Need for Training

If you're working in your backyard, some of these things will be right at hand. However, if you're training at a park or other places away from home—as you should as your dog progresses—you need to be prepared. Here's what you'll need:

- **Your dog's regular flat nylon or leather collar.** Test the collar before going out in public. If you can pull the collar over the dog's head and toward and off its nose, it's too loose, and you need to tighten it. However, you should always be able to insert four fingers–width between your dog's throat and its collar. If you can't, it's too tight and you need to loosen it.
- **Your dog's regular walking leash.** It should be four to six feet long, made of nylon or leather, have a loop handle on one end and a buckle

to clasp onto the collar at the other end. Be sure to avoid chain leashes as they can fracture your hand or fingers.

- **A long (twenty- to thirty-foot) lunge-line leash.** Avoid the retractable kind; they can break, jam, or pull out of your hand and hit the dog in the head. And most of them are made with a thin cord that can slit your hand open if the dog lunges while you're holding onto it.

- **Water.** Dogs get thirsty. They wear a warm coat year-round and they can only sweat and breathe through their mouths. So please provide them with plenty of water.

- **Water bowl.** Some dogs will only drink out of their bowl and are not comfortable with lick sticks or bottles.

- **Beach towel or blanket.** This isn't for your comfort. This is used for the "stay" command. It allows you to see right away if the dog has inched its way out of a "stay."

- **Plastic bags or a scooper.** If you're going to a public place, you'll need these to clean up the dog poop.

- **Food treats.** The treats need to be relatively small, no larger than a sugar cube. Some suggestions: doggy beef jerky, Redi freeze-dried liver treats, Ken-L-Ration Pupperroni treats, Scamp liver snaps, cut up pieces of cooked hot dog or string cheese. It is important that there be no crinkling bags or containers during training and that the treats remain out of sight until the dog has earned its "paycheck." If the dog hears crinkly bags, it may become bag-cued and only work for food. Therefore, the treats need to be hidden in pockets or a fanny pack.

The Overall Approach

When setting out to train your dog, it is important to recognize that dogs of different ages have varying degrees of the mental ability and maturity required to obey your commands. (For this reason, I divide my dog-training classes into three levels: Puppy Kindergarten for dogs between twelve weeks and sixth months of age; Older Dog Class for mature dogs with little or no training; and Advanced Training Class for mature dogs with a good foundation of training or that have passed the Older Dog Class.)

Dogs six months and older can be worked harder than puppies. They can be expected to perform longer "stays," quicker "sits" and "comes," and snappier "heels."

In general, younger dogs need to be given more latitude and need more encouragement with voice commands and food treats. Puppies need more frequent breaks from training; you never want to work a puppy for more than ten minutes without a break, whereas a mature dog can handle twenty minutes straight. Where appropriate, throughout this section we will clearly mark which methods should be used for older dogs and which ones should be used for puppies.

Remember, your dog already knows how to sit, lie down, come, and stay on its own. What we are attempting to do in a fun way is to have the dog do these behaviors on your command. One thing that helps us do this is the fact that dogs find praise, petting, and food treats rewarding. We use this to get and keep their attention, to raise their motivation and learning rate, and to guide their bodies into the sit, down, and stay positions. This is called positive reinforcement.

Positive reinforcement is anything added to a person's or dog's environment that will make a particular behavior happen again. For humans, many times we do what we do partly because we receive praise, hugs, kisses, grades, and money. This concept of positive reinforcement also works for our dogs. However, money and grades are not seen as reinforcing by our pets. Praise, petting, and treats are.

Remember a rule of training: It takes three to four weeks of practice to lock in a new behavior and six to eight weeks to extinguish or eliminate an undesirable behavior. Sometimes our dogs don't "get it" right off the bat. They may resist sitting or lying down in the beginning, or the "come" command may have a bad association to it, (especially if someone used the "come" command and then punished or isolated the dog when it came to them). So oftentimes, we must shape, or through baby steps, lead our dog to a final goal behavior. If need be, go in increments and be patient.

Begin training your dog in the order in which these commands appear. Introduce a new command each week while continuing to practice the old ones. After eight weeks, your dog should have the basics down. And one last tip before we begin: Since we rely on food treats early on in training, it helps if the dog is a little hungry. Avoid training sessions just after it has eaten.

PUPPY KINDERGARTEN

I. THE SIT COMMAND

FROM LARRY'S CASE FILES:
"Cassie" the Wiggle-Butt Golden Retriever

FILE # 92-00024-CL
DOG'S NAME: Cassie
BREED: Golden retriever
AGE: 2.2 years
PROBLEM: Won't sit still

In 1992, Cassie, a two-year-old golden retriever, and her family entered my Older Dog Class. Cassie's owners had gotten her from a breeder when she was two months old. She liked everyone but wouldn't sit still and frequently jumped and knocked people over. Her owners had tried on their own to teach her the sit command—the old-fashioned way, by pulling up on a choke chain and pushing down her rear end. However, wiggle-butt Cassie would scoot her back end out from under their hands and would then proceed to jump and pull. It was time to try another way to teach Cassie to sit—a more positive and fun way.

With very few exceptions, owners *need not* touch their dogs to get them to sit, lie down, come, and stay. Hand signals, verbal commands, praise, and treats can accomplish the same results, but without the undue side effects of fear and aggression.

In two weeks, Cassie was sitting with no problem. No excessive wiggle and without force or choke chains. Cassie successfully graduated with the other dogs and performed her sit command with great etiquette.

I'll tell you how it was done.

SITS

Your dog is longer than it is wide or tall. We use this physiological fact to our advantage and create a seesaw or teeter-totter action to get it to sit. With puppies, or if there are other people around, you may want to practice the sit command with your dog on leash. Later, in a secure environment, practice off leash. Here now are the step-by-step instructions for how to get your dog to sit without using brute force.

The Six Steps for Teaching Sit

1. Put the leash loosely around your left wrist and stand in front of your dog.
2. Place a food treat in your right hand and close your fist around it.
3. Make a clicking sound with your tongue, or pat your leg with one hand, and begin walking backward, baiting the dog to come toward you. Keep your closed right hand in front of you, below your waistline, between you and your dog.
4. Stop. Slowly move your right fist from either under your dog's chin or from the tip of its nose in an arch that goes past its eyes, over its head to the back of its skull while saying the word "sit."
5. The dog, either right away or after some practice, will follow the bait hand up with its head, which causes the rear third of its body, including its butt, to hit the ground. It's sitting!
6. Excitedly say, "good sit!" pop the treat from the bait hand into the dog's mouth, and pet your dog. Repeat six times for puppies (under six months) and ten times for older dogs (six months and up). After completing the repetitions, take a water break.

With a treat in your right hand, make a clicking sound and begin walking backward.
Keep your hand below your waist, as shown by Larry and "Yukon."

Stop walking, and begin to move your right fist from the dog's nose, past its eyes, to the back of its head.

The dog will follow the bait hand with its head, causing its rear end to hit the ground.

After the dog is in the sitting position, say "good sit" and reward it.

One of the great things about this method is that you never have to touch your dog to get it to sit. It is so much better for your dog than the traditional method, in which the owner is urged to place his hand on the dog's back and push down while giving the command. This simply won't work for some dogs who, like Cassie, will pop up or wiggle out from under the hand that is pushing.

With our method, the hand gesture must be precise, however, and go back over the dog's head. Some training manuals have tried similar gestures with poor results. A wrong gesture, such as the hand flipping back toward the person training the dog, can induce the dog to jump up or climb on the person. In addition, a hand signal that leaves the hand open allows the dog to see if there is a food treat. This may set up the dog for responding only to food. Some trainers give the hand signal too high above their waist, which might teach the dog to stand on its rear legs to beg, or to jump.

For puppies, do three sets of six sits each day. For older dogs, do three sets of ten sits per day. Do a set in the morning, one in the afternoon or early evening, and one before bed. In the first two weeks, give a treat reward for each sit. Starting the second week, do not have a treat in your hand before the dog sits. Instead, give the "sit" voice command and hand signal, wait until the dog sits, and then reach into your fanny pack, and reward the dog. Starting the third week, give a treat every other sit. Gradually mix it up, so that the dog never knows when it will get a treat for sitting. Increase the praise and petting you give as you decrease the food treats.

Continue to practice sits (and the other commands you'll learn) throughout your dog's life. It keeps your dog sharp and reinforces the notion that the human members of its pack are dominant. Before you or any family member gives your dog any attention (eye contact, petting, letting it in or out, playing, or feeding) make the dog sit first. All social reinforcement is contingent upon a sit.

Also, whenever the dog approaches you in a situation in which it usually starts jumping on you (i.e., arriving home from work), give it the sit command first, *before* it jumps. This trains it to come up to people and sit rather than to come up and jump.

Practice the sit command for at least one week before starting on the lie down command. When you do not give a treat, pet the chest. Each subsequent week after that, gradually phase down the treats to two times out of ten. The dog is now on an intermittent reward schedule which will lock in the behavior. Also around week three, mix up the commands; sometimes only give your pup the sit hand signal. Sometimes only say "sit," and at other times, do both.

Harry, the reluctant Shih Tzu who had refused to lie down.

II. THE LIE DOWN COMMAND

FROM LARRY'S CASE FILES:
"Harry" the Reluctant Shih Tzu

FILE # 96-00012-CL
DOG'S NAME: Harry
BREED: Shih Tzu
AGE: 6 months
PROBLEM: Refuses to lie down

In January 1996, Harry, a six-month-old Shih Tzu, and his owners enrolled in my Older Dog Class. Harry's owners had gotten him from a breeder one month before. They wanted a Shih Tzu because they had had one previously for eighteen years. Other than having been neutered and being treated for a hernia, Harry was in healthy condition. Occasionally, Harry would act shy around strangers. In addition, he would pull on the leash and would not follow general commands. One of the commands Harry chose not to follow was the lie down command.

Harry epitomized the laid-back attitude of a California dog. He'd slowly scan the horizon, look up at the birds, and calmly trot around without a care in the world. However, for three weeks, he refused to lie down in our class. (Why should he? He was already pretty low to the ground.) Finally, during the fourth week of our class, by using our positive-reward techniques, we got Harry to lie down. His owners and I were so happy, we let out cries of joy and praised Harry up and down. Harry graduated with success and aced his lie down command when it counted. Go Harry, go.

Why do many dogs refuse to lie down? What does it mean when they finally do? Why is this command so difficult? How can you get your dog to lie down in five easy steps?

LIE DOWNS

The lie down is often more difficult than the sit for two reasons. First, having your dog lie down places it in a more vulnerable position. This has a psychological effect on the dog, for whom being beneath something means acknowledging weakness and surrendering authority. *Dogs who think they are equal to or higher in the pecking order of the pack than their owner will refuse to lie down.* I have seen a chocolate Labrador growl at its female owner when she attempted to give a lie down command.

Also, some owners have inadvertently spooked their dogs by trying to force their pet to lie down by pushing, pulling, or plastering down the dog, evoking pain. Therefore, lie downs take some time.

The Five Easy Steps To Get Your Dog to Lie Down

1. Bait the dog as you would in the sit command described above.
2. Have it sit. This gets half of its body already down.
3. While keeping the bait hand at its nose, pivot to your left (going backward) with your right foot, ninety degrees, so you are now alongside your dog's right ear and face, off to its side. This allows the dog's front legs to slide out unencumbered. Using your knees as if putting down a heavy box (not bending your back), slowly squat down, while saying the word, "down," or "lie." At the same time, slowly draw your bait hand down in a straight line from your dog's nose, past its chest, to the ground.
4. When your closed-fist bait hand is on the ground, and the dog, still in sitting position, is bent down sniffing it, slowly pull your hand out and in front of the dog, sliding it on the ground, palm down. This will cause the dog to slide forward—and down.
5. When the dog is lying down fully flat, reward it with the treat, praise "good down," and pet the dog. Immediately repeat six times for puppies and ten times for older dogs.

If your dog's rear pops up from the sit position before you complete Step 4, re-sit the dog immediately and break down the exercise into baby steps. First, have the dog merely bow from a sit position while you say "down" and reward it. Get it to bow lower and lower without its rear leaving the ground until it finally slides into a full down. You may want to first practice on a blanket or rug before practicing on hard or cold surfaces.

Puppies and small breeds already low to the ground can present a problem because your bait hand travels very little distance from the dog's

LARRY AND YUKON DEMONSTRATING
LIE DOWNS.

1. Have the dog sit.

2. After pivoting, bait the dog
straight down to the ground.

3. Bend your knees as you bend down with the dog.

4. When the dog is completely down, praise and give it a treat.

nose to the floor. The distance may be so small that the dog won't really notice it and find it necessary to go into a full down. To counter this, place the dog on a bed or high curb and have it sit. Do the regular "down" hand gesture and continue to move your hand past the dog's feet to the floor or ground. This artificially provides you with more distance for your bait hand to travel and to elicit a sliding-into-a-lie-down response from your dog. The dog usually plops down while watching your hand make its way toward the floor.

ADDING LIE DOWNS TO THE HOMEWORK

Continue practicing sits, three sets a day. Take a five-minute break after a series of sit practices before launching into your new lie-down practice. As with sits, do three sets of six lie downs for puppies or three sets of ten for older dogs each day, rewarding each time. A word of caution: Don't try to save time and combine your sit practice with lie-down practice. If you attempt to have your dog sit only in order to get it to lie down, then when you say "sit," it will begin to lie down instead. Wait the five minutes.

Whenever you notice the dog lying down on its own accord, say "good down," and pop it a treat, even if you did not command it to do so. This will help the dog understand what the lie-down body position is.

Start picking different things to have the dog sit and lie down for. For example, before you put the dog's leash on or throw the ball, have it sit. For other activities, such as riding in the car or placing your dog's food bowl on the ground during mealtime, have it lie down.

For the first week of practicing lie downs, tell the dog to sit, pivot to the side, command it to lie down, and reward it. After the first week, continue to pivot to the side and bend down, but give your dog the down command without having it sit first. From now on, the dog is to drop *directly* into a lie down without first sitting. Beginning week three or four, tell the dog to lie down while you remain in an increasingly higher and higher body position, until you can have your dog drop into a down while standing fully erect. You should no longer have to bend down with the dog. And finally, at week four, start skipping the food treats, first to every other time, then to every two times, until you reach two out of ten times, replacing the treat with lavish petting.

III. JUMPING UP

FROM LARRY'S CASE FILES:
"Susan" the Cheerleading Bearded Collie Mix

FILE # 93-636311
DOG'S NAME: Susan
BREED: Bearded collie mix
AGE: 4 years
PROBLEMS: Jumping up

In 1993, I went out on a consultation involving a four-year-old bearded collie mix named Susan that was jumping on people and eating cat feces (not necessarily at the same time). Susan was obtained by her owners from another family when she was two months of age. Her digging may have reflected a long-standing family history of this behavior, because when her owners went to get her, Susan's daddy doggy barked ferociously while her mom was hard at work digging a hole. Like mother like daughter.

When I arrived at the home, Susan's owners reported their lack of success in getting her to stop jumping on visitors. (I always have the dog put away first before I enter the home to bypass this whole event.) Not surprisingly, Susan had attended a traditional force-method obedience class when she was a year old. Her jumping was never successfully treated in that class. The only thing she still remembered to do from the class was sit. Other than having been spayed and having an anal gland removed, Susan was in good health.

I outlined an anti–stool eating program (discussed later in the book) and an anti-jumping program for Susan and her owners. Within a few weeks, her owners reported her jumping was cured and the stool-eating had ceased.

Jumping: The Downside

Allowing a dog to jump up on people can be dangerous. A large dog can easily knock down a child or elderly person. Even a small dog can startle or frighten someone. Many strong, able-bodied people simply don't want your dog jumping on them, scratching their legs, tearing their stockings, or making their pants dirty—no matter how cute you may think your dog is. Owners who allow their dogs to invade someone's personal space without invitation are not being responsible.

Even jumping up on inanimate objects such as furniture has its pitfalls. Besides damaging such items, jumping frequently goes along with overly aggressive nipping and stealing things off the kitchen counter. The misbehavior can spread. Allowing the dog to jump communicates to it that it is equal or superior to you in the pack. This can lead to further challenges to your superiority, which can manifest themselves in behaviors such as growling, humping, and biting.

Excessive jumping can harm the dog physically as well. Repeated sudden stops and starts and Slinky-like jumping creates repetitive stress on your dog's back end and can cause early arthritic conditions and spinal or hip problems.

For all these reasons, you should eliminate jumping from the start. You can start by recognizing why dogs attempt to jump up in the first place.

The Three Main Reasons Dogs Jump

1. **Dogs like to jump up to give facial greetings,** like their wolf ancestors. Dogs have scent glands around their face that give off identification information like the magnetic strip on the back of your American Express card. By simply getting down to the dog's level to greet it, and letting it sniff and lick at that point, you can remove a lot of the dog's incentive to jump.

2. **Dogs jump up on other dogs to assert dominance,** or superior position, in the pack. The dog that is literally on top is politically on top, too.

3. **Dogs jump up because their owners have accidentally rewarded the jumping behavior** by giving the dog inappropriate attention when it jumps. Take the typical owner. She returns home after a day at work. The first thing she does after entering the front door is greet the dog, pet the dog, feed the dog, and let it out or take it for a walk. All the while the dog is flying through the air, hyper and jumping, like Susan, our cheerleading bearded collie. This, in effect, rewards the dog for jumping up through several types of powerful reinforcements: verbal, kinesthetic (touch), food, and freedom—all administered in an intense fifteen- to twenty-minute period.

HOW TO STOP YOUR DOG FROM JUMPING

THE FIFTEEN-MINUTE RULE

Owners must switch their response and only reward quiet all-four-paws-on-the-floor behavior. As soon as you come home, ignore the dog for the first fifteen minutes. If your dog jumps, use the Startle-Redirect-Reward technique and squirt it with water, shake the penny can or press the ultrasonic device. Continue to wait out the fifteen minutes. Then and only then, when the dog is quiet and calm, start lavishing it with attention, petting, feeding, and walking. The dog quickly learns that if it greets you calmly, without jumping up, it will receive your attention and affection sooner.

BEAT 'EM WITH A SIT

Another highly effective, preventative technique is one I've dubbed "beat 'em with a sit." Follow the sit command instructions given earlier in the chapter. Get to the point where you are doing three sets of sits, ten repetitions each, for a couple of weeks. When you and your dog have mastered that you're ready to practice this technique.

Whenever your dog approaches you or any other member of the family, immediately give it the sit command with the hand signal. This will back the dog away from you and position it in a sit. Reward with a treat and verbally praise, "good sit." Do this every time your dog approaches you *before it gets a chance to jump*. This will teach your dog to come up to you and sit instead of coming up to you and jumping.

REMOVE ALL ACCIDENTAL REWARDS FOR JUMPING

Remove all play or rough-housing that induces jumping up. Instigating the dog to jump through play and love will counteract your attempts to get the dog to stop jumping up on people and furniture. For every step forward you take with disciplining the dog for inappropriate jumping, you take two steps back with play-induced jumping. You're sending a mixed message.

Lap dogs should be taught to walk into your lap while you are sitting or reclining on the floor. Or, if you're sitting in a chair or sofa, have the dog sit first, then pat your lap and say, "up." The dog is then allowed to jump up.

S-R-R

If a dog jumps up without the up command, it is disciplined using the S-R-R technique. In the act of jumping, tell the dog "off!" or "phooey!" and startle it by blasting it in the face with water, shaking a soda can of pennies, depressing an ultrasonic device, or depressing an air horn. After waiting five minutes, redirect the dog to the sit position—*without* giving it a reward. Being repeatedly startled in the act will make your dog associate jumping up with a negative feeling and it will cease doing so. Remember, it is important to use a specific discipline word when you use your startle device so that the dog begins to make an association between the word and the device. Before long it will react to the word alone, allowing you to stop using the device. Two to four weeks of startling the jumping behavior, giving consistent rewards for good behavior, and removing all accidental rewards should eliminate the jumping.

WHAT NOT TO DO

Do not knee your dog in the chest to stop it from jumping! Do not step on its rear feet. This commonly recommended technique could crush or fracture its feet. Do not reach for a choke chain and hang your dog. Do not push your dog or strike it in any way. You may inadvertently hurt your dog or traumatize it to the extent that it will never trust you again.

Of course, much depends on your lifestyle. If you don't mind your dog jumping up on everything and everyone all the time, no matter how you are dressed or undressed, then removing the behavior problem of jumping up won't be a priority for you. Just warn your guests.

However, by allowing the dog to jump up on Monday and Wednesday, but not on Tuesday or Thursday; or by allowing the dog to jump on you when you are in your jeans, but not in your three-piece suit; or by allowing your dog to jump on the green chair but not on the blue chair; or by allowing your dog to jump up on Uncle John and Aunt Mary, but not on Uncle Fritz or Auntie Ann, you are locking in the jumping behavior and confusing the heck out of your dog. Intermittent reinforcement or once-in-a-while rewards are strong enough to lock in any compulsive behavior, be it gambling or your dog, jumping. Allowing your dog to jump sometimes, on some people, at some locations, is enough to lock in that misbehavior for life. It also does little for your dog's psyche, creating mass confusion in its attempts to figure out any consistency in the house rules.

BASIC OBEDIENCE FOR OLDER DOGS

I. COME-WHEN-CALLED COMMAND

FROM LARRY'S CASE FILES:
"Ellie" the American Gladiator Pomeranian

FILE # 97-000419
DOG'S NAME: Ellie
BREED: Pomeranian
AGE: 4 months
PROBLEM: Not coming when called

In 1997, I went out on a consult involving a four-month-old Pomeranian named Ellie that would not come to her owner when called. This was very frustrating for Ellie's owner, who was a senior citizen. She needed to have Ellie come to her without hesitation to avoid danger. Since Ellie had no fear and was truly a canine American Gladiator (proud, puffed-out chest and all), it was crucial we teach her to come on command.

In taking her history, I learned that Ellie's owner had gotten her at five weeks of age from a family. She chose Ellie because her daughter also had a Pomeranian and because she wanted a small dog (see Chapter 20, "Matching Your Personality with the Right Dog," for detailed information on which dog might be right for you). Ellie had no history of illness or surgery, and she was friendly to all. Her problem was that she would dash off, frequently toward a street, putting herself in danger of being hit by a car. We needed to fix this right away. I worked with Ellie and her owner, first on the come command at home and later in class on general obedience. Ellie ended up being the fastest and best come-command dog in the whole class. Victory for the Gladiator!

WHY DOGS MAY NOT COME

Dogs love to explore. They love to chase and be chased. Fast-moving objects and alluring sounds catch their attention. If older dogs have not had a history of being told to come for negative results (they were punished, for example), they react similarly. We use these traits to our advantage when we teach them to come to us on command. Older dogs may have to be reconditioned to like the word "come" if they have already made a negative association with it. Training our dogs frequently involves not only adding something new and desired, but removing something old and undesirable so that the dog can learn a new command.

You can unintentionally instill a bad association with the word "come" by not adhering to the following rules:

Four Things Not To Do
1. Do not call your dog to come for punishment.
2. Do not call your dog to come for grooming or medical procedures.
3. Do not call your dog to come so you can isolate it somewhere it doesn't want to be.
4. Do not call your dog to come from the shade into the sun, especially on hot days.

Get in the habit of calling your dog to come for its food, to play, to come in, to go for a ride, and so on. If you have to get your dog from point A to point B for a potentially traumatic situation, have it sit, give it a treat, attach its leash, and walk it or heel it there.

FOUR NATURAL BEHAVIORS IN TEACHING THE COME COMMAND

There are several techniques you can use to get your dog to come to you on command. All of the techniques rely on the following guidelines:

- Be in motion with the dog. This provides a more alluring target to chase.
- Make unique, friendly, and alluring sounds to trigger and maintain the dog's attention.
- Do not pull or yank the dog's leash when practicing.
- When the dog begins to come toward you, drop down or squat and extend your bait hand with the treat.

For the first week or two, reward the dog for merely coming. Do not add on the sit command until week three of practice.

THE SIX COME-COMMAND TRAINING TECHNIQUES

Good-Bye Comes

Good-bye comes are a fun way to introduce the come concept to puppies because puppies love to chase and be chased. Instead of letting them grab our underwear and then chasing them, however, we grab their "underwear," and they chase us. This exercise takes two people.

1. The two people stand together with the puppy. One person holds the leash.

2. The second person pets the dog and says "good-bye," and runs twenty to fifty feet away, stomping loudly. This will trigger the pup's tendency to chase. But that urge is temporarily frustrated by the person holding the leash.

3. The second person stops, turns around, squats down, and gestures with a closed fist using a come-to-me movement to his or her chest, while calling out the dog's name and the come command: "Bruno, come!"

4. The first person relaxes the leash and jogs behind the puppy when it runs to the second person.

5. When the dog arrives, the person who called the dog rewards the dog by saying, "good come," and gives it a treat. Repeat this six times and practice it three times a day.

Warm-Up Comes

Warm-up comes are for mature dogs, especially those that have repeatedly been called to come for traumatic events and do not want to come. The idea is to teach the older dog that the word "come" is indeed a good and positive word, and to prepare it to come more reliably. A word of warning: This procedure makes no sense to humans since no one, including the dog, is moving. This is just to condition the dog to like the word "come." Here's what you do:

1. Have the dog sit in front of you.

2. Place the leash loop around your left wrist and have a supply of treats in that hand.

3. With your right hand, make a fist. Gesture your right arm out and then hinge it back to your chest (or beltline if your dog has a propensity to jump up)—using the come-to-me hand signal. At the same time, say your

dog's name and the come command: "Bruno, come!" Reach with your right hand into your left hand and give your dog a treat. Repeat ten times in a row, at a rapid pace. Take just long enough between commands for your dog to chew and for you to reload.

4. If the dog moves or gets up from its sit position during this procedure, re-sit the dog and continue. Do three sets of ten a day, coupled with the long-line solo come exercise described below, and your dog will soon associate a positive experience with the come command.

Long-Line Solo Comes

These are for both puppies and older dogs. The purpose of long-line solo comes is to create a realistic scenario of the dog getting away from you. It will teach your dog to come back to you from a long distance.

When practicing these, it is important to remember to *not* yank the leash (because when your dog gets away from you it usually has no leash to yank); to give the dog a moving target (yourself); to use a friendly and unique tone of voice; and to squat low to the ground with your closed bait hand extended. The lower you get, the more of a doggy magnet you are. The higher you are, the more threatening you appear. Then, do the following:

1. Put the dog on a twenty- to thirty-foot leash.

Call the dog to come and move back, using the come hand sign without pulling the leash.

2. Hold the leash and let the dog wander off. (It's artificial and contrived to first put the dog into a stay position and then call it to come, since most real-life situations in which you need the come command involve the dog galloping away from you showing you its rear end.)

3. Wait for the dog to be distracted and almost at the end of the leash and *not* looking at you. Without pulling or tugging the leash, excitedly and loudly call your dog to come, "Bruno, come," and begin moving quickly backward. As the dog responds, keep moving until the dog is just about to reach you, then squat down, extend your closed-fist bait hand and reward the dog for coming with praise and a treat.

For puppies, repeat six times in a row, three sets a day. For the older dog, repeat ten times in a row, three sets a day. Give treats each time.

If, after two or three weeks of practice, the dog ignores you after being issued two commands to come, try depressing a hand-held air horn behind your back and yelling "No!" to startle and interrupt the ignoring behavior, and reissue the command. Or you can gradually and gently begin reeling in the dog with the long line, while continuing to back up and call it until the dog comes to you.

As the dog begins to chase you, stop, squat down, and give the come hand signal again.

Once the dog arrives, give it the sit command.

Once the dog sits, praise and treat it.

With continued practice and success, you can put the dog on increasingly lighter and longer lines to better simulate the dog being completely off leash. Also, you can practice this same technique, without the leash, in an enclosed, safe area. Practice with the leash attached to its anti-pull harness if your dog wears one on its walks.

Run Away Comes

This is a variation of the long-line solo comes. Put the dog on the twenty- to thirty-foot long line (or two long lines hooked together). Wait until the dog is at least twenty feet away. With enough slack on the leash so you don't yank on it, turn your back on your dog and begin running away. As you run, call your dog to come, "Bruno, come!" and keep running until the dog is about to reach your legs. Then bend down and reward the dog for coming without telling it to sit. The faster you run, the better your dog's come response will be. Remember what we mentioned above: Dogs like to chase and be chased and will run after fast-moving objects.

Doggy Volleyball Comes

This is a variation on the good-bye come, and the long-line solo come, and works for puppies and older dogs. Here's what you do:

1. Put the dog on its long line. You and an accomplice stand twenty to thirty feet apart, each with treats in your pockets. You hold the leash. Your partner squats down and calls the dog to come and uses the closed-fist hand signal.

2. When the dog comes, your partner rewards it with praise, petting, and a treat, and then stands up and ignores the dog.

3. At that moment, you bend down and call the dog to come. When it does, reward it likewise.

4. Repeat back and forth ten times, getting the dog to go back and forth between you—like a volleyball. You'll find the dog is soon enjoying the game, anticipating the command and volleying itself back and forth.

Do this once a day, six repetitions for the puppy, ten for the older dog, with a treat each time.

Hide-and-Seek Comes

This technique is especially helpful in incorporating children into the training of your dog and strengthening their bond with the dog.

1. When the dog is in the house or outside in the yard with the family, a member of the family slips away unnoticed by the dog and hides.

2. The family member calls out, "Bruno, come find me! Bruno, come!" When the dog successfully locates the hiding family member, it is rewarded with praise and treats. Family members can take turns being the person who hides.

If you're following my seven-week plan (see chart at the end of the chapter), in the third week your practice schedule should look like this:

- Continue with sit repetitions. Treat *every other* repetition. Pet and praise when not issuing a treat. Only reach for the treat after the dog sits. Mix up your commands: Give hand signals only, verbal commands only, and then both together. Have dog sit before giving it any attention.
- Continue with lie-down repetitions. Treat each time. Reward the dog when it lies down on its own, saying, "good down." The dog should now be dropping directly into the lie-down position without having to sit first. Only reach for the treat after it lies down. Start working on being taller and taller when you give the command.
- Start the new come commands. For puppies, do the good-bye comes and long-line solo comes, three sets of six a day, with a treat for each repetition.
- For older dogs, do the warm-up comes and the long-line solo comes, three sets of ten a day, with a treat for each repetition. Choose between the volleyball and hide-and-seek methods as optional practice for puppies or older dogs.

II. THE HEEL COMMAND

FROM LARRY'S CASE FILES:
"Midnight" the Black Labrador Who Took His
Owner Water Skiing on Asphalt

FILE # 96-000291-CL
DOG'S NAME: Midnight
BREED: Labrador retriever
AGE: 1.5 years
PROBLEM: Pulling on the leash

In April of 1996 Midnight, a year-and-a-half old Labrador, and his owner joined my Older Dog Class. When they arrived, Midnight had his six-foot-six, 200-pound owner practically flying in the air like a kite! Midnight liked dragging his owner down the street while gagging on his choke chain and slingshotting mucus, phlegm, and saliva on storefront windows. Smoke would be coming from Midnight's owner's shoes and his right arm seemed a few inches longer then his left. This had to stop.

Midnight was obtained from a breeder when he was eight weeks old and was a healthy dog. He was friendly toward people and dogs, and his owner could remove bones or food from him without a problem. His biggest problem was being uncontrollably wild when taken for a walk—even on his choke chain. Midnight desperately needed to learn the heel, or "no pull" command.

After reviewing the sit command, I instructed Midnight's owner and the other students how to use the Halti headcollar, a humane alternative to the choke chain. Within twenty minutes, Midnight was heeling at his owner's side, without pulling or gagging.

WHY CHOKE CHAINS ARE HARMFUL
—AND DON'T WORK

As you may have gathered, in teaching thousands of dogs and their owners throughout Southern California, I have never and will never use choke chains or prong collars. They are barbaric and antiquated, especially given the following:

1. Dogs still pull on the choke chain, even at the discomfort of gagging themselves (witness Midnight and his flying owner!).

2. Children and elderly people can be pulled off their feet by holding onto a dog on a choke chain.

3. Dogs still have six to ten feet of lunging ability and can attack when on a choke chain.

4. Choke chains can become "discriminative stimulus," which means the dog will tend to respond *only* when the choker is on and will completely ignore you when it is off.

5. Yanking too forcefully, or too frequently, high up under the jaw with a choke chain can damage the auditory nerves leading to a dog's ears and gradually deafen it.

6. Frequently, a dog develops a head shyness–fear aggression response after repeated painful choking episodes. It retreats, growls, or snaps whenever someone reaches for its choke chain or head (another example of how antiquated force-method training can create behavior problems that were not there to begin with).

Thanks to modern technology, there now exists the alternative anti-pull devices mentioned in the beginning of this training chapter. Before you begin teaching your dog to heel, you must assess how much your dog naturally pulls on the leash when you walk it. That will determine whether you'll need an anti-pull device, and if so, what kind.

Many young puppies do not have a significant pulling problem, and if you merely walk at a steady pace with both hands on the leash and your hands at your sides, the dog tends to stay alongside you. Why fix what's not broken?

But some dogs constantly pull on the leash and take their owners water-skiing on asphalt. Other dogs tend to walk along fine and then suddenly dart in an unanticipated direction, taking their owner's arm with them. And some dogs constantly zigzag in front of or behind their owner, frequently causing the owner to trip over the dog or step on it.

If you have a dog that exhibits one of these pulling problems, you need to begin the heeling exercises by fitting it with a special collar. The K-9 Pull Control, 4 Paws Anti-Pull Harness, and Martingale Training Collar, seem to work best on puppies that pull mildly to moderately and on older dogs with "pushed-in" faces. The Halti Headcollar and Gentle Leader Promise Halter seem to work best on larger dogs and dogs that pull severely. For dogs without a pulling problem, practice heeling without any anti-pull collar.

Remember, you do not need to make your family pet heel like it is an obedience trial champion. Heeling for family pets should be defined as when the dog is walking at your pace with its shoulder even with your knee and heel. It doesn't really matter whether the dog heels on your left or on your right. (It only mattered in the days when dogs frequently accompanied equestrians.) As long as you practice on the same side all the time and do not let the dog lag behind or pull ahead, that's what counts.

HEELING WITHOUT AN ANTI-PULL DEVICE

If your dog will be heeling on the left, securely place your left hand about twelve inches up the leash from the buckle on the collar. The loop of the leash, and the rest of the leash, will be around your right hand. Your right hand will be the hand giving the hand signals and reaching for treats. Your left hand does not let go of the leash. Simply reverse the hand positions if you plan to heel your dog on your right side. (This leash-holding instruction also applies when you use an anti-pull collar.)

Next, have your dog sit on your heeling side by giving it a verbal command, "sit," and the appropriate sit hand signal. Reward the dog with a treat and praise, "good sit." Say "heel" in a firm but friendly voice and begin to move forward with the leg that's closest to the dog, without yanking the leash. Keep your hands at your sides, your head up, look straight ahead, and say to the dog "good heel" as you walk. The dog should be alongside your leg, heel and knee.

Every thirty steps, give the sit command, reward the dog for sitting and give the heel command again. Continue this heeling, stopping and heeling routine for twenty-five minutes, twice a day.

If your dog pulls away from you during these walks, you need to consider an anti-pull device.

HEELING WITH THE K-9 PULL CONTROL, 4 PAWS ANTI-PULL HARNESS, OR MARTINGALE TRAINING COLLAR

The first step is in using the K-9 Pull Control, 4 Paws Anti-Pull Harness, or Martingale Training Collar is to get the right size. Make sure the personnel at the pet shop size your dog's neck for the Martingale collar. For the K-9

Pull Control, if your dog is twenty pounds or lighter, you will probably need a small; twenty to fifty pounds a medium; fifty to ninety pounds a large; and above ninety pounds extra large—although I have my doubts about how effective the K-9 Pull control or the Martingale collar would be with a dog that large. In classes, I use the K-9 Pull Control or Martingale collar primarily for smaller dogs, or dogs with a less severe pulling problem.

The first day with the device, just put it on your dog while you're home and let it get used to it. For the K-9 Pull Control, make sure the straps around the front shoulders are loose enough for you to insert your hand between the strap and your dog's limb. It should be loose enough so that it doesn't cut into your dog's armpit, but snug enough so the strap doesn't droop down your dog's leg, causing it to trip. Encourage the dog to walk around the house. Play the dog's favorite games. Do not leave the dog unattended with either device on; it may chew up the K-9 Pull Control or get the inch of chain on the Martingale collar caught on an object.

Beginning on the second day, take the dog out twice a day for twenty-five-minute walks with the device on. Follow the steps in the previous section.

From now on, *never* take the dog out for a walk without its anti-pull harness. Each time you do, you set yourself back two weeks because the dog is inadvertently rewarded for pulling.

With both the K-9 Pull Control and the Martingale collar, keep both hands at your sides and walk at a brisk pace, sitting your dog every thirty steps, and then popping the treat. When you resume walking, give your dog the command to heel, make a clicking sound with your tongue and begin walking. With the K-9 Pull Control harness or the 4 Paws Anti-Pull Harness, if the dog pulls ahead, the shoulder straps will tighten. Your dog will slow down. With the Martingale collar, if the dog starts pulling ahead, make a snapping sound with the leash and chain (it won't be able to choke your dog) and say "No!" Have the dog sit, wait five minutes and then resume your walk.

HEELING WITH THE HALTI OR GENTLE LEADER

The Halti Headcollar and Gentle Leader resemble a horse's halter, minus the bit. Both are designed so the owner can control the dog without having to yank on the leash. The dog has no room to lunge and elderly family members and children can walk sizable dogs that are wearing it. However, the Halti and Gentle Leader take more getting used to for most dogs, so there is a warm-up program before you begin.

Again, with either of these collars it's important to get the correct size. This is easier with the Halti because the sizes are broken down into more specific categories. The Gentle Leader comes in three basic sizes: small, medium, and large, with an adjustable plastic slider to fit around the dog's muzzle.

The Halti comes in four commonly used sizes. Cocker spaniels, miniature poodles, beagles, and dogs with similarly sized heads take a Size 1. Brittany spaniels, collies, boxers, Dobermans, and Australian shepherds, a Size 2. Labrador retrievers, German shepherds, Rottweilers, and pit bulls, a Size 3. Irish wolfhounds, St. Bernards, Newfoundlands, great Pyrenees, or great Danes, a Size 4.

In the first week, do the following warm-up exercises each day to get your dog acclimated to the Halti or Gentle Leader being near and on its face. Do these exercises one right after the other.

Halti and Gentle Leader Preparation Exercises

1. Take one of the Halti (or Gentle Leader) straps and *lightly* tap your dog's nose with it with one hand, while popping a treat into its mouth with the other. Do this ten times.

2. Lightly rub your dog's nose with one of the Halti straps with one hand while giving it a treat with the other. Do this ten times.

3. Hold the Halti from the nose loop, so it hangs naturally in one hand, and stick your other hand through it with a treat. When the dog takes the treat, completely slide the Halti up on your dog's muzzle, halfway between the tip of its nose and its eyes, and then slide it right off. Do this ten times.

4. Put the Halti on the dog, clasp it closed behind its neck, and play your dog's favorite game for ten minutes.

Also, during this week, feed your dog only when you put the Halti on it.

During this first week, do not attempt to walk your dog with the Halti on, or even attach the leash to the dog while it has the Halti on. Through the warm-up exercises, your dog should begin to develop a positive association with wearing the Halti and become primed for actually heeling with it on.

After one week of this warm-up, you are ready to begin. Repeat warm-up exercises 1 through 4, but reduce the number of repetitions to six for each exercise.

HALTI WARM-UPS

Warm Up #1: Tap nose with Halti strap and give treat.

Warm Up #2: Rub nose lightly with the strap and give treat.

Give treats.

Warm Up #3: Give treat and slide Halti loop on the nose.

Give another treat and then slide Halti off nose.

Warm Up #4: Put Halti on muzzle.

Tuck one fastening strap under and through regular neck collar.

Clip the two fastening straps together behind the neck.

Gently pull down the lowest ring of the Halti.

Hook leash onto the lowest ring and make sure dog can open mouth to full yawning position.

Important Safety Tip for Securing the Halti or Gentle Leader

Keep your dog's regular collar on. Before you secure the seat belt–like Halti straps that attach behind the dog's head, tuck the loose end of the Halti— the end you're going to plug into—under and through your dog's regular collar. Then attach the Halti straps as the directions dictate and tighten the Halti. Running the Halti (or Gentle Leader) straps through the regular collar will prevent the dog from escaping if it manages to paw the Halti off the top of its head, because the Halti—and therefore the leash—will still be attached to the collar. This is preferable to hooking the leash through the Halti and regular collar rings. That tends to artificially loosen the Halti or Gentle Leader, thereby making it easier for the dog to either slip or paw out of the nose part of the device.

The Halti should be tight enough so it cannot come off the nose or slide into your dog's eyes. However, it should be loose enough so that your dog can open its mouth to full yawning position so it can breathe—and bark! The leash is attached to the bottom-most ring of the Halti. Now you're ready to walk.

Heeling with the Halti or Gentle Leader

1. Position your dog on whichever side you want it to learn to heel on. That same-side hand clamps down tightly, four to six inches up the leash from the dog's head, with the arm relaxed at your side. The rest of the leash and the loop handle are around the opposite-side hand.

2. Have the dog sit and give it a treat.

3. Say "heel" and begin walking, repeating "good heel" as the dog walks by your side. Walk at a steady pace, allowing enough leash so the Halti is not unduly tight if the dog is not pulling on it, but not so loose that the dog can bow its head down and paw the Halti off its nose. Walk at a mild to brisk pace for at least twenty minutes so the dog can get used to it.

4. If your dog resists the Halti in a frantic bucking manner, walk a few steps, stop and have it sit before it begins to protest. Reward the sits and increase your steps gradually between each sit.

5. Walk the dog twice a day for twenty-five minutes, always with the Halti on.

Give the dog lots of treats when putting the Halti on and taking it off. Continue to feed the dog only when the Halti is on. Do a third of your entire dog's sits, comes, downs, and stays with the Halti on.

HALTI OR GENTLE LEADER WEAN-OFF

Your dog becomes a candidate to be weaned off the Halti if it begins to heel without struggling against the Halti and demonstrates after a period of time that it has no aggression problem toward other dogs or people. If at any time the dog regresses by pulling during walks, go back to the Halti.

Your dog may be ready to wean off the Halti as soon as six to eight weeks or as long as a couple of years, or you may just enjoy the hassle-free experience of walking your dog with the Halti and not care to put in the extra work to wean it off. Whatever suits you is fine. Look out for uninformed choke chain enthusiasts who comment on the aesthetic appearance of the Halti and how you should use a choker and jerk your dog. Ignore them.

There are four wean-off steps:

1. For the first week, walk the dog with the Halti and leash fully attached. The dog should be perfect on it, never jerking, never pulling.

Larry and Yukon demonstrating heeling with Halti headcollar.

2. In the second week, walk the dog with the Halti on, but attach the leash to its regular collar. Give the same commands, walk at the same pace, hands in the same position, and leash relaxed.

3. In the third week, slip the nose part of the Halti off, but keep it attached around your dog's neck, with the leash attached to its regular collar. Same commands, signals and pace.

4. In the fourth and last week, take the Halti completely off the dog, and walk the dog with the leash attached to its regular collar.

If at any point during this four-week transition program the dog begins to pull again, go back to the previous step for at least two weeks before trying it again.

III. THE STAY COMMAND

FROM LARRY'S CASE FILES:
"Daisy" and "Jones" the Door-Bolting Poodles

FILE # 97-000592
DOGS' NAMES: Daisy and Jones
BREED: Standard poodles
AGES: 1.5 years
PROBLEM: Bolting out the front door

In July of 1997, I went out on a consult involving a pair of standard poodles, Daisy and Jones. These dogs were familiar to me. During a consult in 1996, we concentrated on getting the dogs to pay more attention to the owners without distracting one another. We also outlined a come-command program. Later, Daisy and Jones's owners took them both through my Older Dog Class, partially to desensitize them to other dogs and also to add distractions to their training.

In the summer of 1997, I received a call from the owners stating that Daisy and Jones were not following the "stay" command and were bolting out the front door whenever it was opened. This was dangerous for the unsuspecting UPS carrier and for the two dogs, who were in danger of being hit by a passing motorist.

I went out to the home for a second visit and outlined the following stay command program and applied it particularly to situations involving the front door. By the end of my hour visit, Daisy and Jones were no longer trying to bolt out the door.

Three months later, I followed up with a phone call. The wife reported the dogs were doing well and instead of trying to bolt out of the door whenever it opened, they would either stay or run into the kitchen. Case Closed.

PROBLEMS WITH STAYS

When starting to teach the stay command, many people make a common mistake. They try to get their dog to remain still longer than it is capable of. The dog repeatedly gets up. The owner gets mad. The dog gets frustrated. And the dog learns that stays stink! To avoid this, you must start out with very short stays and work your way up.

Stays should not be strictly expected out of puppies less than six months old because of their low attention spans. With puppies, we shoot for a two-minute stay after four or five weeks of practice.

Daisy and Jones, the door-bolting poodles, are now reformed.

With dogs six months and older there can be a different problem. As with the down command, if your dog has come to believe it is equal or higher than you in the pecking order of the pack, it will refuse to stay. Stays force the dog into prolonged compliance and demand great attention and self-control. For this reason, we like older dogs to do lots of lie downs and long stays. With older dogs, we ultimately expect a thirty-minute stay.

The stay hand signal is the only hand signal in our approach that is not a fist. Rather, it involves thrusting your hand straight out from your body, toward the dog, with the palm facing out. Until the dog locks in the concept of the command, keep your hand signal up during the length of the stay and repeat the command "stay" over and over.

STAYS—THE FIRST WEEK

1. Put a short leash on the dog. Put the loop handle around your left wrist and have a handful of treats in your left hand.

2. Have your dog sit in front of you by giving it the sit command with your right hand.

3. Open your right hand into the signal described above and say "stay."

4. Almost at the same instant you give the command, take a quick quarter-step to your right, and then immediately step right back to your dog before it has a chance to move.

5. If the dog has remained in the sit, say "good stay," reach into your left hand for a treat and give the dog the treat with your right hand.

6. Immediately, as the dog is chewing the treat for the previous stay, open your right hand again and give the "stay" command.

7. Keep your right hand open and up as you take another quick quarter step to the right and return to the dog before it gets a chance to move. Reward again. Repeat six to eight times for puppies, and ten to fifteen times for an older dog. Do this once a day, three days in a row.

The idea is to have such a short stay—about one second—that the dog does not have the opportunity to blow it. It learns that when you say "stay" and give the hand signal it will get a treat for just sitting there. A key here in the early stage is to move quickly away no more than a small step and then quickly back. Moving any farther, any slower, will entice the dog to follow you and blow the stay.

Larry demonstrating the stay hand signal with Yukon.

Increasing the Distance

Beginning the fourth day of the first week, begin to increase the distance. Take two small steps away from the dog, this time at a forty-five-degree angle from it, and return quickly before it can move away. On the fifth day, take three steps, on the sixth day, four or five steps. At the end of the first week, you should be able to get to the end of the short leash and immediately back to the dog without the dog getting up and following you. If you don't reach this point by the end of the first week of practicing stays, practice for one more week and achieve successful results before moving on.

STAYS—THE SECOND WEEK

Increasing the Time

Once you have established some distance, you will try to get the dog to stay for increasingly longer periods of time.

1. Have the dog sit.

2. Go to the end of the short leash, put your hand up in the stay command, and repeatedly say "stay, stay, stay. . . ." Do this for ten seconds for a puppy and fifteen seconds for an older dog.

3. If the dog stays, walk back to it and reward with "good stay" and three treats, given one at a time.

4. Repeat Step 2 but increase the time to twenty seconds for a puppy, thirty seconds for an older dog.

5. If the dog stays, reward it with a "good stay" and four treats. The longer the dog stays, the more treats it will get. Add one treat for each additional timed period. If the dog attempts to get up, say "no" and place the dog back in its original spot and start over with the last successful timed interval.

6. Continue the session. Raise the time period by ten seconds for a puppy, concluding with a thirty-second stay. For an older dog, increase by fifteen-second intervals until it achieves a one-minute stay.

During the second week of stay practice, add ten seconds a day to each stay for puppies, so that when you reach week three you're up to a two-minute stay. With an older dog, once you reach a full one-minute stay increase the stay by one minute each day for the rest of the week.

Stays—The Third Week and Beyond

Starting the third week of practicing stays, begin increasing your distance from the dog by using the long line instead of the short leash. Continue to increase the duration of the stays.

By the third week of practicing stays with an older dog, you should be integrating the stay command into your heeling walks, which we will discuss a little later.

Corrections

As the stays increase in duration, the dogs can either sit or lie down, or begin from a sit position and slide down into a down position. The only thing the dogs can't do, once you begin timing them, is get up and walk away. If your dog tries that, say "no," go back to it, gently place it *exactly* where it started, and begin again at the last successful timed point. You may have to repeatedly put it back and start over until the dog figures out that "If I keep getting up, we're going to start all over again, and I'll be here all week. I might as well settle in for the duration and do it." Then you have it.

Do not call your dog to come to you out of a stay command until the dog has achieved a solid fifteen-minute stay. If you do, the dog will begin to anticipate the come command sooner and sooner, and will break its stay sooner and sooner.

Puppy owners should shoot for a five-minute stay by the end of seven weeks. For dogs six months and older, the goal is a half-hour stay. Older dogs have greater attention spans and are capable of even longer stays.

After your dog achieves a stay command (for a minimum of fifteen minutes), start practicing at new locations. This way, your dog learns to respond with distractions and in novel locations. This helps you to avoid one of the pitfalls in Myth No. 4 of traditional dog training: If you practice at home and at the class site, the dog will respond equally well in all situations and environments.

Working on these obedience commands each day over eight weeks should produce a happy, well-trained family pet. Practice, however, should continue throughout the dog's life.

Working on obedience commands, it must be noted, is totally *distinct* from working on behavior problems. Practicing obedience commands generally addresses the dog's *voluntary* movements and makes the dog a "good mechanic" in responding. Behavior problems generally involve emotional attitudes and involuntary or spontaneous behaviors, such as aggressiveness, jumping, barking, and destruction of property. Those types of problems are handled much differently.

Puppy Kindergarten Class

(Throughout this practice program, whether you give a treat or not, always pet and praise the behavior and notice it when the dog does it on its own.)

Week 1
- Sits: 3 sets of 6 per day, treat each time
- Comes: good-bye comes and long-line solo comes, 3 sets of 6 per day, treat each time
- Practice anti-jumping: the 15-minute rule, "beat 'em with a sit," and S-R-R after the fact

Week 2
- Sits: 3 sets of 6 per day, treat each time
- Downs: 3 sets of 6 per day, treat each time
- Comes: 3 sets of 6 per day, treat each time
- Practice anti-jumping

Week 3
- Sits: 3 sets of 6 per day, treat every other time; treat stays in pouch until command is done
- Downs: 3 sets of 6 per day, treat each time; treat stays in pouch until command is done
- Comes: 3 sets of 6 per day, treat each time; add run-away comes
- Stays: 2 sets of 6 per day; get to end of short leash by end of week
- Practice anti-jumping

Week 4
- Sits: 3 sets of 6 per day, treat every third time
- Downs: 3 sets of 6 per day, treat every other time; dog goes straight down without sitting
- Comes: 3 sets of 6 per day, treat each time; add doggy volleyball comes; practice in one new location every week

- Stays: start timing at end of a short leash, and shoot for one full minute
- Practice anti-jumping

Week 5
- Sits: 3 sets of 6 per day, treat every fourth time
- Downs: 3 sets of 6 per day, treat every third time; dog drops straight down without sitting; owner standing fully upright
- Comes: 3 sets of 6 per day, treat each time; add hide-and-seek comes
- Stays: work up to 5-minute stay, treat each time
- Heeling: twice a day for 25 minutes; sit every 30 steps, treat each time
- Practice anti-jumping

Week 6
- Sits: 3 sets of 6 per day, treat every 2 out of 10
- Downs: 3 sets of 6 per day, treat every fourth time
- Comes: 3 sets of 6 per day, treat each time
- Stays: up to 5 minutes on short leash, treat each time
- Heeling: twice a day for 25 minutes; sit every 30 steps, treat each time
- Practice anti-jumping
- Review everything

Week 7, Graduation
- Sits: 2 with treat, 1 without
- Downs: 1 with treat, 1 without
- Comes: 1 with treat, 1 without
- Stays: up to 5 minutes on short leash, with treats
- Heeling: solo, with sits and treats
- No jumping

Older Dog Class

(Throughout this practice program, whether you give a treat or not, always pet and praise the behavior and notice it when the dog does it on its own.)

Week 1

- Sits: 3 sets of 6 per day, treat each time; have dog sit before receiving any type of attention
- Heeling: twice a day for 25 minutes on Halti, Gentle Leader, K-9 Pull, or 4 Paws; dog not allowed leash without it

Week 2

- Sits: 3 sets of 10 per day, treat every other time; treat stays in pouch until command is done
- Downs: 3 sets of 10 per day, treat every time; treat in hand
- Heeling: twice a day
- Practice anti-jumping: S-R-R after the fact

Week 3

- Sits: 3 sets of 10 per day, treat every third time; treat stays in pouch until command is done; mix up hand signals and verbal commands
- Downs: 3 sets of 10 per day, treat every other time; treat in hand; dog drops straight down without sitting
- Comes: warm-up comes and long-line solos comes, 3 sets of 10 per day, treat each time
- Heeling: twice a day
- Practice anti-jumping: S-R-R

Week 4

- Sits: 3 sets of 10 per day, treat every fourth time
- Downs: 3 sets of 10 per day, treat every third time; dog drops straight down without sitting; owner standing fully upright
- Comes: 3 sets of 10 per day, treat each time
- Heeling: twice a day

- Practice anti-jumping
- Stays: 2 sets of 10 per day; start on a short leash and get to the end of a long leash by the end of the week

Week 5

- Sits: 3 sets of 10 per day, treat every fifth time
- Downs: 3 sets of 10 per day, treat every fourth time
- Comes: 3 sets of 10 per day, treat each time
- Stays: work up to 10 minutes on long leash
- Heeling: twice a day for 25 minutes
- Practice anti-jumping

Week 6

- Sits: 3 sets of 10 per day, treat every 1 out of 10
- Downs: 3 sets of 10 per day, treat every 2 out of 10
- Comes: 3 sets of 10 per day, treat each time
- Stays: work up to 30 minutes on long leash
- Heeling: twice a day for 25 minutes; if ready, begin to wean dog off Halti
- Add stay command to sits when heeling to prevent dog from popping up on its own
- Practice anti-jumping

Week 7, Graduation

- Sits: 1 with silent hand signal, 1 with verbal command, 1 with both
- Downs: 1 with silent hand signal, 1 with verbal command, 1 with both; owner stands upright
- Comes: 1 with treat, 1 without, using both verbal command and hand signal
- Sit-stay on sit
- Heeling: solo and with group, no treats

PART TWO:
MODERATE THERAPY
AND ONGOING
TRAINING

5

NUISANCE BARKING

"We came home and found this nasty note on our door from our neighbor, who said that Buffy was barking all day. He threatened to poison our dog if we didn't do anything about it. We're desperate. Can you help?"

"We received a citation from Animal Control. We have thirty days to take measures to stop our dog from barking. If we don't, they said they'd take us to court. Can you help us? If not, we plan to give our dog away."

FROM LARRY'S CASE FILES:
"Brandon" the Collie Who Was "Framed"

FILE # 94-88882
DOG'S NAME: Brandon
BREED: Collie
AGE: 1 year
PROBLEM: Nuisance barking

It made the front page of the local newspaper: A collie in a quiet suburban neighborhood was creating quite a ruckus because of its barking. The owner had been advised by the county's animal control officials to put an electric shock, no bark collar on the dog. Humane Society officials, local animal-rights organizations, and dog lovers were up in arms over this recommendation. Brandon was caught in the middle.

After reading the article, the dog's veterinarian, Dr. David Gordon of the Arroyo Pet Clinic in Lake Forest, California, and myself offered our services free. I felt the shock collar would be abusive and ineffective. Brandon's owners were adamant: Brandon was not the culprit.

Another dog in the neighborhood was the actual barker. It was my job to go into the home and find out exactly what was going on and remedy the situation. A few days after the article ran, I went out to the home.

Upon visiting Brandon's home, and taking an extensive medical, behavioral, and nutritional history, I learned that Brandon really didn't bark that much and was often mistaken for a dog that lived nearby—an incessant nuisance barker. In fact, Brandon did not bark at all when I knocked on the front door, nor when someone else rang the doorbell after I arrived. Brandon did, however, bark at inappropriate times, and this had to be corrected.

I discovered several reasons for his barking: First, Brandon was isolated from his pack—the human family members—for too long of a time period. Second, Brandon was inadvertently rewarded for whatever barking he did do, by receiving attention and being egged into chase-me games by the children in the family. Third, for several weeks construction was being done just outside Brandon's yard fence, which stimulated him to bark along his territorial perimeter.

Also, upon observation, Brandon seemed to be suffering from some stiffness or awkwardness in his gait as he walked. Upon subsequent referral to Dr. Gordon, it was confirmed that Brandon was experiencing a painful hip condition that could contribute to increased vocalization when he was forced to move.

Once I learned these things, in addition to finding out that the shock collar merely caused Brandon to whimper all day instead of emitting a full-blown bark (which still irritated his neighbors), I began to formulate a behavior-modification plan that included medical treatment for his hip condition.

In a letter I wrote summarizing my observations and treatment recommendations, which I sent to the director of the county's animal control, the family veterinarian, and the property-management company, I partly concluded by saying, "If the behavior-modification plan is implemented fully, Brandon will not have the opportunity nor reason to engage in nuisance barking. . . . he is *not* a hyperactive dog. He is not a yapper. . . . He does not require a shock collar nor does he require de-barking (having the vet surgically remove his vocal cords). His barking was triggered by two specific underlying situations: first, isolation and frustration barrier-induced barking; and second, play-induced barking in interaction with the children. . . . I think the family is fervently working on remedying this barking complaint situation and is in good faith willing to implement this behavior-modification program."

Barking Is Natural

Dogs bark, canaries don't. This is one way—but not the only way—dogs communicate. Dogs most frequently bark to express needs, to request responses of their human owners and to stake out their territory against intruding animals or humans. So it's appropriate for dogs to bark. It is nuisance barking that is inappropriate.

Nuisance barking can be defined as barking when there's no trigger or reason for barking, the dog continuing to bark after the owner wishes the dog to stop, or the dog continually barking when the owner is away. There are some common threads that run throughout our nuisance barking cases, and recognizing them helps illuminate proper intervention strategies.

The Reasons Dogs Nuisance Bark

ISOLATION

One of the main reasons dogs nuisance bark is that they are isolated from the pack. Dogs are pack animals. They are descendants of the wolf. The two most important things pack animals do together is eat and sleep. If you work all day and your dog sleeps outside all night, that leaves three to four hours of contact with your dog. It's enough for a hamster, fish, or canary, but not nearly enough for a canine. When dogs are isolated like this they suffer uncontrollable anxiety and the way they relieve this anxiety and boredom is not by having a beer or watching MTV, but by nuisance barking, digging, chewing, escaping, and self-mutilation. Hence, the dog must be integrated into the pack.

BARRIER FRUSTRATION

Dogs tend to nuisance bark if they are constantly stimulated while trapped behind a barrier they can see through. It would be as if you went to a drive-in movie but could not hear the sound track: very frustrating. For dogs the barrier is commonly a fence—cyclone, wrought iron, or wood slat. By being behind this barrier all day, and by being sporadically stimulated by people, animals, and vehicles passing by, the dog experiences overwhelming frustration because it can't pursue the object. So, out of this frustration, it barks. In addition, the dog does not credit the fence for its frustration. It ascribes its feelings to those people and dogs who walk by and stimulate it. Therefore, untreated frustration barrier-induced nuisance barking can lead to aggression toward those people and dogs who stimulate the nuisance barker.

EXCESSIVE VISUAL STIMULATION

Similarly, dogs can be stimulated to nuisance bark when they are inside the home, perching on a sofa and looking out the front window. Such locations are viewing "hot spots" that provide excessive visual stimulation. In a comprehensive anti-nuisance barking program, this visual access needs to be removed to reduce and eliminate the nuisance barking.

ACCIDENTAL REINFORCEMENT

Most nuisance barkers have actually been accidentally rewarded for their excessive barking. The owner often rewards the barking by petting or holding the dog (touch reinforcement) in an attempt to calm it; or by giving the dog attention or yelling or barking back at the dog, which creates a dialogue that pleases the dog. Or the owner accidentally rewards the dog's barking by giving the dog something else it wants, such as freedom, a treat, or a toy in an attempt to divert its attention away from barking.

There is also non-accidental reinforcement. Some owners try to create watchdogs by egging on their dogs to bark—usually in an attempt to wrap their own egos in a dog's macho veneer. A majority of problem barkers began their misbehavior this way and have maintained it through continuous accidental or intentional reinforcement.

SEPARATION ANXIETY

Some barking might not merely be nuisance barking. Rather, it might be one symptom known as separation anxiety, in which the dog has uncontrollable anxiety whenever the owner leaves. This is a more complex behavior problem that is not responsive to discipline or merely bringing the dog into the home. We address this behavior problem in Chapter 8.

ANTI-NUISANCE BARKING PROGRAM

One of the first things we do in a nuisance barking case is to remove all incidental reinforcement for the dog's barking. The owner must *not* look at the dog, pet the dog, talk to the dog, let it in or out, or give it a treat or toy if it barks.

Next, we look at the environment. Most problem barking dogs have excessive visual access. This means for too long it has had too great a view outside the yard or home—a view that allows it to see pedestrians, bicyclists, skateboarders, mail carriers, dogs, cats, birds, and so on all the time.

It's not always easy, but it's vital to eliminate these stimuli. This might mean turning a see-through fence into a solid one or putting up a wall, building a run on the side of the house away from the stimulus, keeping the dog in the house when things are active outside, or closing the blinds or shades.

THE CRUEL USE OF SHOCK COLLARS AND DEBARKING

Shock collars or debarking the dog are cruel and unusual punishments. If the dog is barking because of separation anxiety or fear, shocking it will only increase the fear and the dog will redirect its activities elsewhere by beginning to dig, chew, destroy, or self-mutilate.

Shock collars are quick-fix remedies that do not address the underlying problem, which could be loneliness, anxiety, frustration, or teasing from the other side of the fence. In addition, some collars frequently misfire because of ham radio waves or remote television controls and cause the dog to whimper and cry. What's more, these collars quickly become a "discriminative stimulus"—the dog lessens or ceases its barking when the collar is on, but quickly resumes barking when it is off (even if a dummy practice collar is used interchangeably).

And finally, debarking and shocking are cruel, not only because they do nothing to correct the behavior, but because frequently the owner is punishing the dog for behaving the way any normal dog would when it is isolated. Keeping the dog isolated or tied up day and night will lead to isolation-induced anxiety that can lead to nuisance barking. Shocking or otherwise punishing a dog for a reaction to conditions *the owner has created* is cruel.

Also available are noxious odor-releasing no-bark collars and ultrasonic no-bark collars. Although these alternative collars are seen as not being cruel, the same problems come up with these devices as with the electric shock collars: They frequently misfire, punishing the dog for breathing hard. They frequently end up causing the dog to whimper all day and still be a nuisance, even without emitting a strong enough bark to trigger the smell or sound response.

Again, this alternative collar does not address the underlying cause of nuisance barking: the isolation, the barrier frustration, the accidental reinforcements, and so on. I must change these root causes in addition to modifying the owners' behaviors through family systems therapy techniques to successfully eliminate the problem. If I don't, the dog will continue to nuisance bark or possibly redirect its underlying anxiety to other behavior problems: digging, chewing, escaping, or self-mutilation.

NOTICING AND REWARDING QUIET BEHAVIOR

Next, we need to acknowledge that our dogs, like even the worst criminals, cannot engage in their misbehaviors twenty-four hours a day. We need to avoid falling into the practice of only noticing our dog when it misbehaves. We need to *notice and acknowledge good, quiet behavior*. Randomly and throughout the day, notice when your dog is quiet. Tell it "good quiet," give it a treat and keep on walking. The dog will quickly figure out what gets rewarded. The nuisance barking will decrease; the quiet, good behavior will increase.

CATCH THE DOG IN THE ACT AND STARTLE-REDIRECT-REWARD

When the dog is in the act of unacceptable and continuous barking, use the Startle-Redirect-Reward technique: Tell the dog "off," and depress an ultrasonic device, blast it with a sudden stream of water, or depress an air horn. The startle is only done during the act of the nuisance barking and should be sufficient to stop the barking but not so potent as to make the dog uncontrollably anxious. This should be effective if the dog is engaging in regular nuisance barking and not the more serious and complex behavior problem of separation anxiety.

Your dog may engage in nuisance barking after you leave the house, usually within the first forty-five minutes or so. If this is all there is to it, you can drive off, sneak back on foot, and use your startle technique when you catch it barking. Or, have a neighbor act as an accomplice and assist you in doing this. The key is that the dog is startled, or corrected, in the act of barking.

ACCESS TO INSIDE THE HOUSE

A dog's anxiety is reduced if it is allowed access to the house to smell its owner's scent. This also reduces the barrier-frustration and boredom components of nuisance barking. Also, the dog should be sleeping inside with its owners to help reduce the pack-isolation anxiety responsible for much of the nuisance barking episodes.

ZERO TOLERANCE TO DOG VOCALIZATIONS

In an effective anti-nuisance barking program, the owner must not respond to *any* of its dog's vocalizations, whether it is a cry, grunt, bark, or whimper. By subtly responding to a low-level vocalization, the owner is unwittingly training the dog to vocalize more than it needs to and is thereby reinforcing and maintaining the nuisance barking behavior on a higher level. For a nuisance barker, never look at, pet, speak to, feed, play with the dog, or let it in or out if it vocalizes in any way.

In addition to randomly rewarding quiet behavior throughout the day, only give the dog attention when the dog is not seeking it and only when it has been absolutely quiet. By doing this, we extinguish the accidental reinforcement for the barking behavior and positively reinforce the quiet behavior instead, causing the dog to become more and more quiet-natured.

THE SIX-BARK RULE

No judge in small-claims court will throw the book at you and your dog for normal barking. If a person is prowling around your property, or an animal has invaded your dog's territory, or someone rings your doorbell, the dog should be allowed to alert its owner through barking. Therefore, owners of nuisance barking dogs should allow their dogs a six-bark limit. That is enough time for the prowler to ascertain that indeed you do have a dog and for you to investigate. Beyond the six barks, the dog is told "off!" If it doesn't turn off its barking, then the Startle-Redirect-Reward discipline technique is used. Tell the dog "off!" again and back up the verbal reprimand with a startle stimulus: the water, the can of pennies, or the air horn. After five full minutes of quiet, have the dog sit and reward it with praise ("good quiet") and a treat.

GIVING THE DOG SOMETHING FUN TO DO

As with the more difficult separation anxiety cases, owners with nuisance barking dogs should not only integrate them more into the family, but should also give their dogs something fun to do when they leave the house. Give the dog three Redi-Gimborn Natural Sterilized Bones (the seven-inch plain versions), one stuffed with cheese, one with peanut butter, and one with doggy beef jerky. In addition to the other steps outlined above, the bones give the dog something positive and constructive to occupy its time with. Chewing also serves as an anxiety-lowering activity, which should reduce the frequency and likelihood of the dog engaging in nuisance barking.

MEDICATION POSSIBILITIES

In rare cases, especially those approximating full-blown separation anxiety, some temporary anti-anxiety medication from the dog's veterinarian may be helpful. This will help the dog get through six weeks without having anxiety attacks and will allow the anti-nuisance barking behavior therapy techniques a chance to kick in.

Treatment Summary

Most nuisance-barking cases rapidly respond to the following treatments:

- reducing pack isolation
- giving access inside the house
- eliminating see-through barriers by making them solid

- removing all accidental rewards for barking and vocalizing
- catching the dog in the act of barking and using Startle-Redirect-Reward
- providing positive activities for the dog to engage in, such as chewing bones
- randomly throughout the day noticing and rewarding "quiet" behavior with praise and treats
- implementing the six-bark rule

With some effort, you can eliminate nuisance barking, better integrate your dog into your family, and keep peace with your neighbors.

Case Study Postscript

Unfortunately, within a couple of years Brandon found himself isolated in the back yard again for long stretches of time. This, of course, led to Brandon experiencing isolation-induced anxiety, leading him to nuisance bark. This points out how the entire family system must be changed if the nuisance-barking dog is to be successfully treated. When one link in the system fails to function, or does not comply with the anti-nuisance barking program, the entire system falters, and the behavior reemerges.

6

DESTRUCTIVENESS

"My husband and I were at home. I was upstairs with the dog and he was downstairs with our children. I went into the closet momentarily to look for something and when I came back into the room, Amber had chewed up the chair cushion I had been sitting on. I couldn't believe my eyes. I was livid. Why would she do this?"

"I had just come home from shopping and gave our dog a new chew bone. After unpacking the groceries in the kitchen, I came back into the hallway and found Buster chewing on one of our throw rugs. He had completely ignored the bone. What should we do?"

FROM LARRY'S CASE FILES:
"Sue" the Lab–Pit Bull Mix Who
Redecorated the Living Room

FILE # 92-000484
DOG'S NAME: Sue
BREED: Labrador–pit bull mix
AGE: 11 months
PROBLEM: Destructiveness in the house

In 1992, I went out on a behavior therapy consult regarding an eleven-month-old Lab–pit bull mix named Sue who was destroying her owner's home. Sue had destroyed the following: four eyeglass cases, an eye-drop bottle, a paperback book, five throw pillows, two bed spreads, one chair leg, a variety of hardcover books, and much of the wife's clothing. What's more, this all occurred while the owners were at home! This meant it was not separation anxiety. In addition, Sue was almost a year old, and therefore her chewing was not related to puppy teething. Part of Sue's destructiveness, I felt, stemmed from the fact that in essence she was a foster child, with little known prior history.

Sue's owners had recently adopted her from an animal shelter. There was no information on the first ten months of her life. We didn't know what kind of disruptive upbringing she might have had. In inquiring about her medical background, I learned that Sue would frequently have loose stools. This condition was unrelated to parasitic worms and was felt to be caused by nervousness. Finally, right after they adopted Sue, her owners put her through a traditional force-method obedience class that taught harsh choke-chain corrections. All this did was teach her to sit and become even more nervous. It had no curative effect on her destructiveness. In fact, it made it worse.

Sue's owners further reported that she seemed to be unable to settle down and relax while at home. She was always on the move and appeared nervous throughout the day. They tried to calm her by petting and giving her biscuits, but this only served to reinforce or reward her nervous state. From their description, it seemed that Sue was suffering from Generalized Anxiety Disorder, and required an anti-destructiveness program, along with anti-anxiety medication.

Causes

The four reasons why dogs engage in destructive behavior are:

1. The dog is bored.
2. The dog is anxious.
3. The dog is imitating.
4. The dog has been reinforced for such behavior.

Of the four, anxiety or boredom are the most likely reasons for a dog's destructive behavior. Most dogs that destroy things when their owners are home, as in Sue's case, suffer from some form of anxiety. Occasionally this anxiety is a side effect caused by a drug or disease, but in Sue's case, like most others, the destructiveness was a manifestation of Generalized Anxiety Disorder, which is characterized by the following:

- Excessive anxiety and worry
- Difficulty in controlling the worry
- Restlessness
- Difficulty concentrating
- Muscle tension
- Sleep disturbance
- Impairment in social functioning

With humans, Generalized Anxiety Disorder, or GAD, is frequently treated by addressing the person's anxiety-producing thoughts, called automatic thoughts. This process of addressing the anxious person's automatic thoughts is referred to as cognitive restructuring. A therapist helps the GAD patient decrease his perception of danger and increase his confidence in coping. With human patients who have GAD, and with our anxious or fear-aggressive dogs, distorted perceptions that overestimate danger and underestimate resources or safety are what lead to and sustain the anxious state. By keeping track of the situations and thoughts that occur when the person is anxious, the therapist can train the human to alter his thoughts. Similarly, the animal behaviorist tries to get the dog to alter its perception or meaning about the situation, which will reduce overall anxiety.

In addition to cognitive restructuring, treatment of GAD with humans can include relaxation training, techniques to overcome avoiding the feared or anxiety-producing situation, and medication. Traditionally, benzodiazepine drugs like Xanax, Valium, and Klonopin have been used. However, and as described in greater detail in Chapter 20, these drugs can lead to nasty side effects, including liver toxicity and dependence. An alternative is BuSpar, which is a serotonin-focused anti-anxiety agent with fewer side effects.

GAD patients often exhibit what is referred to as the anxiety profile. This profile includes four categories: Physical Reactions, Behaviors, Thoughts, and Moods. Dogs with GAD, because of their different physical makeup and capabilities, usually manifest symptoms in the Physical Reactions, Behaviors, and Moods categories. Common anxiety reactions, in both people and dogs, include:

- **Physical Reactions**
  Muscle tension
  Racing heart

- **Behaviors**
  Avoiding situations where anxiety might occur

- **Moods**
  Nervous
  Irritable
  Anxious
  Panicky

In Sue's case, and with the two examples cited in the opening quotations, the dogs were "acting-out" or demonstrating their anxiety through their destructive behavior. Humans act-out, or demonstrate anxiety, by talking quickly, exhibiting shallow, rapid breathing, engaging in frantic movements, pacing, biting their nails, running away, screaming, and self-medicating with alcohol or barbiturates. However, unless the underlying cause of the anxiety and the entire family system is addressed, the symptoms reappear and the anxiety continues. In addition, the long-term use of the depressants to self-medicate leads to addiction and further anxiety. Frequently, the repetitive acts of pacing or chewing bring temporarily relief for the person suffering anxiety.

The same applies to our GAD dogs. By chewing or digging, the dog, through repetitive behavior, helps channel or express its anxious state. In addition, by selecting objects that are closely associated with its owner and the owner's scent, the GAD dog is in effect self-medicating. The smell of its pack leaders helps reduce the dog's anxiety, and by engaging in the repetitive behaviors of chewing or digging, the dog is aerobically releasing its pent-up tensions and lowering its overall anxiety.

In Chapter 8 on separation anxiety, we address the dog's anxious state, which is a direct result of being incapable of being alone or separated from its pack leaders. In Chapter 1 on nipping, we cover the young puppy's tendency to play nip as it grows and cuts a second set of teeth.

This chapter, however, focuses on dogs that are sporadically or constantly destructive throughout the day and night and most often when the owners are home. This ever-present or free-floating anxiety is more characteristic of a generalized anxiety and requires ongoing treatment and longer behavior therapy—eight to twenty weeks.

Anxiety Triggers

Frequently, the triggers for this generalized ongoing anxiety are the following:

- The dog is sleeping separate from its owners.
- The dog is receiving overly harsh punishment.
- The dog is being constantly yelled at.
- The dog is being punished after the fact, and therefore for the wrong behaviors.
- The owners are giving inconsistent, and often, contradictory commands.
- The dog has no "time-out" sanctuary place where it can go, nap, and relax.
- The dog was shuttled from home to home during the first six months of its life.
- The dog was confined in an animal shelter or pet shop for an extended period of time.
- The dog is getting insufficient exercise.
- The dog is getting insufficient overall attention.
- The dog has inadvertently been rewarded for acting out to get negative attention. To dogs, negative attention is better than no attention.
- The dog has been given clothing and household objects to chew on.
- The dog is excessively roughhoused by the owner(s).
- The dog's routine has been severely disrupted or changed (people divorcing, moving in or out, feeding and sleeping times changed, etc.).
- A new animal has been added to the home.
- An old animal has been removed from the home or has died.
- A baby has been introduced to the home and the dog is banished from the house.
- The dog gets constant attention from its owners when they are home.
- The dog's demands for attention are responded to instantly.
- The dog has experienced a traumatic event.
- The dog has been chronically sick, necessitating extensive medical treatment and hospitalization.

- The dog's owner is sick.
- The dog's primary caretaker dies.
- The dog is undergoing violent traditional force-method training, including techniques such as kneeing in the chest, hanging, and "helicopter" spins.

Treatment

Many of the causes of the anxiety suggest which treatment approach to use. For example:

- Have the dog sleep inside with the owners. Fully integrate it into the pack.
- Do not use harsh or after-the-fact punishment. Instead, use the S-R-R technique described in Chapter 4.
- Talk to your GAD dog in a calm, soothing voice, instead of yelling. Remember that dogs have more sensitive hearing than we do.
- Be consistent. Have all the members of the family give the same commands and do the same things.
- Stabilize the GAD dog's routine as much as possible: Be consistent on feeding, sleeping, playing, walking, and exercise.
- If previously overly confined in a shelter or pet shop, take the dog out to open areas, such as parks and enclosed tennis or basketball courts, to play.
- Take the dog on walks twice a day for a minimum of twenty-five minutes.
- Each day the dog should have an aerobically taxing fifteen-minute romp, chasing after a ball, jogging or swimming.
- Notice when the dog is behaving nicely and calmly, and reward it by saying "good quiet" and popping treats.
- Train the dog using positive, nonviolent obedience techniques to increase its stimulation and reduce anxiety. See Chapter 4 for details.
- Avoid falling into a "punishment rut" and only acknowledging your dog when it has acted up through destruction to get your attention.
- Do not give your dog any clothing to chew on.
- Do not give your dog any household items to chew on.
- Cease all rough play.
- Make any major changes in the home in little steps, gradually, instead of launching them all at once.

- If there is to be another animal or a baby added to the home, refer to Chapters 7 and 11 on introducing babies and new pets, and follow the behavior-therapy programs outlined there.
- If your dog is grieving the loss of its owner, or a fellow pet, refer to Chapter 13 on pet loss and follow the relevant procedures given there.

As stated in the beginning, if there is no drug or disease causing the generalized anxiety, and if you follow these behavior-therapy techniques in treating and training your GAD dog, within eight to twelve weeks you should notice a significant (at least fifty percent) drop in your dog's overall anxiety and destructiveness. If necessary, consult with your veterinarian about the possible benefit of prescribing an antianxiety drug for your dog (such as BusPar, Valium, Elavil, or other psychotropics listed in Chapter 20) to help along the behavior-modification steps outlined above.

Case Study Postscript

Two weeks after my visit, Sue's owners reported that her anxiety seemed to be less and her destructive behavior had been reduced. They were still working on the program and had made an appointment with their veterinarian to get Sue some medication. For some reason, Sue began urinating in the house (possibly another indication of anxiety), so I outlined the housebreaking program contained in Chapter 2.

7

INTRODUCING A SECOND PET INTO THE HOME

"We thought our two-year-old Labrador would enjoy having another dog to play with. So we went down to the shelter and adopted this older German shepherd. We brought the dog home and the two dogs began ferociously fighting. Now, as soon as they see one another, they attack! Should we bring the shepherd back?"

"Our son wanted to have a puppy ever since we got a cat for our daughter. So we brought home this golden retriever puppy who is as cute as can be. However, our cat went ballistic. She hissed, raised her back, and now refuses to use the litter box. Help!"

FROM LARRY'S CASE FILES:
The Unhappy Newlyweds—The Wife's Dog-Repulsed Cat, "Tara" and the Husband's Cat-Chasing Schnauzer, "Hugo"

FILE # 97-001021
DOG'S NAME: Hugo
CAT'S NAME: Tara
BREEDS: Schnauzer and domestic shorthair
PROBLEM: Introducing the dog to the cat

In 1997, I went out on a consult regarding a three-year-old schnauzer named Hugo who was having a hard time adjusting to living with an adult domestic shorthaired cat named Tara. Within five minutes after arriving at the home, I heard the ultimatum loud and clear: "Help us get my cat and *his* dog to get along, or this marriage is over!" Talk about pressure.

Hugo had never lived with cats before and he was having a hard time adjusting. He thought Tara was something to be chased and eaten. Of course, the wife and her cat had other ideas. They subscribed to the catch phrase from the movie *Homeward Bound*: "Cats rule, dogs drool!"

Hugo was eight weeks old when the husband got him from another family. He had been a friendly puppy, other than when he charged the front door after hearing the doorbell ring or when he saw a cat. He had a history of lunging and growling at cats. Hugo was a healthy dog with no major illnesses, and he was neutered. The husband could take bones away from him and handle his food bowl while Hugo ate. However, Hugo had never attended an obedience class. This was part of the problem.

I outlined for Tara's and Hugo's owners the program that follows, and demonstrated some of its key components. In twenty minutes, I had the wife's cat, Tara, lying down by my left knee (I was sitting cross-legged on the floor) rolling in catnip, and the husband's dog, Hugo, in a down-stay by my right knee, snacking on cheese treats. They were a foot apart with no growling, chasing, or running. The owners were amazed.

Introducing a Second Dog into the Home

Several issues arise when people have one dog and want to get another, or have a cat and want to get a dog. It is important for pet owners not to make an impulsive decision that can lead to having to give one animal away or having an animal severely injured or killed by another.

If the reason you want to get another dog is to keep your first dog company, don't do it. Many owners fail to give their dog enough attention. The dog feels isolated from its pack and pack leaders and engages in destructive behavior. As a quick fix, the owners decide to get another dog so that they don't have to bother giving the first dog more quality time and attention; the new dog will do it for them, they think, and the new dog won't require any attention either. Wrong! Very frequently, the first dog still misbehaves, and frequently it teaches the second dog to do the same thing. Now the owners have two dogs that need their attention. Often the owners end up giving one or both of the dogs away.

Sometimes owners run out and get a second dog that is incompatible with their first dog. Upon arriving home one evening after work, they discover that the two dogs have been in a vicious fight and they have to medically treat or bury one of the dogs.

Now, if you have the time, energy, space, and financial wherewithal for a second dog, there are several things you can do to increase the chance that the new animal will be a success in the home.

Tips on Getting the Two Dogs to Hit it Off

Get a dog the opposite sex of the one you have now. Same-sex dogs fight far more frequently than do dogs of the opposite sex. Almost ninety percent of my sibling dog-fighting cases involve same-sex dogs. Establishing which dog will be dominant—and make no mistake, one has to be dominant—is more problematic between same-sex dogs. Male pairs are more likely to fight over turf and territory. Female pairs are more likely to fight over possessions and toy objects.

Make sure both dogs are spayed or neutered. Unspayed and un-neutered dogs fight more frequently and more intensely. Much of the fighting is hormone-based, involving territorial marking and heat cycle–related aggression. Of course, you also want the dogs to be fixed to avoid a never-ending cycle of puppies.

Select a second dog **equal in size to or smaller than your first dog.** This reduces the likelihood of continual contests over which dog will be dominant, since size plays one important factor in that issue. Whether it is smaller or larger than the newcomer, your first dog will be reluctant to give up its dominant position. If it is the bigger dog, that is not as likely to be a problem because the smaller newcomer is unlikely to issue a challenge. However, if the first dog is the smaller of the two, the new dog may well use its size advantage to become the top dog and fights can ensue.

Select a second dog from a breed that has not been bred to be an attack or fighting dog. These dogs will naturally be more dominant and will not back down if your first dog puts up a fight over leadership.

Have the two dogs meet several times on neutral turf to see whether they get along before even thinking of a meeting on your old dog's turf. If the two cannot get along on neutral turf, the likelihood of them getting along on your old dog's turf is practically nil.

There will be a honeymoon period of approximately four to six weeks before the new dog's true personality will show itself. The way the dog is behaving and adjusting after that period is a good indicator of its future and continued behavior.

One Leader of the Pack

You can reduce the chance that the two dogs will fight if you remember that dog packs are inherently totalitarian. (See Chapter 10, "Sibling Dog Fighting," for more detailed information.) Only one dog can be the top dog. This will only change if the dominant dog becomes injured or too sick to defend its dominant position. Then the second dog will slide into the spot. You can support this necessary hierarchy and keep the peace in several ways:

- Do not treat the dogs as equals. By trying to treat the dogs fairly, equally, and democratically, you will anger and frustrate the true dominant dog and force it to reassert its dominance in increasingly forceful ways, including fighting and attacking the No. 2 dog.
- You want to actively support your first dog as dominant dog by petting it first, greeting it first, letting it exit and enter first, feeding it first, and so on. The exception to supporting the first dog is if you see clear and ever-present signs that the two dogs have switched things around and the second dog is dominant. There are several indicators.

DOMINANT DOG INDICATORS

1. The dominant dog will always successfully cut off the less-dominant dog at doorways and get in front of the other dog when greeting the owner.

2. The dominant dog will hump and climb up on the back of the less-dominant dog, creating a T-stance. The submissive dog will not.

3. The dominant dog will jealously guard and keep the toys to itself and prevent the other dog from eating its food.

4. The dominant dog will frequently go to where the less-dominant dog is resting and force it to relinquish its place so the dominant dog can use it. The reverse does not happen.

Look out for these behavioral indicators on who is the dominant dog and actively reinforce the pecking order to preserve the peace between your two dogs.

Cats and Dogs

When mixing cats and dogs, it's helpful to get the cat first. Let it mature, socialize it, maintain its claws, and then get the dog, preferably as a puppy. This way, the puppy will grow up being around the cat and see it as a fellow pack member. The cat—which can always escape and go high, leap over obstacles the dog cannot, or let the dog know when it's had enough with a smack on the dog's nose—will set the tempo and rules of the relationship. The dog and cat have a good chance of being friends.

It is not impossible to do it in reverse, but if you haven't socialized your dog with cats when it was younger, it may be aggressive toward the cat, fearful of it, or play too rough with it and inadvertently injure or kill it.

Other tips for getting your cat and dog to get along:

- Protect the cat's feeding area and its litter box area from intrusion by the dog. Feeding the cat in a high location works well.
- Rub each animal with a towel, getting the scent on it, and exchange towels, placing the cat-scented towel under the dog's bedding and/or food dish and vice versa. This will foster a greater positive association between each animal and the other animal's scent.
- When you first bring the puppy home, crate it or put it on a leash so the cat can investigate the dog without being chased or trampled.
- Caress and give verbal praise and assurance to the cat and provide it with some catnip and cat treats whenever it is around or approaches the contained puppy.
- Then reverse the roles, and let the dog sniff. Give the dog petting and treats when it is behaving appropriately around the cat in the cat carrier.
- After a month of these carefully structured socialization sessions, gradually give the cat more and more freedom around the dog, with the dog going from short leash or crate to a twenty-foot leash and no crate.
- Fixing both cat and dog will help to create a more amicable relationship.
- If the dog becomes too rough or begins to chase the cat (even if the cat instigates it), startle the dog with a silent startle technique (to not inadvertently punish the cat for simply breathing), such as a water

blast, and tell it "No!" When the dog is behaving appropriately with the cat, give lots of praise and treats.

- Obedience training for the dog, and possible nutritional adjustments in diet for both dog and cat, can also help foster a harmonious relationship between the two. Try a lamb-and-rice-based diet for the dog; if the cat seems stressed, some veterinarians and behaviorists recommend a beef-and-chicken-based diet.

The Dog-Cat Re-Conditioning Behavior Therapy Program

As outlined for Hugo's and Tara's owners, if you have a cat-chasing dog or a dog-repulsed cat, you need to "switch condition" these attitudes for the pets to get along. Here is what you do:

PRELIMINARY STEPS

- Separate the cat and dog when you aren't home.
- Only give the dog and cat attention together, not separately, and only when they are in view of one another.
- Before introducing them in the daily socialization sessions, (with the dog being on leash) give the dog a week of sit and sit-stay practice (refer to Chapter 4 for details).
- Give the dog lots of scrumptious treats and praise for its obedience practice, which should consist of three sets of sits and one half-hour stay a day, initially on leash.
- During this time, give the cat one-on-one focus sessions with one of the owners. The session should include catnip toys, catnip, and gentle caressing in a specific part of the home.
- Rub a towel on the dog and put it where the cat sleeps and eats, and vice versa. This is done so that the dog and cat further develop a positive association with each other's scent.
- If the dog misbehaves, whether the cat is around or not, give it the S-R-R discipline technique outlined in Chapter 4.
- Don't allow the dog to jump up on furniture.

After these preliminary steps, begin twice-a-day reconditioning "socialization happy hour" sessions for the dog and cat by doing the following:

1. Bring in the cat, sit down, and start its one-on-one catnip session.
2. Bring in the dog from a greater distance. Have it sit-stay at several points along the way—first at thirty feet from the cat, then twenty feet, then ten feet, then finally, side by side with the cat. The dog must be on leash and anti-pull collar.
3. If the dog breaks its stay, growls, barks, or snaps, blast it in the face with water and say "Off!" After a five-minute respite, resume the practice.
4. Give both the dog and cat lavish attention, petting, playing, and treats when they are in the room together—always with the dog on leash control. Beginning the second week, do not give the dog and cat attention except when they are participating in these reconditioning sessions.

Over the eight-week program, the dog starts looking forward to being with the cat and no longer chases it or growls at it, and the cat no longer runs away. The dog is then able to be weaned off its leash and anti-pull collar and maintain its behavior free in the house. The dog and cat should at the very least tolerate one another, and at the very most be the best of friends.

This program tends to work best with dogs who are merely undersocialized versus those who are engaging in predatory hunting aggression. Such dogs would not be amenable to the program outlined above. For information on aggression, see Chapter 9.

Case Study Postscript

A month after the initial consult, I followed up with a call to see how Hugo and Tara were getting along. The wife reported that things were much better. The animals were beginning to like one another and Hugo no longer chased or growled. Even visitors noticed the difference in his demeanor.

PART THREE:
LONG-TERM THERAPY
AND RE-PARENTING
THE PERSONALITY

8

Separation Anxiety

"You have to help us! We came home today and found that our dog had chewed through the dry wall of our garage into our kitchen. We can't believe it. If we can't fix this, we'll have to get rid of him."

"We came home and found that our dog had chewed her legs raw to the point where they were bleeding. She only does this when we're gone. What should we do?"

From Larry's Case Files:
"Ellen" the Christmas-Tree-Eating Pit Bull Mix

FILE # 95-000289
DOG'S NAME: Ellen
BREED: Pit bull mix
AGE: 8 months
PROBLEM: Separation anxiety

In early 1995, I went out on a behavior-therapy consult regarding an eight-month-old pit bull mix named Ellen who had been digging crater-like holes in the backyard whenever her owners were gone. Ellen's owners had adopted her two months before my visit from the local animal shelter. They selected Ellen because the wife wanted a large mixed-breed dog that was playful and sweet. Ellen was that and more.

Ellen was friendly toward people and dogs. Other than a recurring ear infection, she was in good health.

Ellen slept with the family at the foot of the bed. She had a variety of toys, including balls, rubber rings, Nylabones, and rawhide. For discipline, all that Ellen's owners needed to do was raise their voices and she would lie down, roll over, and urinate. Ellen was being fed a high-quality commercial dog food and had not yet attended any type of obedience class.

Her main problem was digging, which she did not do when her owners were home. Therefore, I felt her behavior reflected a moderate case of separation anxiety, as opposed to puppy digging or boredom.

Initially, I suggested the family give Ellen greater access inside the home instead of confining her to the yard. Dogs and cats tend to experience less anxiety if they have access to areas of the home that most smell like their owners. Since Ellen was housebroken, and could refrain from urinating and defecating all night, I thought giving her access through a dog door into the home would reduce her anxiety and thereby curtail her digging.

I also had the family implement parts of my separation anxiety treatment program (outlined below) to comprehensively treat Ellen's anxiety-based destructive behaviors.

Within the first week, I began receiving distress calls from the wife. During the first couple of days, Ellen had done fine with having access to inside the house. However, around the third or fourth day, she and her husband came home to find the Christmas tree and presents had been attacked and chewed up! Needless to say, they were upset. We needed to revise our plan immediately. Ellen's separation-anxiety symptoms had spread from digging holes to chewing up items in the home. We made two revisions; first, we placed her fiberglass kennel crate right up against the dog door entrance. When she went through her dog door, she went right into her kennel and didn't have access to the rest of the house. Second, I referred her owners to their vet for a few weeks' supply of an antianxiety medication. (See Chapter 20, "Puppy Prozac," for more details.)

Later that spring, I called for an update. The wife said things were good. We decided to progressively give Ellen more freedom into the house again and phase out the crate limitation. Again, within a couple of weeks Ellen engaged in more chewing destruction. This time, she put a hole in the couch. Ouch! In addition, the owners observed that the traditional doggy tranquilizer the veterinarian had put Ellen on was only making her "goofy" and anxious, and had not remedied the anxiety.

So we revised the plan again. I had the owners implement the entire separation anxiety program, consistently, for an eight-week period. Then, I referred them back to their veterinarian for a temporary prescription of the psychotropic antidepressant Elavil. We also put the kennel crate back against the dog door and gradually over the eight-week period phased it out again. Finally, we decided both Ellen and her owners would benefit from going through one of my older dog obedience courses.

From Larry's Case Files:
"Rasta" & "Bandit" the Houdini-esque Lab and Hound

CASE FILE # 95-000018
DOGS' NAMES: Rasta and Bandit
BREEDS: Labrador retriever mix and hound mix
AGES: 8 years and 4 years, respectively
PROBLEMS: Separation anxiety and escaping

In August of 1995, I went out on a consult involving an eight-year-old Lab mix named Rasta and a four-year-old hound mix named Bandit who had recently begun showing signs of separation anxiety and were escaping from the backyard. Rasta and Bandit were obtained from some friends who couldn't keep them any longer. Their current owners brought them home at one-and-a-half years and four months of age, respectively. Rasta and Bandit had demonstrated sweet dispositions, and besides being spayed and having occasional urinary tract infections, they were healthy.

Rasta and Bandit peek out of the door they chewed up during their days of separation anxiety.

A few weeks before my visit, they had chewed up some window blinds, furniture, and wall molding. Although Bandit appeared more anxious than Rasta, the owners couldn't be sure which dog was doing what. After the destruction inside the home, the owners placed the dogs in the fenced-in backyard. However, within a few days the dogs had chewed things up in the yard and had escaped. They would be in the front yard when the owners would arrive home from work. For a while, the owners couldn't figure how the dogs were escaping. Both the destructive behavior and the escaping from the yard only occurred during the owners' absence. Neither dog would engage in this behavior if the owners were home. Diagnosis: moderate to severe separation anxiety.

We immediately implemented the entire anti-separation anxiety program outlined later, which included giving them limited access into the home, securing the fence they were leaping over, and drastically changing how the owners interacted with both dogs.

Separation Anxiety: Don't Leave Home Without Me

"We are not only gregarious animals liking to be in sight of our fellows, but we have an innate propensity to get ourselves noticed, and noticed favorably, by our kind. No more fiendish punishment could be devised, were such a thing physically possible, than that one should be turned loose in society and remain absolutely unnoticed by all the members thereof."

—WILLIAM JAMES, American psychologist-philosopher

Separation anxiety is a condition in which young children or animals experience undue fear and nervousness when separated from their parents or pack leaders. Many nursery school children or kindergartners experience this anxiety when they are first separated from their parents. They cry, shake, throw a tantrum, and experience a variety of psychosomatic and physical symptoms such as stomachaches or vomiting. When dogs experience this anxiety, they often attempt to relieve it through chewing, digging, barking, escaping, or self-mutilation.

The American Psychiatric Association's Diagnostic and Statistical Manual of Mental Disorders-IV (DSM-IV, 1994, pp.110–113) states that the essential feature of Separation Anxiety Disorder is excessive anxiety concerning separation from the home or from those to whom the person (or dog) is attached.

With humans, Separation Anxiety Disorder may develop after some life stress, such as a death of a relative or pet, an illness, change of schools, a move to a new neighborhood, or immigration. Among the several diagnostic criteria for human Separation Anxiety Disorder is the presence of recurrent excessive distress when separation from home or major attachment figures occurs or is anticipated.

Separation anxiety in dogs is difficult to treat because it takes place only when the dog's owners are gone. Heavy-handed punishment techniques recommended by traditional-method trainers frequently make the problem worse because they raise the dog's overall anxiety rather than lower it. These methods also often fail because the root cause isn't always mental; underlying medical disorders, sometimes involving improperly functioning thyroid or adrenal glands, may contribute to the dog's anxiety.

Dogs suffering from separation anxiety go absolutely nuts whenever they are left alone by their owners, whether it is outside or inside, whether it is for ten minutes or ten hours. They destroy their immediate environment, continuously bark, frantically dig, and/or self-mutilate various parts of their bodies. These symptoms get progressively worse with age—as opposed to simple boredom or teething-induced chewing, which progressively fades away with age and time. Most separation-anxiety cases come from the extreme ends of the age spectrum. Either it is a young puppy that cannot tolerate being left alone by its family and begins to destroy things or cries, or it is an older dog that, after being left alone for years with no problems, suddenly cannot tolerate it anymore and begins to engage in destructive activities. Each separation anxiety case requires a tailor-made program to fit the frequency, duration, and intensity of the problem, as well as the personality characteristics of dog and owner.

In addition to behavioral treatment, many severe separation-anxiety cases require antianxiety medication prescribed by a veterinarian. The type of medication and the dosage will depend on the facts of the case and the medical history of the animal. Both veterinarian and animal behaviorist should assess the data. Often, the antianxiety medicines are temporary and are used to allow the behavioral techniques to take effect. Each case is different.

Goals of the Separation Anxiety
Treatment Program

The chief goal in treating separation anxiety is to reduce the dog's anxiety response through counter-conditioning. The idea is to make the dog see that its family's leaving is not purely a bad thing. At the least, we want the dog to view being left alone as a mixture of both positive and negative experiences. At best, being left alone would be seen as positive and fun.

I also want to eliminate accidental reinforcements for the dog's anxiety states and adjust exercise schedules, nutrition intake, and medication levels to reduce the dog's anxiety.

Owners should keep departures low key so that they don't leave the dog in a hyped-up state. Arrivals must also be kept low-key—no lavishing of praise or petting upon entrance—to prevent the dog from feeling anticipation anxiety.

I begin to desensitize the dog to the customary cues that its family is getting ready to leave by having the people act out the cues and then not go anywhere, but rather play ball, give treats, or go out the door and immediately come back in again. Then I have the family vary its time away so the dog is not left for a full day every time the family gets ready to leave the home.

I make sure the dog is getting sufficient attention and exercise to avoid unnecessary isolation from its pack and that it is sleeping inside at night with the family. I have the owner work with the dog on some gentle obedience exercises to channel excess energy.

I reduce the extreme contrasts of attention. Many dogs suffering from separation anxiety get an overload of attention when the owner is home—constant petting, exercising, and roughhousing. This sets them up for major withdrawal symptoms when the next morning or Monday comes and the owner is suddenly gone for ten hours. The extremes of non-stop attention and no attention are just too much for some dogs to handle. The extremes must be moderated to help these dogs obtain a happy medium.

Of course, a cornerstone of the treatment is reconditioning the dog to look at being left alone as something positive. It involves giving the dog some irresistible food items, prepared to sustain prolonged attention, and only giving them to the dog when the owner leaves. Although the dog will experience some anxiety that the owner is leaving, it begins to realize that owner departures are the only times it gets these super treats. The dog, it is hoped, will gradually make more positive associations with its owner's departure than negative ones.

But even all these techniques don't guarantee success for the dog that is suffering from severe separation anxiety. Some dogs just need to be around a family member most of the time—something that is not always possible. So curing this problem is an iffy prospect. One thing is certain, however: Merely looking at the surface symptoms of separation anxiety, such as nuisance barking and chewing destruction, and focusing on them with heavy-handed punishment techniques will only make the problem worse.

Separation Anxiety Treatment Program

- Keep arrivals and departures low-key. Riling the dog up before you leave or immediately greeting it upon coming home when it's excited will reward and trigger the anxiety. Ignore the dog fifteen minutes before you leave and upon coming home. When coming home, only start giving the dog attention after it is calm and not excited or anxious.
- Do not respond when the dog demands attention. This rewards the need for constant attention. Ignore the dog when it barks at you, paws at you, nose-nudges you, or turns around and backs its butt into you.
- Only give your dog attention during the moments when it is not actively seeking it. When it is lying down, or looking elsewhere, call it over and have it sit, and give it as much attention as it wants.
- Reduce the contrast: Most of our separation-anxious dogs cannot tolerate the "either-or" conditions of receiving all of the attention when the owner is home and no attention when the owner is gone. It's akin to the divorced-child syndrome of getting cotton candy, amusement parks, and movies on the weekend and then going back to being the latch-key kid after school during the week. For dogs, this type of contrast will drive them nuts and contribute to their separation anxiety. Reduce the contrast by doing the following:
  1. Pick two days out of the week when you are home.
  2. Ignore the dog for six to eight hours on those days, matching the time you are away at work.

3. Only feed or let the dog out to go to the bathroom during this time. The dog will quickly learn to think, "What's the big deal when my owner is gone, even when he's home, he still sometimes ignores me."

- Practice departure "fire-drills:" Separation-anxious dogs begin to experience anxiety when they notice the cues emitted by their owners signaling that they are about to leave. So, let's mix 'em up. Do all the cues that you are about to leave (grooming yourself in the bathroom, dressing, packing lunch, setting the microwave, grabbing the car keys, opening the garage, etc.), and don't go anywhere. Instead, play ball with your dog. Next time, step out and come right back in. Play a game. Next time, go out for five minutes, then twenty minutes, then in and right back, then an hour, then ten minutes. You get the idea. Vary the time you're gone and teach the dog that your departure cues don't always mean you will be leaving for the entire day all the time!

- A half-hour before you leave, take the dog on a fifteen-minute vigorous heeling-on-leash walk in which you walk at a quick pace, having the dog heel at your side and sitting every thirty paces. This will help channel and vent pent-up tensions in your dog before you leave it.

- Counter-condition your dog to see your departure as being a good thing. Fifteen minutes before you leave the home (for whatever duration—even if practicing the fire drill departures), do the following things:

  1. Confine your dog in one area of the house instead of giving it access to the entire home. The confined area should be a "safe zone": floor instead of carpet, no access to pillows, cushions, television remote controls, clothing, etc.

  2. Provide the dog with three natural sterilized bones of the type described in earlier chapters. Only give these bones when you are preparing to leave the home—no matter for how long! Upon returning, remove the bones, wash them out and put them away until your next fire-drill practice or actual departure.

  3. Put on a tape recording of your voice, calmly reading a newspaper or magazine, for at least an hour's duration, or use a tape player that has continuous play. This way, even when you are not at home you're still there. Make sure you play the recording when you are

home too, so the recording does not become associated solely with you leaving.

- Make off-limits chew objects undesirable. If the dog previously has destroyed certain objects in the home as a result of its separation anxiety, you want to prepare those items in a way that will make them repulsive to your dog. Pet stores' bitter-fruit flavored products usually don't work; they merely serve as icing on the cake and induce your dog to go after these objects even more. Instead, try this: Have the dog smell and lick an end of a Q-tip coated with hair spray. (*Do not* use the come command to get the dog to do this.) The dog should make a face, sneeze, or back its head away after smelling and tasting this aversive agent. Then liberally spray the hair spray on the cushion, wood molding, or dry wall where the dog has chewed before. When you leave and the dog moseys over to the off-limits chew area, it will smell and taste the same distasteful agent it had on the Q-tip. It should back off and turn to the natural sterilized bones full of goodies instead.

If digging was one of the symptoms of your dog's separation anxiety, implementing some of the treatment strategies contained in Chapter 3 on digging will be helpful. You might want to provide the dog with a digging play box (similar to a sand box for kids) with buried treats and toys. That way the dog has an acceptable place to dig and the rest of the yard is saved from looking like the surface of the moon.

Also, either set the dog up with a dog door or another way of accessing the yard, or arrange to come home at lunch time or have a dog-walking service come by.

If barking is a part of your dog's separation anxiety, I have to add additional treatment techniques:

1. Do not give the dog any attention for *any* type of vocalization. This includes whining, barking, crying, or growling. If you give the dog eye contact, petting, feeding, freedom, or play during or immediately following any sound it makes, you are adding gasoline to the fire and maintaining your dog's separation-anxiety-caused barking.

2. Reduce your dog's visual access to things it will bark at. See Chapter 5 on nuisance barking for explicit instructions.

3. Catch the dog in the act of the crime of barking. Again, with

fear-based or anxiety-based behavior problems, punishment won't do. However, during those times when you are home, and ignoring the dog as instructed above, the dog may begin to engage in the same anxiety-related behaviors it does when you're gone. If it begins to incessantly bark (ten minutes-plus, non-stop), tell it "Off!" and blast it in the face with water, shake the penny can, or depress an ultrasonic device. After the dog is startled and has stopped barking, wait one to five minutes, and begin to reward the dog's quiet behavior.

4. Randomly throughout the day, notice when your dog is not vocalizing in any way. Go by, toss a treat, and say "good quiet." The dog begins to learn that it gets paychecks for good quiet behavior and pink-slip startles for noisy behavior. However, since separation-anxiety-based barking is fear or anxiety based, these discipline techniques are not to be used with great frequency, nor should they be relied upon as the sole way of stopping the barking.

- Set up another tape recorder or a video recorder, or have one of your neighbors monitor for sounds of barking when you are away for the day, especially during the first couple of weeks. You want to chart the time it occurs, the frequency, duration, and intensity.
- If your dog continues to incessantly bark because of its separation anxiety after it has access to go in and out of the house, you must place your dog inside, in order to have a cooling-off period for your neighbors and avoid complaints. If need be, come home at lunch to walk it, have a dog walker come by, or make some other arrangement so the dog can still relieve itself. You don't want to create a new problem (house-soiling) while trying to treat an existing one.
- When you do give your separation-anxious dog attention, dole it out in ten-second increments. Part of what contributes to the intolerance of being alone or ignored is that the separation-anxious dog is constantly being petted for marathon periods of time. Instead, always have your dog sit before giving it attention and then only give your dog ten seconds of petting. If it wants more attention, wait until it is not actively seeking it, have it sit again, and give it another ten. You can end up giving as much or even more petting or attention than you were giving to your dog before the program. The only difference is now it has to earn it by sitting, and you ration it out in digestible bites so as to not create an overly dependent dog.

Medical Issues

You also need to rule out any underlying medical disorder contributing to your dog's anxiety: low thyroid levels, improperly functioning adrenal glands, or tumors. Your vet can check for these.

If your dog has moderate to severe separation anxiety, then temporary (eight to twenty weeks) of antianxiety medication may be needed from your veterinarian (see Chapter 20 for details). Often, this allows the dog to become sufficiently relaxed so the behavior-modification and counter-conditioning techniques can work. The four antianxiety agents most often prescribed are: the canine neuroleptic, Acepromazine; the human tricyclic antidepressant, Elavil; the serotonin anxiolytic, BuSpar; or the antihypertensive medication (beta-blocker), Inderal.

Each of these agents has potential side effects, and your veterinarian has to first determine that your dog is healthy enough to withstand them—no heart, thyroid, or seizure problems—in addition to taking a blood panel to assess liver function. Negative behavioral side effects stemming from the use of these agents need to be considered. For example, if you have more than one dog at home, do not use Acepromazine. One of the possible side effects is to create aggression between dogs. It's not worth taking the chance that your dog's anxiety levels will drop if it might begin viciously fighting with its sibling dog or other dogs. In addition, Elavil and Inderal are human drugs, only experimentally used for dog-behavior problems. You will have to sign a release acknowledging this.

Dogs Especially Predisposed to Separation Anxiety

Dogs with the following histories or characteristics seem especially susceptible to developing separation anxiety:

- Dogs taken away from their parents and littermates too early (prior to eight weeks) or too late (after fourteen weeks).
- Dogs not fully integrated into their new home that end up being relegated to the yard or garage.
- Dogs bred to be on a heightened alert, such as the herding breeds.
- Dogs being "triangled"—used as an emotional replacement "sponge"

for someone else in the family. If there is a dysfunctional marriage, an acting-out, run-away child, or a recent divorce, the dog is sometimes drafted to try to fulfill the survivors' relationship needs in an excessive way. The excessiveness is manifested through:

1. Giving the dog constant attention.
2. Giving the dog constant petting.
3. Always responding to all demands for attention from the dog.
4. Spending all free time only with the dog.
5. Having the dog situated where humans customarily are: in the front passenger seat of the car, at the dinner table, on the couch, and in bed on the opposite pillow.

This triangle scenario creates an overly dependent dog that will suffer overwhelming anxiety if the owner is absent for any period of time. As soon as the survivor in our scenario changes jobs or becomes re-employed, or begins a new relationship with a human partner, the dog is relegated to where it once had been, and the separation anxiety symptoms begin to crop up.

In general, if owners can consistently implement the separation-anxiety program, it will take roughly eight weeks for the anxiety-related behaviors to subside, be under control, or be eradicated. Most of the dogs, especially those with moderate to severe separation anxiety, will require some type of medication for some period of time, to achieve success.

Separation anxiety, like its cousins fear aggression and phobias, is a fear-based behavior. It cannot be emphasized enough that harsh punishments, yelling, ostracizing, and standard obedience training will not have any effect in curing this behavior. In fact, using punishment techniques will make the behavior worse, because they will raise the dog's overall anxiety and thereby contribute to the very problem you're trying to fix.

Case Study Postscripts

ELLEN

Six months after my initial consultation and following a seven-week non-violent obedience class, Ellen continued to do well without engaging in any destructive behavior. She is now off the Elavil.

RASTA AND BANDIT

Two months after my initial visit, Rasta's and Bandit's owners reported all destructive behavior and yard escaping had stopped. For two years, Rasta and Bandit did fine. In early 1997, their owners called and said there had been one significant relapse in their behavior. One of the two dogs had chewed some window blinds. I instructed them to put into practice key components of the separation-anxiety plan and consult with their veterinarian about possible medication. I followed up two weeks later and the owners reported no further incidents of destructive chewing.

9

AGGRESSION

"My husband leaned over to pet our dog and the dog showed his teeth and growled. I've never seen him do that before. We then disciplined him, but he tried to bite us."

"My daughter went to take a bone away from our dog and he bit her hand. Now, whenever we try to approach him when he has a toy, he growls and runs under the bed where we can't get to him. I can't have this going on in my home with my kids."

FROM LARRY'S CASE FILES:
"Rocky" the Front Door Bouncer Rottweiler

FILE # 95-003108
DOG'S NAME: Rocky
BREED: Rottweiler
AGE: 2½ years
PROBLEM: Dominance aggression

Rocky was facing doggy heaven in September of 1995. His new owners had Rocky for one month when they called. It seemed that after they brought him home, he would not accept any new person, family member, or stranger without trying to viciously attack them. Rocky was a whopping 110 pounds. When around anyone other than his new owners—a young married couple and one of their relatives—Rocky would growl, show his teeth, lunge, and try to bite. In a panic, and based on a referral from their veterinarian, Rocky's owners called me. If I couldn't help, they would euthanize him.

I took an extensive history over the phone. It seems the previous owners had isolated Rocky in the backyard, with no socialization and minimal attention for the first two years of his life. His only companion was another dog. In addition, his previous owners had gotten Rocky from a backyard breeder. We therefore had no credible information on the temperament of his parents. However, it was pretty obvious his previous owners had gotten him just to be a guard dog, stuck him in the backyard, and that was that. Bye-bye Rocky.

In addition, Rocky had early experiences involving pain with strangers. He had a congenital shoulder condition that had given him much pain and necessitated surgery (association: veterinarians and animal health technicians = pain). In my opinion, Rocky was also neutered way too late, at eleven months of age, allowing him plenty of time to lock in aggressive tendencies, many testosterone-based. To top it off, Rocky had once been sent away for "training." It was not clear whether this was guard-dog training or general obedience, but the method used brute force (association: male trainers and kennel attendants = pain).

In most of my aggression cases, I go to the home so I can see the family and dog in the environment in which the behavior in question takes place. However, in Rocky's case, the aggression was quite dangerous. Plus, I didn't think we'd accomplish very much at home. Most of his troubles were due to a lack of socialization with other people during the entire two years of his existence. We needed to make up for lost time and attempt to desensitize or re-condition him to at the very least tolerate, if not enjoy, strangers. I decided to have Rocky run through my Older Dog class, umpteen times if necessary, until we systematically desensitized and exhausted his aggressive response and helped the owners reinforce desired behaviors.

Rocky came to my training class in October. As with other dogs this aggressive, I had his owners set him up across the street from the other dogs. I instructed them to place a Halti headcollar, choke chain, and regular collar on him (the choke chain and regular collar served as safety backups for the Halti). The leash hook would be buckled through the rings of all three collars. This is an extra precaution so he couldn't slip through, chew through or break through a collar and get loose.

Rocky barked from across the street. I instructed the owners to use a non-force method to startle him. After five minutes of good behavior, they rewarded him with praise, treats, and petting for being quiet while in the sit position.

When I approached Rocky, he growled and tried to lunge at me. I was still twenty feet away. Clearly we had our work cut out for us.

In addition, I gave the owners an in-home anti-dominance aggression program (outlined following) to implement strictly and consistently when someone came to visit. I also referred them to their veterinarian for a prescription of the antidepressant psychotropic medication Elavil. We were pulling out all the stops in Rocky's case; the alternative was death. Potential side effects of the medication was an acceptable risk in this case. (See Chapter 20 on Puppy Prozac and the risk-benefit ratio for further explanation.)

By the end of the first series of seven classes, Rocky was allowing me to feed and pet him while he was in the sitting position. During the second series of sessions, and concurrently with the in-home dominance aggression program and medication, he began to exhibit friendly and happy behavior. (Sometimes I am just as surprised as the owners are with the power of these behavior modification techniques.) He actually began enjoying coming to class and upon seeing me, would wag what was left of his tail. I ended up using him as my demonstration dog in that class and in the next series of classes.

In addition, he was allowing people to enter the house without growling, lunging, and trying to bite them. (Of course, initially he was on leash, Halti, and in a down-stay.) After two or three visits, he would be happy to see them and would seek them out for petting and play. Over an eight-week period, we phased out the medication and after a fourth series of classes, the owners decided he was doing well enough to solely focus on the in-home program.

From Larry's Case Files:
"Ray" the Limb-Devouring Spitz

FILE # 97-003118
DOG'S NAME: Ray
BREED: American Eskimo dog (spitz)
AGE: 4 years
PROBLEM: Fear aggression

In late 1997, I went out to visit a four-year old American Eskimo dog that had bitten two adults and tried to bite a child. Ray had been rescued from a local dog pound when he was two and a half years old. We had no idea what happened to him for the first two years of his life. As I discuss in detail in Chapter 18, "Your Dog's Mental Health Needs," it is crucial that a dog be adequately and positively socialized with other people and animals during the first six months of its life. Otherwise, the dog will tend to be either fear aggressive or dominant aggressive. This appeared to be the case with Ray.

His owners adopted him from the shelter because he was cute. Ray also had been neutered late and was observed to have epileptic-like seizures. He would become fear aggressive (tail and ears down, standing still or backing away, and barking) when people came over. If they tried to reach out and pet him (frequently around the head area) he would lash out, bite, and retreat. Ray also exhibited fear of children and would hide when the owners' young nephews came over. If they pursued, he would bite.

With others in the family, Ray was showing mild dominance aggression. He would growl and bark at Grandma, especially when she tried to get him off the furniture. Ray would ignore attempts by the family to discipline him. Ray's owners would either try to verbally reprimand him or close his mouth shut—a standard force-method dog trainer's technique. The mouth-clamping exercise would only rile him more and contribute to his snapping. He had not attended any obedience classes.

His biting incidents seemed to have escalated around the time he began to have seizures, roughly one year prior. In taking his bite history, there were three clear incidents reported to me.

Incident one: Six months prior to my visit, after one of his seizures, Ray lashed out and bit a family member on the leg. He then ran and hid.

Incident two: Four months later, he growled and attempted to bite a visiting eighteen-month-old nephew who was approaching Ray.

Incident three: A few weeks prior to my visit, Ray had bitten an adult female visitor who had showed him her hand to sniff and then attempted to pet near his face.

After each incident, Ray would be verbally scolded and ostracized for a period of time.

Although we didn't know what happened to Ray during his first two years, it seemed obvious to me that he either lacked sufficient socialization during his early development, or had experienced a traumatic encounter with a stranger or child. He was afraid of strangers and children and out of that came fear aggression. The family was inadvertently reinforcing his aggressive behaviors by allowing him on the furniture and responding to his barking demands. The corporal punishment technique of clamping the mouth shut was also contributing to his mouthiness and nipping. Finally, his seizure activity had coincided with the onset of his aggressive episodes, and therefore I referred the family to their veterinarian for a neurological assessment and anti-convulsion medication. (He was subsequently placed on Phenobarbital.) I then proceeded to outline and implement a gradual re-conditioning and desensitizing anti-fear aggression program for Ray and his family.

FROM LARRY'S CASE FILES:
"James" the Biting-the-Hand-That-Feeds-You Springer Spaniel

FILE: 96-0004201
DOG'S NAME: James
BREED: Springer spaniel
AGE: 18 months
PROBLEM: Dominance aggression
toward his owner

In 1996, I went out on an in-home behavior therapy consult involving a 1½-year-old male Springer spaniel named James who had bitten his owner three times in a three-month period. One of the most dangerous scenarios I can think of is one in which an elderly owner with physical limitations is paired with a dominant-aggressive dog that is physically agile. (I often see severe mismatches between the personality of the owner and the breed-personality of the dog. I discuss this point in more depth in Chapter 16, "Knowing When to Adopt Out," and in Chapter 19, "Matching Your Personality to the Right Dog.")

James's owner got the dog from a local breeder when James was ten weeks of age. His new owner had had no interaction with either of James's parents and could not attest to their temperaments. Nor did she observe James interact with his littermates to compare activity levels and hierarchical behaviors.

At the time of my consult, James was sleeping at night on the bed and was frequently jumping on furniture and guests. He exhibited aggression toward strangers at the front door (one of the reasons I never enter a home with a dog—especially an aggressive dog—at the front door) and toward children. James's owner did not know how to punish James so there were no consequences for his actions. In addition, she could not remove a bone or toy from James without him growling or biting her. She could not be near him when he ate his food without him growling or biting.

Prior to my consultation, James's owner had hired a traditional force-method trainer who put a choke chain on James and hung him until he was gagging. This only caused James to become more aggressive, especially toward male strangers. Big surprise.

James's bite history:

Incident one: March 1996. After James's owner gave him a steak bone to eat, she bent down to remove it and he bit her on the arm.

Incident two: April 1996. While going for a ride in the car, a relative was getting into the front seat but James jumped in before he could sit down. When attempting to grab his collar to move him to the back seat, James bit him on the hand.

Incident three: June 1996. While James's owner tried to tether him in the car before beginning a drive, he bit her on the hand.

Before I entered the home, I had James's owner put him away so she, her daughter, and I could talk. Once I saw her, I remembered she had once brought James to one of my older dog classes. I remembered an incident in which I went to check whether James's collar was on adequately and he lunged and growled at me. Fortunately, I was quicker and was able to restrain him with his leash and Halti.

After taking the bite history on James, it was clear to me that he was exhibiting dominance aggression and object guarding, and that his owner was deathly afraid of him and had inadvertently (through an enmeshed family system) reinforced his dominant behavior. She had unwittingly done this by allowing him up on furniture and beds, allowing him to jump on both her and guests, backing off when he growled at her, and not having any disciplinary consequences for his misbehavior.

We immediately implemented a strict anti-dominance aggression program. She was given obedience assignments, non-corporal punishment techniques, and was referred to the veterinarian for a prescription of a psychotropic medication. It was either this or James was going to be put down.

Aggression

Aggression cases are dangerous and anxiety-provoking. There is always a risk for the behaviorist, owner, and dog. In trying to treat such cases, owners and trainers should expect to be bitten. I all too vividly remember one of my very first aggression cases. It involved an unspayed two-year-old German shepherd that was referred to me after she body-slammed a wrought iron gate off its hinges and charged across the street, pinning a mother and her two children against their van.

When I arrived, I saw that the dog's owner still allowed her to charge out the front door. After fending her off and having the owner put the dog away, I spent the following three hours taking a social, medical, and behavioral history. The shepherd had never experienced visitors coming to the home nor had it been socialized outside the house during its first two years. All of its human contact after leaving the breeder was with the elderly father and his live-in teenage daughter. The dog was never formally obedience trained nor was it spayed. Twice a year when it came into heat it became quite agitated, even with the owners, and aggressive around food.

In addition, the dog was kept in the backyard day and night, and for the last two years had been harassed and teased by children coming home from school through an adjacent alley. They would taunt, yell, and throw stones at the dog from behind the wall.

After hearing this deplorable history, I had the owner bring the dog in on leash and collar. The dog immediately growled and lunged. The owner gave her some commands and got the dog to be quiet. While I remained sitting, we gradually got the dog closer and closer to me, with praise and treats, until after almost an hour, the dog was eating treats out of my hand and allowing me to pet her gently on her chest. At this point, the daughter was relieved and asked if she could take the dog off the leash. I had a very strong intuitive feeling, however, that the dog was still not safe. I asked her to move the dog back a few feet, so I could get up and increase my potential dominance while getting more food treats out of my bag.

As soon as I stood up, the dog without warning lunged in the air and snapped its teeth together a few inches from my throat. I could feel the heat of its breath! The owner was flabbergasted. He saw that in spite of the almost three hours of desensitizing and non-threatening interaction the dog had just had with me, she had gone right back to square one, with full ferocity, without provocation. She was unable to sustain the desensitization association (one of the criteria I use when evaluating shelter dogs declared vicious), and was therefore dangerously unpredictable. The dog was later euthanized. A very sad and tragic case pointing out how serious dog aggression can be. This seriousness is also reflected in national statistics.

STATISTICS

- Estimated amount paid out by U.S. insurance companies in 1994 for dog-bite claims: $1 billion. (Insurance Information Institute, Inc.)
- Average amount of a dog-bite insurance claim: $12,000. (State Farm Insurance)
- Chances that a bodily injury homeowner's insurance claim will involve a dog bite: 1 in 3. (State Farm)
- Chances an American will be bitten by a dog this year: 1 in 50. (Centers for Disease Control)
- Likelihood a biting dog will be male: 8 in 10. (Humane Society of the U.S.)
- Likelihood a biting dog will not have been neutered: 6 in 10. (HSUS)
- Chances the bite will require medical attention: 1 in 5. (CDC)
- Chances the bite victim requiring medical attention will be a child: 3.2 to 1. (CDC)
- Average number of fatal dog bites every year: 9 to 12 (HSUS,CDC)
- Ratio of households keeping a dog because of fear of crime, 1981 compared to 1993: 2 to 1. (HSUS)
- Chances the victim of a fatal dog attack will be a burglar: 1 in 177. (HSUS)
- Chances the victim of a fatal attack will be a child: 7 in 10. (CDC, HSUS)

There are close to five million dog-bite incidents in the United States each year. Most of the victims are children under ten years of age, with the highest subgroup being children from five to nine years of age. More boys than girls are bitten. What's worse, most dog bites are committed by dogs known to the victim! Either it is the family dog or a friend's dog. In the United States (as opposed to countries like England and Australia), most dog bites are committed by mixed-breed dogs. Following mixed breed dogs, German shepherds are identified as the purebred dog most reported in biting incidents, followed by poodles. In severe-bite incidents, pit bulls, German shepherds, chow chows, and other dogs from the sporting and working breeds are the most frequently cited biters.

Is Your Dog Aggressive?

Do you think your dog might be dangerously aggressive? Here's a checklist of questions to ask yourself:

- Has your dog ever attacked another animal totally unprovoked?
- Has your dog ever attacked another person totally unprovoked?
- At the sight of *any* other dog or animal, does it immediately go into a growling, snarling mode and strain on its leash so that you can barely contain it?
- Has it ever attacked you or any member of your family?
- Are you or other family members ever scared of your dog?
- Does your dog growl or bite if you try to take away one of its bones, pet it while it's eating, restrain it by the collar, or after it wakes up from a nap?
- Does your dog pull away from someone reaching for its head and then snap or bite?
- Does your dog whip around, growl or bite when children force it to run or get up from a lying position?
- Does your dog bite or growl when you attempt to remove it from the couch or chair?
- Does your dog lunge out the window of the car and attempt to bite gas station attendants or toll booth operators?
- Does your dog attack its sibling dog every chance it gets?
- Does your dog bite or growl when the veterinarian is examining it or the groomer is attempting to groom it?

If the answer to *any* of the above is yes, you might own an aggressive dog.

There is no "one type" of aggression or aggressive dog. In fact, there are several different types of aggression. Any breed can be aggressive, although breeds successfully developed for guard or attack work are more susceptible. Examples of such breeds are the German shepherd dog, sharpei, chow chow, pit bull, Rottweiler, Doberman, and akita. Successful treatment for aggression depends on which type of aggression your dog has. There are different treatment strategies for the different types.

Twelve Types of Aggression

1. Dominance aggression: The dog sees itself as equal to or higher than people inside or outside its dog pack, and is aggressive out of a controlling position. Frequently, overly enmeshed emotional boundaries between owners and dog can lead to this dysfunction in the family system.

2. Fear aggression: The dog behaves aggressively to keep those people, objects, or situations it fears away from itself. This usually is the result of either not being exposed or socialized to the feared stimuli, or having been traumatized in some way.

3. Food-related aggression: The dog reacts aggressively when approached while eating or when food drops on the floor while the family is eating.

4. Possessive or object-guarding aggression: A form of dominance aggression in which a dog inappropriately guards its toy objects from its owners.

5. Territorial aggression: The dog protects an inappropriate location, or protects an appropriate location but in the wrong context or situation. The dog attacks anyone near, on or in its property without due cause. This includes dogs that, while sitting in their owners' cars, lunge at gas station attendants or pedestrians walking by.

6. Predatory aggression: The dog stalks, stares, and silently pursues small animals or infants. Often the small animals are killed.

7. Play or learned aggression: Through rough play or intentional teaching, the dog learns to be aggressive.

8. Inter-dog aggression: Dogs in the same home fight with each other, frequently over which will be the dominant dog (see Chapter 10, "Sibling Dog Fighting," for more information). Or a dog may exhibit aggression toward all dogs, including those outside the home.

9. Maternal aggression: The dog protects its puppies by showing aggressiveness while in heat and during pregnancy. This is normal and is usually temporary.

10. Pain aggression: Usually an inappropriate response due to an underlying physical condition that causes the dog pain. Example: A child chases a dog that has painful arthritis; the dog shows aggression toward the child to stop it from triggering the pain.

11. Idiopathic-biological aggression: A genetic, or inherited, aggression. The dog is aggressive, apparently without cause, toward everyone and everything, most of the time. Or the dog, without warning or apparent cause, engages in spurts of aggression toward family members or people it knows. The condition usually appears between one and three years of age and can appear in any breed. In some breeds there is a special label for this phenomenon. For example, in springers it is referred to as Springer Spaniel Rage Syndrome. While idiopathic aggression is rare, the prognosis is poor and the dog usually must be euthanized.

12. Redirected aggression: A dog redirects its aggression toward another object or person. Often this occurs when it is interrupted while engaging in another type of aggression. Example: You try to break up a fight between two dogs and one of them attacks you.

Recognizing an Aggressive Dog's Body Language

A dominant-aggressive dog will try to appear bigger than it really is by leaning forward in its stance and having its hair stand on end (piloerection) from its neck to its rear end. Its tail will be up stiff, or stiffly wagging. Its ears will be up or pointed forward. It will establish direct eye contact. Its lips will be pulled back exposing teeth. It will be coming toward its target and it will be barking or growling.

A fear-aggressive dog will try to appear smaller than it is by getting low to the ground or crouching. Its tail will be tucked or stiffly wagging. Its ears will be down or back. It will be standing still or backing away from its target. Its lips will be retracted back to expose teeth and it, too, will be growling or barking. However, it is important to note that in some cases, the dog may be exhibiting a mixture of aggression types and could be alternating back and forth between these two sets of behavioral indicators. With pain and predatory aggression, there may be *no* warning or growling until the bite attempt has already been carried out.

With all these types of aggression, it is recommended that you attempt to reduce the dog's overall levels of built-up tension. Changing to foods with fewer chemical additives can help. Many dogs do well, both behaviorally and physically, on the natural lamb-and-rice diets. In addition, daily fifteen-minute aerobic exercise sessions can help. You could take the dog jogging (with proper anti-pull collars and restraints if it is aggressive and if it doesn't have hip or heart problems), throw tennis balls in the yard, or do some laps together in the pool. Doing at least one twenty-five-minute heeling obedience walk per day, often in the morning, will also help to reduce tension. It's important you stay as calm and relaxed as you can while holding your dog's leash so you don't communicate tension and anxiety to your dog. Although you hold the leash securely, you want to remain relaxed so as not to set it off into an aggressive on-guard mode.

With some dogs, having the owners conduct daily one-on-one stress-management focus sessions can help reduce tension. Twice a day, for at least fifteen to thirty minutes, just you and the dog are situated in a quiet room without other people, animals, or distractions. Talk soothingly to your pet. If its aggression does not prohibit touch, give it a gentle caressing petting or massage session, keeping your voice low and relaxed. This can go a long way, for both you and your dog, in reducing overall tensions that might contribute to your dog's aggressive tendencies.

This chapter will focus on the two most common types of aggressive disorders in dogs: fear aggression and dominance aggression. Food-related and object-guarding aggression are included with dominance aggression.

A Review of Aggression

When people engage in chronic aggressive behavior, they are frequently diagnosed with either a Conduct Disorder or an Antisocial Personality Disorder. Conduct Disorder is defined as a repetitive and persistent pattern of behavior in which the basic rights of others or societal norms are violated. This includes: bullying, threatening, or intimidating others (as our dominant-aggressive dogs do), initiating physical fights, and being physically cruel to people or animals (as our predatory or inter-dog aggressive dogs do).

Antisocial Personality Disorder is defined as a pervasive pattern of disregard for and violation of the rights of others. This includes: failure to conform to social norms, impulsiveness, irritability, and aggressiveness (as with both the dominant and fear-aggressive dog).

Much of the aggression in dogs is learned during their first six months of life. It can come from the dog being attacked by another dog, abused by a toddler, cut by the groomer, or being insufficiently socialized with other people and dogs.

Some traditional trainers use electric shock, muzzles, prong-collars, and physical violence in attempt to "counter-dominate" an aggressive dog—to "show the dog who's boss." These approaches aren't sound. If things have gotten so out of hand that muzzling, shocking, or beating the dog is the only way to counter aggression, the dog needs to be euthanized—for everyone's safety and quality of life. This is dealt with in greater detail in Chapter 13.

Don't use electric shock or muzzles or violence. Pain can increase aggression in dogs (and people). It might make some dogs overly submissive. Many times, the dog will personalize the fear of the trainer who brutalizes it, but will still be aggressive—often more aggressive—toward others it does not view in the same way.

Who wants to live in a self-imposed prison where you have to lock down your dog or avoid having guests or children come and visit? Who wants to have to go through the daily trauma of watching one's dog going crazy when it sees another dog out on walks? Who wants to live with the constant fear that their dog will jump through a plate glass window or screen door and severely injure or kill a delivery person or child? It would be like living with a loaded, hair-trigger weapon sitting on the coffee table all the time. That is not our view of dogs and the human-animal bond.

When dealing with an aggressive dog, there is considerable emotional anxiety on the owner's part. There are also aggressive tensions and physical danger on the dog's part. And of course, there is risk to the veterinarian and behaviorist working with the dog and its family. There are liability and public safety issues to also consider.

Treating the Whole Family

Echoing one of the main themes of this book is the need for the animal behaviorist to treat the entire family system when trying to change a severe dog-behavior problem. It is insufficient to merely focus on the dog—no matter which techniques you use. The humans in the family must change the way they relate to their dog if the dog's behavior is to completely change. The structure and emotional boundaries of the family must be altered to effect a complete "cure" in the problem dog's behavior. This approach is referred to as Structural Family Therapy.

Structural Family Therapy was originally outlined by family therapist Dr. Salvador Minuchin and is based on changing the organization of the family. The assumption is that once the structure of the family group is transformed, the positions of members in that group are altered. As a result, the individual family member's (or dog's) experience or perspective changes.

The family structure is defined as the invisible set of demands that organizes how family members interact with one another. In this case, the family structure is synonymous with the structure of the wolf-pack hierarchy in the home. Repeated transactions establish patterns of how each member of the pack is to relate to one another and to those outside the pack. A power hierarchy and mutual expectation of how pack members are supposed to behave underlie the functioning of the group.

The rules defining who participates in which activities and how are established by the emotional boundaries of the family or pack. The two extremes of boundary functioning are termed enmeshed (diffuse boundaries, no clear lines of hierarchical position, or inappropriate crossing of those lines), and disengaged (inappropriately rigid boundaries, which foster lack of feelings of loyalty and belonging).

Dominance aggression is rampant in families in which the emotional boundaries are too enmeshed with the dog, whereas fear aggression is rampant in families in which the emotional boundaries are too disengaged, or rigid. The goal of the animal behaviorist, like the human Structural Family Therapist, is to create change in the family system and restructure the emotional boundaries with the dog in order to eliminate the aggressive behavior.

The tools used to restructure such operations include marking boundaries by making them explicit, assigning tasks to alter transaction patterns, and supporting, educating, and guiding the family in learning new ways of relating to their dog. One axiom of behavior therapy is: Any behavior that has been learned can be un-learned and re-learned.

Aggression-Treatment Programs

Caution: The programs outlined here are not cookbook cures! They should only be implemented with the hands-on assistance of a qualified animal behavior consultant and/or veterinarian. Whenever you work with an aggressive dog you are assuming the risk that you will be bitten and/or hurt. Remember that.

Dominance-Aggression Treatment Program

With dominance aggression, you must benevolently but firmly put the aggressive dog back in its place in the pack. You need to train it to see the humans in its pack as being higher in the pecking order. You also need to correct and discipline the aggressive displays without triggering a counter-aggressive response. Then you want to actively reward submissive behavior and tighten the dog's obedience response to razor sharpness. Lots of lie-downs and long stay commands are usually an integral part of the program. And it goes without saying that the dog should be fixed (neutered or spayed).

You also want to remove the trigger situation (the activities that set off the aggression) for at least two months. If the dog is going to improve with treatment, you will notice it within about eight weeks. Here are the nuts and bolts of the dominance-aggression treatment program:

- Always have your veterinarian rule out any organic or physical disease that could be manifesting itself through your dog's aggressive behaviors. Rule out brain tumors, epilepsy, low thyroid, and so on.
- Completely ignore your dog for a full seventy-two hours, except for feeding it and letting it relieve itself. We want to put the dog in a socially deprived state (starving it for attention) in which it will more likely than not do anything you ask of it to get some attention—including putting aside some of its aggressive tendencies and being obedient. This "shunning" strikes at the core need of a pack animal to not be ostracized from the pack. At the end of the seventy-two-hour period, phase in your attention by having the dog sit first and only giving attention when it's not actively seeking it. This is outlined in greater detail below.
- The dog should have no contact with strangers or other dogs until the fourth week of the program.
- The dog should not be taken out in public during the first four weeks.
- The dog should never be allowed to run or roam off leash.
- The dog should never be tied to a tree in the yard.
- The dog should not be confined all day behind a fence barrier it can see through. Allowing the dog to run free, tying it up in the front yard, or putting it behind a barrier it can see through will only worsen the dominance aggression you are trying to fix.

- No physical punishment.
- The dog must start earning all of its attention—petting, feeding, playing, eye contact, and freedom—by doing one or two obedience commands. Initially, it will be required to sit (refer to Chapter 4) before you: pet it, look at it, talk to it, play with it, feed it, or let it in or out. Starting the second week, and using my non-violent positive-reward methods, teach the dog the lie-down command and begin the three-week process of training the dog to do a fifteen to thirty minute stay (sitting or lying). By week four of this program, your dog should be sitting on command at the first request, lying down at the first request, and achieving a minimum fifteen-minute stay. These three obedience commands are essential for the rest of the dominance-aggression program to be successful. The bottom line: No more freeloading! The dog has to earn everything positive from now on.
- Do not respond to any of the dog's initiations for attention. This includes: the dog whining or barking at you, nose-nudging your hand or arm, pawing at your leg, or turning around and backing its rear end into you. Every time you give the dog attention when it demands it in these ways, you are lowering your status in the pack hierarchy and teaching the dog to be aggressive and dominant. Basically, your dog is saying to you, "Give me attention now, human slave doormat," and many of you do. This is a very dangerous thing to do with a dominant-aggressive dog.
- Only give the dog attention when it is not seeking it and when it is quiet and sitting or lying down.
- Practice the sit command as outlined in Chapter 4 for ten repetitions in a row, three times a day.
- Whenever you notice your dog assuming a submissive position or doing an obedience command of its own accord, notice it ("good sit"), and reward it with a treat and petting.
- Do not allow your dog to jump up on furniture or people. If it does, practice the Startle-wait five-Redirect-and-Reward method of correction outlined in Chapter 4.
- Always be one physical level higher than the dog. In dog street rules, whoever is physically on top is politically on top as well. Therefore, you should be sleeping in the bed. The dog should be on the floor. You should eat at the table. The dog should be lying twenty feet

away on the floor. You should be on the couch, the dog should not. And so on.

- No petting around the dog's head or face for six months.
- No tug-of-war games; that's how they train dogs to be aggressive. It also lowers your dominance position.
- No roughhousing on the floor.
- Any lip curling, growling, talk-back barking, lunging, or biting attempts should be disciplined while they are taking place. Startle-Wait five. With actual growling or aggression, instruct the dog to sit after five minutes following the startle-discipline technique, then ignore it the rest of the day. Over time, the dog will learn, "If I lash out at my owners or their friends, I'll be blasted in the face with water, be made to sit, and then be ostracized." However, when the dog sits and is not displaying the aggressive behavior, it gets lots of treats, reinforcement, and attention. Very quickly, the dog becomes conditioned to behave obediently and more submissively because it learns what behavior earns a "paycheck" and that aggression results in a "pink slip."
- Obviously, to use the above techniques, owners must always be ready for the dog's behaviors during the first six to eight weeks. You must notice and reward consistently, appropriate and obedient behavior when it occurs, as well as noticing and correcting inappropriate or aggressive behavior. This means the owners must have their startle devices on them at all times, as well as their pack of treats. This way the dog knows why it's being rewarded or punished.
- If you are afraid of your dog, carry pepper spray or mace when you are around it, and have it on a twenty-foot leash. When an owner is afraid of his dog, the dog picks up on this and takes advantage of it by further intimidation. The mace or pepper spray is just in case anything goes wrong during the therapy interaction. In addition, if the dog becomes aggressive and won't allow the owner to come near it, the owner has twenty feet of leash to grab, tie-off, and secure the dog. The owner can corral the dog without having to approach its face. It's important the owner supervise the dog if the leash is to be attached so it doesn't get caught on a sprinkler head or similar object and inadvertently choke the dog.
- The dog is not to be given any bones or chew toys until further notice. These toys are often triggers for the dominant-aggressive behavior. I

like to have clients wait until the halfway point of the anti-dominance aggression program is reached (four weeks) before phasing back in the chew toys. When the chew toys are phased in at week four, it is under the following conditions:

1. The dog has to sit and lie down before being given the chew toy.
2. The dog is now taught the "drop" or "give" command. Whenever the dog has its bone or off-limits object, the owner grabs some irresistible treats, bends down six feet away from the dog, extends his hand with treats, looks away, and says "Give!" or "Drop!" The dog must relinquish the chew object in order to eat the unusually scrumptious treats (broken up pieces of string cheese, cooked hot dogs, liver treats, etc.). Once the dog relinquishes the object, tell it to sit, and reward the dog with one hand while removing the object or chew toy with the other. If the dog makes any aggressive displays, blast it with the water or ultrasonic device, tell it "Off!" and remove all toys and ignore the dog for the rest of the day. Start again the next day. This is not bribery nor will it teach the dog to steal. The dog must earn the paycheck or positive reinforcement, by doing the behavior first (dropping the chew object), then sitting, and then receiving the verbal praise ("good drop") and then the treat. Practice this each day, and in two to four weeks, the dog will relinquish the object just by hearing "drop" or "give"—without needing a treat.

Many dominant-aggressive dogs are used to dragging their owners throughout the neighborhood like kites. So, before we work with your dog's dominance aggression around other people and dogs, it should have gone through the first four weeks of implementing the above plan at home. (This includes the possibility of psychotropic medication.) If the first four weeks are successful, you can start the other phase of this program involving other people and dogs. However, the dog must be absolutely secure on leash with a non-abusive but effective anti-pull harness it can't get out of before taking it out in public, before it meets guests in the home, and before it attends a non-force obedience class. If your dog has a snout (in other words, it is not a breed with a pushed-in face, like the Shih Tzu, Lhasa apso, Boston terrier, and the like), you will need an anti-pull Halti headcollar, or a similar collar for safety, socialization, and pulling problems. (See Chapter 4 for details on these special collars.)

Dealing With the Dominant-Aggressive Dog When People Come Over

SOLICITORS

If the person at your door is a solicitor or other person who will not be entering the home, allow your dog a maximum of six barks. That's enough to alert you, but not enough to get the dog worked up in to a frenzy, anger your neighbors, or get you involved in a small-claims court case. Then have the dog sit. If it won't sit or be quiet, tell it "off," and blast or startle it. Wait for five minutes of good behavior and again redirect to a quiet sit. Tell the solicitor through the unopened door you don't want any.

FRIENDS, FAMILY

A friend or family member who does not live with you can be of great help in ridding your dog of its aggression. If possible, practice the following exercises as often as once a day. It goes without saying that you must warn your visitor you are training your dog not to be aggressive, that you need his help, and that the dog may try to bite. Obtain clear consent. Never allow children to participate in these exercises. When your guest arrives at the door tell him, "One minute please!" Put your dog away for a few minutes in a secure room with a bone that has peanut butter smeared on it. How? Recommended method: Have your dog sit. Give it a treat. While it's chewing the treat, hook its leash onto its regular collar. Heel or walk the dog to a room, give it the bone, and close the door.

Here's what to do next:

1. Let your guest in and have him sit down. It should be in a room with lots of space and one that your dog does not often frequent. Tell your guest not to look at or try to pet or approach your dog.

2. Give your guest a handful of irresistible doggy treats.

3. Lay a trail of these irresistible treats on the floor from your guest to the door your dog is behind.

4. Go to your dog. Make sure it doesn't rush through the door.

5. Before you bring it out, have your dog sit. Give it three or four treats while you put on its Halti headcollar or other special collar, securing the Halti straps twice through and around the regular neck collar before

fastening. That way, if the dog paws off the "nose" part of the Halti, it can't run away.

6. Have your dog sit at the heeling position. Place both hands on the leash (as described in more detail in Chapter 4), and tell it "heel."

7. Open the door and proceed forward, encouraging the dog to vacuum up the trail of treats. Act as happy as you can, petting the dog and getting it to wag its tail in a relaxed manner.

8. If at any time it growls or barks at the guest, tell it "Off!" and blast it in the face with water or use another startle device. If the dog barks again, startle or blast it again. This can potentially go on for fifteen minutes or more.

9. Once the dog is quiet and sitting, proceed toward your guest, stopping and sitting down ten to twenty feet away, with both hands on the leash and giving the dog a foot or so of leash.

10. Put your dog into a sit or down stay. (It's had four weeks of this training already and should be up to a half-hour stay.) Reward the dog lavishly with praise and treats. Again, if there is any barking, growling, or lunging, tell it "Off!" and startle. Then wait fifteen minutes more for quiet, non-aggressive behavior while the dog is in a sit or down stay. The dog remains on leash and collar throughout this entire time.

11. After at least thirty minutes of not showing any aggressiveness toward the guest, have the guest toss treats to your dog, using a friendly voice, saying your dog's name and what a good boy or girl he or she is. Make sure the guest does not look straight into your dog's eyes. If there are any aggressive displays, say "Off!" startle, wait five minutes and resume. That's as far as you go until week eight of the program.

12. At week eight—and only if the dog is acting friendly, is not showing signs of aggression, and has met the guest on at least three previous occasions—you can start to heel the dog over to the guest, and have it sit and stay. The dog must be on the leash and special collar. If the dog maintains good behavior, the guest can extend a handful of treats and feed your dog while you hold the leash. You or an accomplice must have your squirt bottle or water syringe aimed at your dog's face the entire time in case of any aggressive displays. The dog must be reprimanded at the earliest signs of aggressive behavior. If it does try to bite, by using the Halti you can pull up on the leash quickly and shut the dog's mouth and pull its head away.

13. Once the dog (at the eight-week point) is taking treats, is friendly

and shows positive recognition of the guest, and is not exhibiting any type of aggression, the guest can try lightly petting the dog away from its face, while giving treats as you hold your dog on leash and Halti. After a fifteen-minute period, return to your seat ten to twenty feet away with your dog, sit down, and put the dog in either a sit or down stay. The dog must remain on Halti and leash for the rest of the visit.

14. When your visitor is ready to leave, heel the dog to a spot twenty feet away from the door and put it in a sit stay, keeping both of your hands on the leash. Say good-bye and allow your visitor to let himself out. Frequently at this point, both dominant-aggressive and fear-aggressive dogs will relapse into an aggressive display when the guest stands up. This is because the guest is now taller, and therefore more dominant or threatening. Some dogs will also try to attack the guest from behind as he leaves, so be sure to hold the leash firmly.

CHILDREN AND OTHER DOGS

The liability risks are too great to have children come over and serve as guinea pigs. Many times, aggression can only be controlled or repressed, not fully cured. Therefore, there's always a risk. With children, you can practice reconditioning exercises at a distance, heeling the dog in public with the Halti headcollar and some back-up collars on. When you take your dominant-aggressive dog out, the safest course is to not only use the Halti headcollar—with straps tucked twice through the regular neck collar before fastening—but to fasten the leash hook through three collar rings: one on the Halti, one on a choke chain, and one on the regular nylon or leather collar. The dog's regular collar must be secure enough so it cannot be slipped over the dog's head, yet you should be able to insert four fingers between it and the dog's neck.

When you are out with your dog, always heel it by your side. Have your treats and startle device with you. Every thirty paces, have your dog do a sit-stay and/or down-stay. When you spot a child or children at a safe distance (no closer than across the street) have the dog sit and stay, praise it, give it treats, and act happy. You want the dog to associate good things and a happy mood when these creatures called children come on the scene. If at any time there is growling, lip curling, lunging, breaking the heel or the stay command, tell the dog firmly "Off!" blast it with your startle device, wait five minutes, do a sit-stay and begin again. Start these heeling walks at the eight-week point of the anti-dominance aggression program.

Finally, to help deal with other dogs, and to further recondition your dominant-aggressive dog, enroll in a non-violent, positive-reinforcement-method obedience class. (For referrals, call the Association of Pet Dog Trainers, 1-800-PET-DOGS.) By attending such a class each week, without it being pained through choke-chain hanging techniques (and by receiving lots of scrumptious treats), the dog starts associating the other dogs, people, and children with something positive, versus something requiring an aggressive response. This will round out the dog's in-home training.

Medication

If your dog is showing serious and dangerous aggressive behavior, and if you are considering euthanasia, consult with your veterinarian about putting your dog on a psychotropic medication. For dominance aggression, antidepressants such as Prozac, azapirones such as BuSpar, and perhaps tricyclic antidepressants such as Elavil, may be of help. However, these medications alone will not cure or successfully treat the aggression. They have to be paired with the extensive behavior-modification program outlined. In addition, your dog's liver enzyme levels need to be monitored for potential side effects of these medications. And these medications can potentially make the behavior more unpredictable, because when the dosage begins to wear off, your dog may rebound with greater aggression. These issues are discussed in greater detail in Chapter 20.

It usually takes six to eight weeks of consistent training (in the home, on daily heeling walks, in obedience class, and with the psychotropic medication) to break bad behaviors and three to four weeks to make new or desired ones. At the end of the eight-week period, you will be able to observe whether or not your dog's dominance aggression is improving, staying the same, or worsening. If there is no improvement or it is getting worse, even with psychotropic medication, then euthanizing the dog should be seriously considered. The dog is too much of a danger. In addition, consider whether a dog that is constantly being aggressive is enjoying its time on Earth. It is, like someone with chronic paranoid delusions, seeing or interpreting things that are not there. How humane is it for a dog to be kept alive in this unhappy state?

Fear-Aggression Treatment Program

With fear aggression, you don't want to be overly firm or use a lot of corrections. This only contributes to the underlying fear that feeds the aggressive behavior. Instead, you want to make the dog less sensitive and less fearful in the situations that trigger the aggression. You do this through systematic desensitization techniques: you counter-condition the dog to view what it once saw as negative as being positive and joyful. Occasional anti-anxiety medication is also warranted, as is some mild obedience training.

Where the fear-aggression program differs from the dominance-aggression program is in what it emphasizes. Much of the technique overlaps. If you have a fear-aggressive dog that is aggressive toward strangers entering the home or toward children in the street, apply the same steps outlined above in the dominance-aggression program. Use treats and keep the dog on leash when greeting visitors. Use a Halti collar with treats and sit commands at safe distances from children when on walks. However, because in fear aggression the behaviors are anxiety-driven, any correction or overly harsh treatment raises the dog's anxiety and will make the problem worse.

We hope to make the dog less sensitive or fearful in the same way we do with humans who have fears and phobias. We present the dog with the feared person, object, or situation in its least fear-producing form, at a safe distance, paired with things that are incompatible with fear. Things such as food treats, toys, and playing activities. With humans, it is hard for a person to remain petrified while feeling relaxed and tranquil. They are incompatible experiences or behaviors. Since dogs lack the language and abstraction abilities of humans, instead of teaching to them to relax, we pair food treats with the fearful trigger. It's hard for dogs to enjoy eating a snack and feel petrified at the same time. After repeated pairings, the dog will start associating pleasant views with what it once saw as fear producing.

As with the dominance-aggression program already outlined, you must have your veterinarian rule out organic or physiological causes to the anxiety. The most frequent such cause is a low-functioning thyroid.

The steps to treating a fear-aggressive dog:

- Remove all potentially fear-producing events from the dog's life. No harsh or physical punishment. No excessive roughhousing. No teasing. Not a lot of handling around the face. Implement a temporary moratorium on grooming if grooming is triggering the fear. Implement a temporarily moratorium on car rides if riding in the car produces fear, and so on. Let's have a cooling-off period.

- As with dominance aggression, it is helpful for the fear-aggressive dog to view you as a secure and trustworthy pack leader. You can raise this trust and improve bonding by having the dog sleep inside the bedroom at night and have it do an obedience command before it receives something positive, such as having it sit before feeding.

- Remove all accidental rewards or reinforcements for the fearful behavior. What locks in and maintains the fearful-aggressive behavior is the dog receiving unintentional rewards when it is behaving fearfully or aggressively. You must not pet the dog, restrain it, hold it, pick it up, give it a pacifying treat, or talk soothingly to it when it is behaving fearfully or aggressively. This only rewards the dog for the behavior. Yes, it's only natural to want to comfort our pets when they appear fearful. However, with a fear-aggressive dog, it is only serving to make the aggression worse.

- Identify what the dog is fearful of, where the fear-aggressive behavior takes place, who is around when it occurs, and what happens immediately preceding its display, during the aggression, and immediately following it.

- Once you identify what the dog is fearful of, grade and prioritize these fear triggers. Identify the most fearful presentation of what triggers the dog and go down from there until you hit the least fearful presentation of the event. Write down ten levels of fear, going from the most fearful to the least fearful presentation of the stimuli or trigger.

- While feeding treats and playing with the dog, gradually expose the dog to each level, starting with the least fearful presentation. So, if your dog is fearful of people reaching for its head to pet, the least fearful presentation would be just seeing a visitor or strange person. Start out then by greeting people at distances while giving your dog treats. The next most fearful presentation might be to have the visitor or stranger within the same room. So, when people come over, instruct them not to reach for your pet's head or stare it in the eyes, but instead to sit down and throw treats until the dog feels comfortable enough (initially on leash) to approach, sit. and take treats out of the hand. (Although excessive punishment will make the problem worse, a squirt of water if the dog tries to bite or growls is helpful to teach the dog that although it is afraid, that kind of display is unacceptable. But, as opposed to the dominance-aggression program, this startle technique with water is the last resort when a bite attempt is being made and is to be used sparingly. The real magic in the fear-aggression program is lowering the dog's anxiety through the desensitizing and counter-conditioning procedures.)

- Gradually work your way through the list of ten steps. Over an eight-week period, initially with the dog on leash, and first with only tossing or feeding treats, the dog is to be exposed over and over again to as many visitors to the home as possible, until it no longer acts fearful or aggressive, and instead starts seeing visitors in a positive light. The dog is on leash and collar, so it cannot escape from what it fears and therefore reinforce the continuance of the phobia. Eventually, you will begin to observe the dog wag its tail and look forward to meeting visitors.

- Once the dog is friendly, relaxed, and safe with guests, have the guests serve as the sole source of positive social attention during the remainder of the visit. You can even have guests put food in your dog's bowl. Have the dog in a sit-stay twenty feet away while the guest puts the bowl down and backs off. Eight weeks of such positive interaction will cause your dog to change its view of visitors from fearful to friendly.

These techniques can be used to cure fears of loud noises and inanimate objects like vacuum cleaners and lawn mowers, as well as fears of animate objects like kids on skateboards and people in uniform. Just use the two basic behavior-modification tools of systematic desensitization (working step by step through the ten levels of intensity of fear) and counter-conditioning (pairing the fearful trigger with something extremely positive so it takes on a positive association).

Case Study Postscript

ROCKY

Rocky has continued to do well. He went off the medication and completed his obedience classes with no further signs of aggression. He and I had actually become good friends. At home, he was no longer growling and lunging at visitors and was beginning to make friends with people who visited frequently.

RAY

Ray did not do well. Even with the anti-seizure medication, he had subsequent seizures and he continued trying to bite various family members and visitors. In addition, the family did not pull together as a team to treat Ray's aggression in a comprehensive manner. Too often, the wife would report tthat only she was implementing the plan and felt quite overwhelmed by the whole situation. At our last conversation, the wife indicated that she and her husband were leaning toward euthanizing Ray.

JAMES

James initially did phenomenally well for an entire six-month period. No more growling. No more biting. No more food guarding. No more object guarding. He had become compliant and affectionate toward his owner.

However, as in many other cases that are going well, James's owner eventually let down her guard. She began to let him get up on furniture and decided to stop his medication. Within a week, James began to growl again.

I immediately put James back on the active case roster. After consultation with the dog's veterinarian, I informed the owner that given James's improvement for an entire six-month period and his sudden relapse after discontinuing his medication as well as key aspects of the behavior-therapy program, he would need to be on his medication long-term and have to go back to square one in the behavior therapy.

James's owner called a short time later and said he was back on the medication and she had begun implementing the program again. James's good behavior was beginning to return. As of this writing, James is still back on track.

10

SIBLING DOG FIGHTING

"We need your help badly. We've had our dogs for five years now, and all of a sudden they're getting into horrific fights! We just don't understand it. Why would they fight after all this time?"

"I just brought the dogs home from the hospital. They needed stitches and antibiotics. My husband says this is the last straw. If we can't get the dogs to stop trying to kill each other, we'll either have to give one away or euthanize them."

FROM LARRY'S CASE FILES:
"Angela" and "Megan" the Battling Dalmatians

FILE # 96-09442
DOGS' NAMES: Angela and Megan
BREED: Dalmatians
AGES: 8 years and 6 months, respectively
PROBLEM: Fighting

In 1996, I went out on a sibling dog-fighting case involving two female Dalmatians. The dog first in the home was a eight-year-old spayed Dalmatian named Angela. The new dog, Megan, which the owners had brought home a month before, was six months old. Within the first five to ten minutes after my arrival and greeting the dogs, they engaged in four full-out fights. These occurred when one of the dogs was under the table, under the owners' legs, or standing beside one of the owners and myself. I had to swing my feet away to avoid being bitten.

In observing Angela and Megan go at each other, it became clear what was happening. The older Dalmatian, Angela, was attempting to establish and reinforce her dominance through eye stares and body posturing. Megan, the younger Dalmatian, would immediately trot over to Angela, challenge her, and not back down in response to Angela's warning growl.

Also, the owners were trying to treat Angela and Megan as equals, thereby cueing Angela to initiate a fight to reclaim her dominance.

One of the first things I did was explain the concept of canine hierarchy (only one dog can be top dog) and to point out how they were setting up the dogs to fight by inadvertently reinforcing Megan as dominant dog, when in fact she was not.

I worked with the dogs' owners in implementing an anti-sibling dog-fighting program. Part of this program included some structured non-force obedience work covering sits, downs, and stays. This was partly necessary for the owners to more clearly establish their own dominance over both dogs, and partly necessary to gain control of each dog so they could call the dominant dog first and the submissive dog would remain in a stay until it was her turn to come.

After spending two hours implementing the beginning of our program, the two dogs began getting along better and engaged in a twenty-minute non-stop play session without any aggressive displays. This was partly the result of having the owners ignore both dogs while I was there, which forced the two dogs to seek each other out for attention.

From Larry's Case Files: "Lily" and "Spring"—the Brittany Spaniel Who Flattened Her Flat-Coated Sister

FILE # 95-00021
DOGS' NAMES: Lily, Spring
BREEDS: Brittany spaniel, flat-coated retriever
AGES: 8 years, 5 years
PROBLEM: Sibling dog fighting

In September of 1995, I went out on a consult involving two female dogs: an eight-year-old Brittany spaniel named Lily and a five-year-old flat-coated retriever named Spring. They had begun to fight—with increasing frequency and intensity. Much was normal about their backgrounds. Both dogs were purchased at eight weeks of age. Both were spayed. Both were healthy. Both greeted guests in an excited and friendly way. The owner could take chew toys out of either dog's mouth without provoking growling or guarding. Likewise, she could approach and handle the dogs while they ate.

The dogs' first fight occurred over a rubber toy Lily was chewing on. Spring approached Lily and began pawing at it. Lily growled and Spring lunged and growled back. They were off and running. The next two fights occurred in the living room when one dog was getting attention from the owner. Lily would growl to assert her dominance and Spring would not back down.

It was clear we had to reorder the pack relationships and teach the owner how to treat the dominant dog differently than she treated the submissive dog. She began to work a program that included non-force obedience training and counter-conditioning therapy.

Spring and Lily now get along after having solved their sibling dog-fighting differences.

Common Characteristics of Sibling Dog Fighting

In a typical sibling dog-fighting situation, the owners already have one dog, and have brought home a second dog, which the first dog begins fighting with. Or, the owners have had two or more dogs from day one and now, three to six years later, they begin to fight.

There are four characteristics common to ninety-nine percent of sibling dog-fighting cases:

1. The dogs are the same sex.
2. The dogs fight only in the owners' presence.
3. The dogs are adult dogs, generally four years or older.
4. The fights involve a struggle for which one will be the dominant dog in the family pack. And in these cases, the owners frequently choose the wrong dog as the dominant dog and begin treating it as such. Or, the owners attempt to treat the dogs equally and democratically, as if the dogs were human children.

Frequently, sibling dogs work out their dominance issues among themselves. This is evidenced by the fact that when the owners return home after being away, there are no signs of fighting or injuries. It's only when their owners interfere that things go wrong.

Signs and Privileges of the Dominant Dog

Owners must figure out which dog is the dominant dog and acknowledge it as such in the ways they interact with their dogs. Owners need to look for various clues.

When a dog is taking a dominant stance, its ears will be fully erect or forward, its tail will be up stiff or stiffly wagging, its hair will be on end from its neck to its rear end, its lips will be pursed forward exposing teeth, and the dog will tend to be rocked forward in its stance. These dominant doggy body language signals are important for the owners to learn and recognize so they can intervene at the slightest hint of a conflict brewing, before a full-on fight ensues.

This parallels working with human patients who have an anger-management problem, or who are victims of domestic violence. The aim in this situation is to help the person learn and sense physical early warning cues that either they or their abuser begin to emit and that signal the beginning of the anger-rage-violence cycle. By helping people identify these human body language signals, the potential for violence is reduced and the opportunity for alternative coping responses is enhanced. It is the same with sibling dogs that fight.

Owners need to know which privileges are to be given to the dominant dog. The dominant dog gets to greet them first, gets attention first, and is fed first. It gets to go in and out of entrances first, and is allowed to horde the toys, guard food, and mount and T-stance the submissive dog.

In Angela's and Megan's case, Megan, the submissive dog, should not have been allowed to have these dominant behaviors. When she did them and would not back off when Angela warned her or counter-dominated her, the owners, in their roles as pack leaders, should have enforced Megan's subordinate behavior on Angela's behalf. This was part of the behavior modification the owners were to adopt in actively reinforcing Angela's role as dominant dog. The owners were to change their behavior by greeting and petting Angela first. In addition, the owners had to enforce Megan's role as submissive dog by intervening with non-corporal punishment startle techniques whenever Megan attempted to horn in on Angela's dominant privileges. The owners were to discipline Megan for trying to be greeted first or for trying to get in and out of entrances before Angela.

The Nuts and Bolts of the Anti-Sibling Dog-Fighting Program

Each case is different. Each owner has a different personality. Each home is laid out differently. Each pair of sibling fighting dogs are different. There is risk. This type of program takes time and effort. Acknowledging this, and that each case needs to be tailored to the particulars of the home in which the sibling fighting is occurring, what follows is the general components of the anti-sibling dog-fighting program.

- Figure out which is really the dominant dog.
- Start treating the dominant dog as dominant and assist the true dominant dog in keeping in check the submissive dog. This is done by greeting, feeding, petting, playing, acknowledging, and letting in and out the dominant dog first.
- Discipline the submissive dog for trying to horn in on the dominant

dog using non-corporal startle techniques. Use a startle that doesn't make noise, like a powerful blast of water, since you do not want to inadvertently punish one dog for the other's offense.

- Only give the dogs attention when they're together; never when they're separate. When you do give the dogs attention, the dominant dog gets it first.

- Do daily reconditioning exercises: one family member with one dog on one side of the yard on leash (and anti-pull device if needed) and the other dog with another family member on the opposite side of the yard. Each dog does ten sits, ten downs, and a five-minute stay. Use the positive-reinforcement methods of obedience outlined in Chapter 4.

- Gradually, bring the dogs closer and closer during these sessions until after a two- to four-week period (still on leash), they are side by side doing their lie downs, sits, and so on. Any growling, lunging, aggressive squaring off, or breaking their stays results in a Startle-Redirect-Reward reprimand.

- After this has been achieved, start adding a fifteen-minute cooling-down session following the yard exercises. This should be inside the home on the same couch with one person with one dog at one end of the couch and another person with the other dog at the other end of the couch. Gradually, bring them closer and closer until (still on leash) they are working through their commands side by side without any provocation.

- At the six- to eight-week mark, start doing these yard and in-home exercises off leash. Remained armed with startle devices in case the dogs fight, and you have to intervene.

- At this point, add a daily fifteen- to thirty-minute heeling walk, with both dogs, with the dominant dog six to ten feet ahead. If at any point the submissive dog tries to get ahead, discipline it by suddenly cutting it off, circling around and ending up in a sit stay, or by startling it with a water blast.

- Rub a towel or old shirt on the dominant dog (getting its scent on it) and put it where the submissive dog sleeps and eats. Do the same with the other dog. This helps establish a positive association for each dog with the other dog's scent.

- Separate the dogs when you leave the home. When you can't give both dogs attention, neither gets any.

- Both dogs need to sleep with their human pack leaders each night. At bedtime, the dominant dog goes into the room first, on leash, and is tethered or crated at the side of the bed. The submissive dog is then brought into the room on leash, and also tethered or crated. (Never tether a dog and leave it alone; it can panic, choke, and die. Only tether under constant supervision so you can untangle the dog if it gets wrapped in the leash.)
- In the morning, the dominant dog is led out of the room first on leash and situated where it can eat in a separate area from the submissive dog.
- Avoid greeting, playing, or petting the dogs for any length of time in tight spaces such as hallways, car entrances, and the like. These are the likely "hot spots" where the dogs will begin fighting.
- If any fights break out, yell "Off!" and blast with the water or air horn or ultrasonic device. If the dogs fail to respond, grab the more aggressive dog's rear legs or tail and lift up, suspending the dog and removing its center of gravity while rapidly moving back. Do not reach for the head area or grab collars; you'll more than likely get bitten.
- Never have either dog on the same physical plane or level as you; it will reduce your dominant position in the pack. The dogs will respect you less and will ignore you if you command them to stop provoking each other or to stop fighting.
- Never respond to either dog's demand for attention. This is also a subtle way to reduce your dominance position, thereby dangerously raising the dog's position to greater authority.

Finally, in some cases, the dogs are so cued to go after each other that some temporary medication from the veterinarian is required in order to take the edge off and give the behavior therapy time to kick in. Some behaviorists suggest giving a sedative to the challenging submissive dog in order to make the dominant dog's work easier, resulting in less fighting. However, there seems to be more success if both dogs are given the medication. The two types that seem to work the best (if they are going to work at all) are the human antidepressant, Elavil (amitriptyline), and the human anxiolytic, BuSpar (buspirone). The medication alone will not do the trick; a comprehensive behavior-therapy intervention, including reconditioning, non-force obedience, and human family therapy intervention—changing the owner's mind-set and behaviors—is also needed to bring about a permanent cure. More information about the use of human psychiatric drugs in this kind of experimental application is found in Chapter 20.

Three out of five cases treated with the methods described above work out. Those that don't, end up with one of the dogs being placed in a home where it can be the only dog. Very often in cases that do not respond, or where the dangers are unacceptable (a great size disparity between the two dogs or young children present in the home), finding a home for one of the dogs leads to a win-win situation. Both dogs are happy, neither is fighting, and the children are safe.

Generally, it will take eight to twelve weeks of consistently implementing this program to lock in lasting results. Once the sibling dog fighting has been treated and eradicated, the dogs will coexist harmoniously until one dies of old age, or one is injured and the dominance roles switch, or a third dog is introduced into the home. Then the pack hierarchy will require additional reordering.

As with human sibling rivalry, it is essential that the owners modify and change their behaviors toward the fighting dogs. Where standard dog training fails, and where some behaviorists fall short, is that they either rely exclusively on heavy-handed punishment techniques that bring out aggression, or they only focus on modifying the dogs' behavior.

This program avoids bringing out aggression and creating new behavior problems while at the same time doesn't skip over the essential component of modifying the owner's behavior through behavior-modification techniques, family-systems therapy, and cognitive behavior-therapy intervention. This program addresses the homeostatic balance of the family system and the crucial part the fighting dogs play in it.

Case Study Postscripts

MEGAN AND ANGELA

Three days after my initial consult, the wife called up to say Megan and Angela were getting along great. They had had only one minor altercation over the last seventy-two hours; before, they had fought every hour or so. She said that the behavioral intervention gave her and her husband hope and improved the relationship between the two dogs. At the end of the eight-week course of treatment, the dogs were still fight free and were getting along well.

LILY AND SPRING

Results were similar with Lily and Spring. A month after my visit, their owner reported that the dogs were actually getting along better than before the fighting episodes began.

11

Introducing a Baby
into the Home

*"Now that Johnny's five, we thought it would be a good time to get a puppy
and teach him responsibility. It would be his dog; he'd be in charge."*

*"Our veterinarian referred us to you. We have a 6-year-old German shep-
herd. He's never liked kids. He was never around them as a puppy. We don't have
any relatives or friends who have young kids. And, well, now I'm pregnant."*

From Larry's Case Files:
"Evan" the Schipperke Who Dared to Growl at Santa Claus

FILE # 91-00021
DOG'S NAME: Evan
BREED: Schipperke
AGE: 3 years
PROBLEM: Dog-child aggression

In July 1991, I went out on a behavior therapy consult regarding a
three-year-old male schipperke named Evan who was aggressive toward
children. Evan's owners did not have any children—but now, the wife was
pregnant.

Evan was a pretty tough dude. The previous Christmas at the mall, he
snapped at a child waiting in line to see Santa Claus, and also growled at
St. Nick himself. I heard Evan received a stocking full of coal that year.

The first time I met Evan, the wife pulled up in her car with him and
his companion schipperke, Sami, in the backseat. When I leaned in to greet
the dogs, Evan growled and lunged at me. This kid had a serious attitude
problem.

Evan and child in sand box.

I was called in to outline a plan to help ensure the safety of the new baby. If this program didn't work, the owners were committed to placing Evan in another home.

Kids and Dogs

There are many things to consider when deciding whether to mix children and dogs in a household. When is a child old enough to take care of a dog? How old should the dog be? Are some breeds better than others for families who have young children?

SITUATION: YOU HAVE A DOG AND YOU ARE GOING TO HAVE A BABY

The ideal situation is for the parents-to-be to have a non-aggressive breed of dog. It is important to socialize it with children in a fun and rewarding manner. Also, they should have fully integrated the dog into the "pack" (existing family members), so it feels it has a secure place in the home. Of course, that is not always the case. What specific things can you do to make your baby's transition into your home with your dog less troublesome?

DO'S AND DON'TS

- Do, before you bring the baby home—weeks before—begin to engage in the same caretaking behaviors, with their accompanying smells, that you will be doing once the baby has arrived. For example:
  1. Using a doll, feed, dress, diaper, and rock the doll.
  2. Get the dog used to the smell of baby powder, diapers, and ointment.
  3. Put the dog through obedience commands with treats as you do this.
- Do, when you bring your baby home, maintain, as best you can, your dog's daily routine.
- Don't banish the dog outside or to the garage and set about lavishing praise and attention on the newborn. Your dog will make a negative association with the baby and that could set up your child to be disliked by your dog.
- Do lavish attention, petting, and special food treats on the dog whenever your baby is receiving attention.
- Do ignore your dog when your baby is being ignored: when it is down for a nap or is temporarily out of the home. Very quickly the dog learns that the only way it will get attention from its pack leaders is when this new squirmy baby is around getting attention too. The child becomes a cue for what is positive in the dog's life. The dog makes a positive association with the child and wants the child to be around as much as possible. The dog believes this is the only way it will receive any attention and affection.
- Do have the dog do lots of obedience responses around the child—sits, downs, and stays. This communicates to the dog that the children in the family are also higher in the pecking order and should be respected. It also provides a structured and safe mode of interaction for both child and dog. Reward the dog with praise and treats for this.
- Do allow the dog to sniff the child but . . .
- Don't allow the dog to lick or handle (i.e., grab, claw, muzzle, nudge, nip, carry, or roll) the baby. Frequently, this will make the dog consider the child its possession or underling, leading the dog to become dominant, overprotective, and overaggressive with the infant. The dog may then growl at or bite other members of the family when they try to approach the baby or take drastic and deadly action if the baby

cries out in distress. Also, the skin of infants and young children is particularly sensitive to dog saliva, and rashes can develop. This drives pediatricians nuts.

- Do, as the child grows older and learns to talk, have him or her share in the obedience training of the dog. This will reduce the possibility that the dog will try to dominate the child—jump up on it, excessively lick it, chase, bite, or mount it.

The dog must see and recognize the parents as strong but benevolent leaders of its pack. This should come somewhat naturally. Adults walk, move, and speak with more authority than children—and are obviously bigger. It's important that the dog sees the parents as the "alpha wolves," so the dog doesn't interfere when the parents are disciplining the children or another pet.

Children should be taught how to approach and handle a dog. Children should not:

- Pet a dog around the face or head.
- Play tug-of-war.
- Tease the dog.
- Bother the dog while it's eating.
- Bother the dog while it's chewing on a bone.
- Bother the dog while it's sleeping.
- Bother the dog while it's receiving medical treatment (includling cleaning the ears and clipping the nails). This is unnecessarily provocative and may lead to an aggressive response from the dog.

However, children should:

- Be involved with training the dog to relinquish objects on command. Everyone in the family should be able to remove a toy or dangerous off-limits object from the dog's mouth without eliciting an aggressive response. This is achieved by teaching the "give" or "drop" command, which is covered in detail on Page 157. Briefly, it calls for rewarding the dog after it relinquishes an object without a chase, tug-of-war, or aggressive response. This should be taught after the dog has been adequately socialized with children and will sit, lie down, and stay on a command from any family member.

A child seven or older can and should be intimately involved in the care of the family's dog. This includes:

- Picking up the dog poop in the yard (with proper gloves and bags so as to not contract toxoplasmosis or parasitic worms).
- Walking the dog after school.
- Feeding it (under parental supervision).
- Participating in fun obedience training. Caring for another creature promotes compassion and empathy in children. The dog should "belong" to everyone in the family and everyone should be involved in its training. In turn, the dog will respond equally to all family members and become equally bonded as well.

SITUATION: YOU HAVE SMALL CHILDREN
AND YOU WANT TO GET A DOG

In general, parents should hold off getting a puppy until their youngest child is about seven. There are several reasons:

- Children younger than this have shaky eye-hand coordination and poor reflexes, making it difficult for them to interact with the dog without stumbling, losing their balance, and being constantly knocked down.
- Children this young or younger have poor impulse control. When they are angry they tend to act it out; frequently their frustration is aimed at the next weakest link in the family system—the pet.
- Young children frequently have nightmares involving animals. This can make them unreasonably timid or fearful toward a real animal.
- Until a child is well into elementary school and develops the ability of basic abstract thinking, the child cannot overcome the natural tendency toward egocentrism. Everything revolves around the child; their view is paramount and there is no other. This prevents many a child from using empathy in understanding how to treat a new puppy without hurting it or from inadvertently abusing the dog. Some children under seven have a hard time differentiating between stuffed animal toys and the real thing. Many young children, therefore, tend to play too rough with puppies. Some hit and twist the fragile young dogs, and some are tempted to pick up and smother or even throw them.

A puppy mistreated in this way very quickly learns to fear the child and other similarly-moving, squeaky, smelly children. One day, the puppy, out of fear and a need to protect itself, turns and snaps, growls, or bites. The child instantly stops tormenting the puppy, which sees that its defensive aggressiveness worked! This reinforces the puppy's behavior ("When

I'm aggressive toward this little terror child, the threat ceases."). The dog-child aggression dynamic is off and running. The pattern continues until the child is injured or becomes noticeably frightened of the dog. The parents must make a choice and naturally, the puppy loses. Hello dog pound.

If you insist on having a puppy in a household with a young child, here are some things to remember:

- You can never leave the dog alone with the child for any reason until the child is seven years of age.
- You must be prepared to give the dog a sanctuary, a place in the home it can go that is strictly off-limits to the child.
- Mature dogs, or older dogs from animal shelters may not be a good pet for a home in which there are children under seven. Many older dogs were not adequately socialized with young children or other dogs when they were going through their formative years. Also, as dogs age, they often develop disorders that can cause them pain when they are forced to move quickly—as is often the case around young children. Therefore, the older dog may be less patient and more aggressive toward younger children or other dogs.

Recommended Breeds for Families

Families with young children should stay away from the guarding/attack/herding breeds such as German shepherds, Rottweilers, Dobermans, Pit Bulls, chow chows, shar-peis, Australian shepherds, and Lhasa apsos.

Families should select a puppy from breeds like collies, Labrador retrievers, golden retrievers, Newfoundlands, beagles, bichon frises and breeds of that nature. These breeds are particularly good with children, especially when obtained as puppies and socialized from early on. Parents who wait until their child is at least seven years old to get a dog, or who introduce an existing, properly socialized dog to a new baby, are providing the potential for the best possible relationship between dog and child. They can produce an unforgettable and enriching experience for both.

Treating Dogs That Are Aggressive Toward Children

As mentioned in the Chapter 9 discussion on aggression, whenever you work with an aggressive dog, you run the risk of getting bitten and injured.

In addition, the risks are that much higher when there are young children or babies in the home. Putting another family's child in harm's way to test your dog is unacceptable and too risky. However, in acknowledging these risks, if parents want to try to train their dog not to be aggressive to their own child or baby, and have the wherewithal to comply with proper safeguards (such as never leaving the dog and child alone together), such training can be successful.

In order to do this, we must counter-condition the dog's aggressive displays so it begins to see the child as something positive. In addition, we must tighten up the dog's obedience responses, neuter or spay it, put it on proper leash control, and frequently use moderate to long-term psychotropic medication from the veterinarian. It takes a lot of time, work, energy, money, and commitment. Many couples with a newborn do not have the time and energy to do this. At that point, options such as placing a dog in a child-free home should be considered (see Chapter 16, "Knowing When to Adopt Out").

The dog-child aggression program includes what has been outlined in the dominance-aggression and fear-aggression treatment plans in Chapter 9. It just depends on whether the dog is exhibiting dominance-aggressive or fear-aggressive behaviors toward the child. It could be a mixture of both, or even a display of predatory aggression.

It is frequently the case that the dog was never adequately socialized to young children and behaves fearfully or in a dominant manner when a baby arrives. With older children, the aggressive dog often has been harassed or traumatized by the child, and is now protecting itself from further abuse. That's why it's important to *never* leave young children and dogs alone together and to provide your dog with a place of refuge your child cannot access. When the parents fail to do these things, the child, either accidentally or on purpose, often hurts the dog when it is sleeping, eating, or chewing on a bone. Or, the child relentlessly pursues the dog and hits, kicks, pinches, or screams at it. The parents must put a stop to these behaviors before the dog does, through an aggressive display.

This recalls a case I had in which a four-year-old girl had been bitten at least three times by the family's fourteen-year-old Shetland sheepdog. Upon taking a history and observing the family, it was easy to see why. The girl would kick at the dog when it was eating its food or chewing on a toy. In addition, the dog was suffering from an arthritic condition, so every time the child would run up to it or startle it, it would jump, feel pain, and show aggression. The parents had failed to supervise the dog and child and had inadvertently allowed this interaction to go on. In this case, once the parents implemented some new rules, including adequate consequences for their four-year-old, the bites ceased and the dog began to slowly trust and warm up to the girl.

When the parents are either incapable or unwilling to implement such consistent and time-consuming rules, the dog needs to be placed in another home.

DOG-BABY RECONDITIONING TREATMENT PROGRAM

For dogs that are either in the home before the arrival of the child, or have never been sufficiently socialized to children, here is what we do:

- Immediately implement either the dominance-aggression or fear-aggression treatment program, as outlined in Chapter 9.
- Never leave the dog and child alone together until the child is at least seven years old.
- Don't allow the dog to jump up on furniture or people. No more on the lap during *World News Tonight*.
- Give the dog attention (positive) when the baby is also getting attention. When the baby is napping, the dog is ignored.
- The dog is to do an obedience command (sit, lie down, and stay) before getting any attention. It must do ten repetitions, three times a day, of the sit and down commands. Use the methods described in Chapter 4.
- The dog must learn to do the stay command and achieve a half-hour stay.
- When you are interacting with the baby, and therefore giving attention (praise and treats) to the dog as well, the dog should be in a down-stay position on a twenty-foot leash, at least ten feet away.
- If the dog attempts to jump up, break its stay, ignores you after the second command, or shows any aggressiveness toward the baby, shout "Off!" and startle it with a water blast. Wait five minutes and resume.
- If the dog is more responsive to one owner or parent than the other, then the parent the dog ignores the most must be the dog's sole source of attention for an entire week, while the other parent totally ignores the dog. This is done so the dog will start becoming equally responsive to both parents.

- The dog should have no contact with the neighborhood kids.
- When adults meet the dog for the first time, have them bend down and feed the dog treats. As the dog warms up, they can pet the dog away from its face without staring directly into the dog's eyes.
- Because the risk to the child is so great, and because the dog is either facing adoption or euthanasia if it continues to be aggressive, the dog should be referred to the veterinarian for a prescription for psychotropic medication to help ease its anxiety or aggressive impulses while the behavior-therapy techniques take effect.
- Whenever the owner is tired, or cannot monitor the dog or child, the dog is put away with a chew bone and separated from the child.
- Do not allow the child to play with or handle the dog's toys. Do not let the dog play with the child's toys.

Within eight weeks, the owners will be able to assess whether the dog is making sufficient progress, staying the same, or getting worse. At that point, the owners may need to decide whether to adopt the dog out to a child-free home or to a shelter, or, if the dog is aggressive toward adults and children, to euthanize it.

Case Study Postscript

After my initial visit, six years went by before Evan demonstrated any aggression toward the children in the home. Evan's owners had a baby boy in 1991, and he and Evan became great friends. The father was so proud of how Evan was tolerating his little boy, he once bragged that Evan remained calm even when his son accidentally grabbed the dog's genitals! I told him, "Let's not push it."

In 1997, Evan's owners called. They now had a little girl as well. One day at mealtime, the girl dropped some food on the floor. When she attempted to pick it up, Evan, who was right by the highchair, growled, snapped, and lunged for the food.

We revised Evan's 1991 plan, adding some rules to keep Evan away from the family's eating area to avoid setting up the same situation. When the owners have the time, they put Evan in a stay or tether him away from the children's eating area. If they don't have the time, he is sequestered outside during mealtimes.

As of this writing, it has been more than six months since the food incident, and no further aggressive displays toward the children have occurred.

Part Four:
Family Systems Therapy:
Changing the Structure
and System of the Family

12

Rescuing the Shelter Dog

"We were thinking of adopting a dog from the shelter. But are they safe? Do they have more illnesses? We're not sure."

"Our friends adopted this cute little Benji dog from the pound. Now the dog is destroying their furniture when they're gone. They're thinking about taking it back. They're just heartbroken over the whole thing."

From Larry's Case Files:
"Fred" the Male-Bashing Border Collie

FILE # 96-00101
DOG'S NAME: Fred
BREED: Border collie mix
AGE: 2 years
PROBLEM: Territorial aggression toward men

In February 1996, in my capacity as an animal-behavior consultant evaluating potentially "vicious" dogs for a shelter, I went out to the home of one of the volunteer staff members. She and her husband had agreed to temporarily house one of the shelter dogs that had contracted the potentially fatal disease parvovirus. Fred needed to be quarantined from the other dogs at the shelter.

I was asked to evaluate Fred because of his tendency to behave aggressively toward men. He had been returned to the shelter twice because of this. The shelter wanted me to determine whether his behavior problem was treatable, or if he was beyond hope and needed to be euthanized.

Knowing this history, and acknowledging that border collies, like other herding breeds, have the potential for territorial aggression, I decided not to meet him on his home turf; the backyard behind wrought iron fencing. As soon as I pulled up to the volunteer's home, I saw the front wrought iron gate. I simulated opening and closing my car door and waited. Sure enough, Fred came running up to the gate and began to bark ferociously and guard his territory. I called the owners on my mobile phone and asked them to put Fred in a different area of the backyard so he couldn't see me until I was ready to meet him—on my terms. They complied.

After taking a brief history from the shelter volunteer and her husband, I had her bring Fred into the living room (a room he'd never been in and therefore hadn't established as his territory) while I laid out a scrumptious trail of treats from Fred's entrance to my feet. I instructed the volunteer to act happy and encourage Fred to devour the treat trail, which he did. When Fred first saw me and heard my voice he barked two or three times and let out a subtle growl. However, over the next ten minutes, while tossing and then feeding him treats, I was able to have Fred sit, lie down, and tolerate me petting him.

Then I took the leash and put him through his paces, getting him more comfortable with me. In less than twenty minutes, he was rolling over to have his tummy scratched and giving me kisses. The male basher was male bonding!

This was a good indicator: Despite Fred's initial guardedness he could be de-sensitized, and he retained that sense of positive association and less sensitivity during my entire visit. I felt, with some minor changes, some obedience, and some socialization under proper safety precautions (like being on leash and the anti-pull Halti), Fred would work out fine.

I visited Fred about a month later at the shelter, this time offering no treat trail. He recognized me immediately and wagged his tail and assumed a friendly body posture. Fred had retained the association over time and in a different situation. Another good sign. These are some of the behavior indicators I look for when evaluating potentially aggressive dogs at animal shelters.

The Decision to Rescue

No doubt about it, rescuing a dog from an animal shelter can be one of life's most rewarding experiences. But it is not a choice to be made without carefully considering several factors. Among other things, you must consider whether you are equipped to handle a dog with an uncertain past or whether that should be left to someone with greater energy and patience. As the trend in animal shelters moves toward a more humane standard (witness the growing number of shelters in Southern California with a "no-kill" policy) you are not necessarily always rescuing a dog. A shelter that has no intention of euthanizing an animal may be the best home for it until the staff there can make a good match of dog and family.

Breed temperament aside, shelter dogs frequently have special needs because of where they have been—and where they are now. If a dog winds up in an animal shelter, whether it is run by a private organization or by a city or county, the dog is there for a reason. Understanding these reasons can help ensure a successful adoption.

If a dog has been given up by its owner, it is often because it has been doing something the owner dislikes or is *not* doing something the owner wants it to do.

The original owner may have tried some half-hearted, home-concocted method to punish or force compliance, such as using a rolled-up newspaper to smack the dog or locking it up all day in a bathroom. Some behaviors that owners try to punish the dog for include house-soiling, chewing off-limits items such as shoes and pillows, nuisance barking, and fence-jumping. Dogs, with these problems, once brought home, may have house-breaking accidents, or chew on household items like pillows or cushions, and may engage in nuisance barking when the owner leaves. Frequently, these behaviors are very natural symptoms of the anxiety the dog experiences because of its isolation.

Violent, quick-fix attempts to remedy these types of behavior problems are temporary solutions at best and usually only make problems worse. Then the owner is stuck with a dog exhibiting the original behavior problem *and* the side effects of the inappropriate remedy. Out of frustration, the owner gives up and brings the dog to the shelter.

Other dogs at shelters are runaways. The dog may have gone house to house, or run the street alone or with a pack of other strays, developing scavenging habits, such as stealing food and jumping fences.

The third most likely history is that the dog was abused, physically and/or nutritionally. Either the abuser gave up the dog or the dog was taken away and turned over to the shelter. A typical sign of an abused dog is head shyness. When someone reaches toward the dog's head, it flinches and pulls away out of fear. Or if you make direct eye contact with it, the

dog submissively urinates in response. Again, with patience and understanding, many of these behaviors can be corrected.

Fourth, sometimes the owner can no longer keep their beloved pet.
Moving to an apartment that doesn't allow animals; contracting a fatal illness; or having a new baby in the home who the dog does not tolerate, are
all reasons a dog might be relinquished by its owner and wind up at the
shelter.

Knowing these four likely scenarios will go a long way toward understanding your new friend. You can see why you might have to alter your
expectations. You might adopt the most perfect, well-adjusted shelter dog
in the world, but you can easily adopt one that requires a lot of extra love
and attention.

Whichever the case, almost every shelter dog needs some corrective
training. It might need some brief lessons to overcome habits such as
house-soiling, chewing, barking, digging, or trying to escape the yard. Or
it might need some special training and exercises to overcome its fear of
strangers, especially men. This is usually true if the dog has been abused.
But even an abused dog can become a trusted, loving best friend with lots
of gentle work.

When thinking about getting a shelter dog, consider its current environment. What is a shelter? It is usually a facility built to house many
dogs, cats, rabbits, and other normally domesticated animals. It is not a
quiet place. Generally, it is jail-like, composed of row after row of double-
or triple-tiered cages into which all manner of dogs are housed. While
shelter workers usually try their best, they are too overwhelmed to deal
with the physical and psychological needs of each animal. The prospective
adoptee, then, is coming from a very unnatural environment. One of the
most important jobs of the new owner is to offset the neuroses inevitably
caused by the shelter experience.

The longer the dog has been in the shelter, the more confinement-
related problems it is likely to have. It might pace nervously, chase its tail,
or gnaw at its front paws. It might act out in more aggressive ways, growling or nipping. It might withdraw in a depressive manner and cower all the
time or lie around, unwilling to get up. The initial four to six weeks in a
new home following adoption is a real test for both dogs and humans.

The longer these behaviors have been allowed to exist, the longer the
dog may take to adapt to you. A thorough intervention plan might be
required. You may need to bring in a competent, non-violent animal behav-

iorist. The behaviorist works with the family and the dog, teaching both to trust and relax. The behaviorist will teach the family how to reward the adoptee's good behavior and avoid rewarding the undesirable.

The sooner the dog understands it has been adopted by a new, loving family, with safe, normal living conditions, the quicker it will settle down into a more relaxed lifestyle. The mere fact that the dog is in a home of its own will go a long way toward relaxing the dog.

Selecting a Shelter Dog

Once you understand the conditions many shelter dogs have been subjected to, you can begin the process of selecting one. Again, you must choose wisely. You do not want to open your heart to a dog only to have to return it. There are no guarantees, but there are some basic guidelines you can follow to ensure the greatest probability of success.

First, do not go by looks alone. Before you give your heart to the cute little mutt in cage No. 32, realize that Benji may actually be Cujo. Conversely, a dog that looks like Cujo may actually be Lassie. It could just need a bath or grooming. Shelter workers can't always keep every dog looking squeaky clean. Go by breed—or breed propensity—and evaluate the traits and likely disposition of the breed of dog you have chosen. This, along with its physical characteristics (coat, activity level, and size) will help you determine whether this particular representative of the breed of dog is mainstream and healthy, and whether or not it is a suitable match for you and your lifestyle.

The health of the dog—especially a shelter dog—is important. Has it been checked for hip problems, ear infections, or other ailments? Is its coat full? Are its eyes clear and nose cold and wet? Most reputable shelters have staff veterinarians who check and treat the dogs up for adoption. If you want outside confirmation, by all means have your own veterinarian check the dog over before making a final decision.

Then comes the aesthetics. After considering all of the above, you can narrow it down using the "adorable" factor to help you pick your dog.

With all other factors considered, have some trial outings or visits with the prospective dog to see how your family and the dog click. If it's okay with the shelter staff, bring some toys and take the dog for a walk. Also, if allowed, feed it. Observe friendliness, activity level, and grooming needs on separate occasions. You can now make your decision knowing you have weighed every factor possible.

We believe we have a responsibility from our Creator to care for the animal kingdom, particularly dogs, since they are social animals who fit especially well into the lives of we humans—shelter dogs, perhaps more so. Just as we have troubled youths and wayward people with dysfunctional backgrounds, we have animals, usually dogs and cats, that find themselves in need. It is especially crucial with shelter animals to consider the probable reasons they ended up in the shelter in the first place, what effect being in the shelter had on them, and what to do when you rescue such an animal to increase the likelihood of a successful living arrangement.

Unfortunately, some shelter animals are returned because the people who adopted them were not adequately prepared.

Bringing Home Your New Pack Member

Try to bring home your new pet at vacation time, before a long weekend, or with some half work days lined up. Why? You probably have just removed the dog from the stressful, crowded conditions of a shelter, kennel, or breeder. You do not want it to go from one extreme to the other: from intense interaction to isolation. For a social pack animal, isolation can lead to anxiety and barking, chewing, digging and self-mutilation.

There is usually a four-to-six week adjustment period any dog goes through with any new home or family until some routine is established, bonding is begun, and the dog's true personality emerges with its sense of belonging and territory. Whether you are adopting a puppy or an older dog, whether is it from a breeder or shelter, the first six months require a lot of training and getting-to-know-you time to integrate the adopted canine into your family. Half-hearted attempts won't cut it.

You want to start by establishing a routine it can rely upon. It's actually pretty easy. Feed the dog at approximately the same time it was fed before. Gradually work toward feeding the dog on your schedule. Use the food the dog was on when you obtained it, unless your vet advises you to switch. Always feed it in the same place. Likewise, take the dog to one specific area outside each time it needs to relieve itself until it gets the hang of it.

Also, to quicken the bonding process between you and your new dog, have it sleep in your bedroom at night for the rest of its life. This not only hastens bonding, but it prevents loneliness-related behaviors such as digging, nuisance barking, escaping, and destructive chewing. You will be there to spot unwanted behaviors and reinforce "no." This will also force the dog to control its bladder, because healthy dogs will not soil where they sleep. The dog is also better protection for you inside where it can safely guard, versus it being outside, constantly raising false alarms and being vulnerable to harm.

Next, take a non-violent, non-force, fun obedience class with your dog so it will see you as a kind but strong pack leader.

Keep in mind, however, that you have an existing set of house rules that are acceptable to you and your family members. You can't expect to bring in a new member of the family and have it automatically conform to your expectations. But, if you try to follow the guidelines I've just given you, the behavior problems we discussed should not come up at all, or if they do, they will be relatively easy to fix.

Case Study Postscript

Two months after the initial consultation, Fred was successfully adopted into a family made up of a husband, wife, and a pre-existing dog: a male husky mix. When I made my final post-adoption home visit, Fred had already bonded to the husband (so much for male bashing) and got along well with the other dog. Fred, the male bashing shelter dog, was a success!

13

Pet Loss and the Grief Process

(Written with Kimberly Whitten Akamine, M.F.C.C.)

"I feel so guilty. I feel I should have done something more to help Amber. Maybe we should have taken her to another vet, gotten another test. I just miss her so much."

"I feel so empty and depressed since Butch died. I find myself looking for him at different times of the day. My husband thinks I'm foolish for making a big deal over a dog. But Butch was more than a dog; he was my constant companion and love. I can't sleep; can't eat."

"I'm worried about my six-year-old. He was very close to our dog. He's been having nightmares and has started wetting his bed. He won't talk to me about Albie's death."

From Larry's Case Files:
"Tozai" the Yellow Labrador and
"Fagan" the Golden Retriever

FILE # 85-00001
DOG'S NAME: Tozai
BREED: Labrador retriever
AGE: 11 years
PROBLEM: Paralysis from the neck down

On August 29, 1985, my dad called to let me know that my dog of eleven years, Tozai, a yellow Labrador retriever, could no longer stand or walk. The medications were not working. Over a forty-eight-hour period, Tozai had become completely paralyzed. I flew from California to New York the next morning.

When I arrived at the veterinary hospital, two veterinary assistants brought Tozai down from the examining table. They left the room. Tozai saw me and perked up. His tail started wagging. His head lifted off the ground, but even though he tried to get up and greet me, he couldn't. He couldn't move from the neck down. Tozai couldn't stand, walk, or drink from his water bowl. He couldn't eat out of his food bowl. He couldn't go to the bathroom without soiling himself. His front paws were licked raw.

It was heartbreaking to see him like this. I broke a large dog biscuit into several pieces and fed it to him while sitting next to him on the floor. He ate all of it with his old gusto; Tozai was there in spirit. I brushed him and lay down next to him and told him how much I loved him; what a good dog he had always been; how sorry I was to see him like this; and that we were not going to let him suffer like this any longer. Toward the end of my visit with Tozai, he whimpered. He cried. His eyes became lifeless and glazed over.

I knew it was time. I said my final goodbye and covered him halfway with his favorite blanket because he was shaking. I kissed him and left. Later, the rest of my family arrived at the veterinary hospital and said their goodbyes and had Tozai euthanized.

Tozai.

LARRY LACHMAN

File # 96-00080
DOG'S NAME: Fagan
BREED: Golden retriever
AGE: 10 years
PROBLEM: Osteosarcoma;
malignant bone cancer

It was something I probably did every day. I kissed my dog, Fagan, on the cheek and told him, "Good boy." But when I did that on June 14, 1996, Fagan cried out in pain. I rushed him to a veterinarian and discovered he had advanced osteosarcoma: bone cancer. A tumor the size of a golf ball was fixed to the back left side of his throat. The X-rays showed that the tumor had already eaten away part of his left jawbone. Horror, shock, and sadness flooded over me. Flashbacks of eleven years earlier with Tozai raced through my mind. Course of action: surgery and possible chemotherapy.

On June 19, Fagan went into surgery and had his left mandibular joint and lower left jaw and teeth removed along with the tumor. In five days, the tumor had grown thirty percent! Another week and he would have been dead. What lay ahead now was a month of post-operative recovery and the decision of whether to pursue chemotherapy.

Fagan and I had a rough time the first two or three weeks. With his left jaw removed and face stitched, it was a difficult feat to get him to eat his food. Gradually, he recovered from the surgery and had his stitches removed. The facts regarding chemotherapy were the following: Given the type of cancer, which has a reputation of spreading and killing quickly, Fagan would have a forty to fifty percent chance of dying within six months without chemotherapy. If he underwent chemotherapy, he would have around a sixty percent chance of living another year or two. Two-thirds of the dogs that undergo chemotherapy have no reaction to it. A third experience a negative reaction and cannot tolerate it. In addition, the quality of life of the dog has to be considered, as well as treatment benefits.

I opted to have Fagan undergo one round of chemotherapy. If he handled it, we'd go on. If his quality of life was good, we'd go on. However, if he had a significant negative reaction or if his quality of life suffered, I'd stop the chemo and let him live out whatever time he had left without the side effects of chemotherapy.

Even with the chemotherapy, Fagan realistically had an expected survival period of anywhere from six to twenty-four months. Our time together had an expiration date. I contacted the local pet cemetery for "pre-need" information. My pre-grieving began. I had gone through the shock and anger and depression. Now I was accepting the inevitable.

Fagan went through two rounds of chemotherapy. He did fine for the first, but had a significant negative reaction to the second. It took a month after that for us to stabilize his functional colitis so that he was no longer throwing up and having diarrhea.

In September, Fagan and I put on a training session for the staff of the Mission Viejo Animal Shelter. In October, we videotaped non-violent training methods for Mission Viejo's community cable television show, Animal House.

On October 23, Fagan began showing signs of deterioration. I had noticed him slowing down. For most of the week, I thought I had seen his jaw swelling up. I had originally made an appointment to bring him into the vet the following Saturday. However, when we woke up the morning of

Fagan.

October 23, he was beginning to show the same symptoms he did when the first tumor appeared. He didn't want to lay his head down on one side, he drooled, he was lethargic.

I made an appointment with his surgical oncologist for that evening. As the day wore on, his breathing became more labored and he looked more and more out of it.

My worse fears were true. The swelling in his jaw was a tumor, and it had spread throughout his body. His oncologist gave him two weeks and said the fast-growing tumor would expand and cause greater and greater suffering.

I decided to have him euthanized later that week to spare him any more suffering. It was mind-blowing how fast this thing had come back. However, we had four good months. Even with the frustrating post-operative recovery, I had spent my summer with him.

Over that night, Fagan's tumor grew significantly. He could no longer place his head down to rest or sleep. He was drooling continuously from both sides of his mouth. His breathing was increasingly labored. He refused food and water. He had difficulty standing. It was time.

On October 24, I had Fagan euthanized at 2:15 P.M. Eric Van Nice, my vet friend, and Deb Varos, a friend from school, accompanied me up to Sea Breeze Pet Cemetery in Huntington Beach, where I picked out a plot, headstone, and casket. A priest friend, Father Rick Sera, met us there. After taking Fagan for a brief walk (even though he was really out of it, in pain, weak, and drooling) Dr. Van Nice and I lifted Fagan up on the table. I stroked and comforted Fagan. I had already told him all the things I ever wanted to over the entire summer we spent together. He and I had taken two long walks alone that morning and spent some time on our favorite couch.

As Fagan lay on the table I continued to pet and console him. Father Sera gave a blessing and a prayer and then Eric gave Fagan the euthanizing injection.

In less than ten seconds it was all over. I was in tears and filled with pain. Father Sera said another prayer and blessing and then Eric and I carried Fagan to a temporary holding area. The next day, he was buried.

The following Wednesday, a gloomy, rainy day, we had a memorial service for Fagan at the pet cemetery. Seventeen of his human friends assembled in the downpour. Each of us shared a memory of Fagan and how he had affected our lives. He was a special dog.

Why You Should Read This Now

Chances are your dog is fairly young, perhaps a puppy, and quite healthy. Its death is something so far down the road you can't contemplate it. You don't *want* to contemplate it. Why ruin the afternoon? Let me make a plea. Invest twenty minutes and read this chapter now. When the day comes that you really need this information, perhaps the last thing you will want to do is dig out this book. Or you may have passed this book on to another dog lover. Also, in the near future, you may be able to assist friends or others outside the family—especially children and the elderly—who are experiencing pet loss.

The first part of this chapter addresses the special roles pets play in our lives and why their deaths are even more painful than those of some of our human family members. The second half of the chapter zeros in on pet loss and children and how a pet's death can affect children of different ages.

Kimberly Akamine, a licensed marriage, family, and child counselor based in Bellflower, California has written an original children's story about pet loss that should help parents of children between the ages of two and six deal with the death of the family dog. Finally, I offer a chart that outlines the psychological and cognitive abilities children are capable of at different ages. This will help parents determine the appropriate way of talking to their children about pet loss.

PART I: PET LOSS AND GRIEF

WHY WE LOVE (AND NEED) OUR PETS

The death of a beloved pet is a uniquely painful situation most of us are not prepared to deal with. To many people, their pets are more than just dogs or cats or parrots. They are true members of the family. And just as when a human member of the family dies, the feelings of loss and grief over a pet can be intense for the survivors.

Think about how you and your friends treat your dogs. Many of us treat them almost like children or siblings. The emotions we experience toward our children or siblings are the same kinds of emotions we experience toward our pets. We love them. We rely on them. We get mad at them.

We become sad if they are ill. We talk to them about our problems. And we express our affection to our pets the way we do with the human members of the family. What's more, our animal brethren can show us unconditional love and acceptance. Therefore, their deaths can hit us even harder than the death of a human friend, since most humans engage in conditional love—there are strings attached.

Animals serve as culturally sanctioned avenues for us to touch and be touched. Research has shown how important it is for all of us to experience this kinesthetic bonding to remain healthy and sane. In a society where physical gestures of affection are embarrassing or taboo, and taking time out to commune with nature and our inner selves is seen as lazy and fuzzy-brained, our pets play a crucial role in our emotional, physical, and social well-being. Many times, having a pet allows an otherwise unaffectionate family to give itself permission to be affectionate, with the animal serving as a permission-giver or catalyst for such displays.

Children with emotional traumas or learning difficulties seem to make better progress when animals are a part of the treatment. And when a husband or wife dies, the family pet may serve as a crucial companion and link to the lost spouse.

Animals are helping developmentally disabled children make physical and emotional breakthroughs in various types of therapy, including institutional visitation programs and therapeutic horse-riding programs. When a parent or relative dies, young children frequently clam up and turn to imaginary friends, puppets, or pets to vent their feelings and sadness.

Several years ago, I was working with hospice patients who had cancer and had fewer than six months to live. One of the hospice volunteers had a rabbit she frequently took to the patients in the home or sneaked into the hospital ward. Being able to see and touch the rabbit would often temporarily relieve the patients' pain. It would trigger fond memories and allow them to be in contact with nature even though they were confined to the sterile environment of the hospital. In one case, a woman had just died of cancer and her young son, a toddler, would not talk to anyone about his feelings or about his missing his mom. A volunteer worker brought in her rabbit and stepped back to watch the boy and the animal interact. It wasn't long before the boy began opening up and sharing his hurt and grief with his new bunny buddy—something he couldn't do with the surrounding adults.

It's easy to see, then, why people become so attached to pets and why they become members of the family; they offer unconditional love, companionship—and uninterrupted listening! As with any family member, when the pet becomes sick, is lost, or dies, the rest of the family may experience hurt, anger, depression, and grief. It is normal, predictable, and expected. The people who would say, "It was just a dog," or "Why are you so upset over this?" are the same people who tell others at funerals, "Now, you must be strong," or "Don't cry, be a man."

Those people who espouse such advice usually do so for two reasons: 1) They are uncomfortable seeing a friend in pain or showing sadness, so they try to heal you and make you and them feel better by squelching your natural emotional reaction. 2) The death and your grief causes them to reflect upon their own mortality, breaking through the Freudian unconscious assumption that we will live forever.

From a medical perspective, following such advice is unhealthy. Dumping one's natural feelings of mourning down a psychological hole creates more and more pressure to deal with the feelings sooner or later. If you do not deal with such feelings emotionally, the body and brain frequently take over and do it for you by manufacturing an illness. Hiding your grief because others say "Be strong" is just sweeping emotional dirt under the carpet; one day, you'll trip on it. Grief needs to be vented.

EUTHANASIA

When is it time to put your dog to sleep? How will you know? What do you need to communicate to the veterinarian? How should you make the decision? How will you live with the decision? How should you say goodbye? Where do you want your pet placed after it is deceased?

First, let's review all the wrong reasons to euthanize your pet. There is no medical, moral, or ethical justification for euthanizing your pet because it won't stop urinating on the carpet, or it chews up a favorite pillow, or you are moving to a new home and cannot take it with you. Too many veterinarians encounter pet owners who bring their pets in to be euthanized solely because of a behavior problem that can be treated. By following this line of thinking, you are guilty of what some ethicists have called "paternalistic euthanasia viewpoint," which means you place your own needs of convenience ahead of the dog's actual welfare.

Another example of the paternalistic line of reasoning is when you or your family *do not* euthanize when you should, simply because you will miss your dog too much or fear how lonely you might end up being. This, again, is putting your emotional needs ahead of the dog's welfare.

So, what are correct reasons for euthanizing your dog? The correct or valid reasons to euthanize a pet fall under what the ethicists call the "preference-benefits" point of view of euthanasia. The preference-benefits view recognizes that your dog has preferences in what it needs physically and emotionally. If your dog's preferred way of being is blocked, through either omission of proper care or an illness, then your dog's well-being is in jeopardy.

Dogs have psychological needs and interests. They seek attention and petting and give attention and touch. They need to eat and go to the bathroom and interact with other people and nature. When your dog cannot fulfill its needs and wants due to illness or injury that causes chronic pain or paralysis, you need to look at euthanasia.

If your dog is in constant or excruciating pain or cannot move, you need to think about euthanizing it. If your dog cannot eat, drink its water, walk, go to the bathroom, or live its life and fulfill its interests, then out of love and care, you are compelled to relieve your dog's suffering by euthanizing it and giving it some peace. If the veterinarians can do no more, or they cannot promise that your dog will no longer suffer and be in pain with their procedures, then you need to euthanize it. Your dog relies on you to take care of its needs even when that means relieving its suffering by ending its life. It's a no-win situation; there is no way to feel good about putting your dog to sleep.

What do you do if the veterinarian brings up the subject of euthanasia first? Listen with an open mind. Get at least two other veterinary opinions. And place your dog's interests first!

The physical body of the dog can only take precedence for so long. How about the inner spirit and the inner turmoil your dog is experiencing? My yellow Labrador had a personality all his own. That personality was not defined by how many pounds of fur the dog consisted of. The physical body was not the core of what made Tozai, Tozai. You could have lined up a million yellow Labs in a row, and he would look exactly like many of them. However, the expression in his eyes and the particular way he related to me and my family was unique. So when his physical body was put to rest, what made up Tozai's personality continued to live and was set free. I knew then that the essence of Tozai lived on. He could hear me then, and he can hear me now.

After deciding to euthanize your dog, there are other decisions you may want to make. Do you want to be present when your dog receives the lethal dose of anesthesia? Or do you want to see the dog before or after the procedure is carried out? Also, have you allowed yourself enough time to say final good-byes?

You should plan for a specific time of day at a specific location to fit your personal preferences and emotional needs. Some mobile veterinarians will come to the home and, with the entire family present, euthanize your pet in its familiar atmosphere, with its blanket and so on. Or, you can have the pet euthanized at the animal hospital. Some people hold their dogs during the procedure. Some say all they have to say before the dog is euthanized. Some people step out momentarily and come back into the exam room after the dog has been euthanized. These choices should be discussed with the entire family and decided upon before the actual day arrives.

In addition to the above considerations, you must ask yourself, "Where do I want my pet to be placed after it is deceased?" Some people prefer cremation and having the ashes interred at a pet cemetery, scattered in the dog's favorite woodsy area, or placed in an urn that is taken home.

Others prefer to have their dog buried in a pet cemetery with a headstone. Some people, depending on their city's zoning laws, bury their pets on their own property. And some people request the veterinarian to prepare the body for county cremation.

If you have children who will be affected by the death of the family pet, then, depending upon their age, a factual and honest explanation of your ill pet's circumstances—in language they can understand—is warranted. Kimberly Akamine, M.F.C.C., helps you with this in Part II of this chapter, with her child development chart, indicating at what age children understand certain terms and concepts.

In addition, following the chart, we offer an original children's story titled, "Chester and Lizzy," which tells of a mouse family whose pet ant dies. This story is for parents to use with children from two through six years of age.

Different people grieve at different rates in different ways. Allow family members to grieve in their own way. Allow them to help decide when and how to euthanize the family pet and what type of mourning services will be held. This provides a rite of passage and allows each member of the family a way to vent their grief.

GETTING IT OUT

Allowing people to express their feelings of loss is one of the main goals of my support groups for people who have lost their pets, or when I counsel them one-on-one. I validate their feelings as being normal and then provide a forum for them to express these feelings so they can move into the mourning process and come to terms with their pet's death.

It is understandable that their pain for their deceased animal may be even greater than past grieving over a relative and that the level of pain is a direct barometer of how much they loved their animal. The pain is a living testimonial to the departed animal and how much they cared for it. It is not unusual to mourn and feel grieving for four, six, or even twelve months. You never forget, but the *intensity* of the pain and disruption of the daily living schedule diminishes with time.

I tell those grieving that from my observations of many terminal cancer patients and chronically sick animals, and from case studies on both, it is not unusual that when the animal dies the owner is not in the room, not home, or has fallen asleep. You should not feel guilty over this. We believe that humans and animals have some control of when they finally let go and die. Both frequently would not want to hurt loved ones by dying right in front of them, so they wait until the person standing vigil goes out of the room, gets a cup of coffee from the hospital cafeteria, or falls asleep. Many times, human patients will wait until after a family member's wedding, graduation, or other such event before dying.

When a loved one does die, prayers, poems, memorials, meditations, and other ways of saying good-bye can be extremely healthy therapy for survivors. When Tozai died, I wrote a six-page tribute to him, reviewing the highs and lows of his life. I ended the tribute by writing a poem in his memory. This poem helped me deal with my grief. Here is the poem:

TOZAI: A YELLOW LAB WITH A GOLDEN HEART

Scratching behind the ears,
Pouncing and bouncing with the favorite ball,
You were there in full spirit,
A spirit of love and kindness
Which I shall cherish always.

You were my friend; you were my baby;
I never regretted having you—even up to the
end.

For it *is* better to have loved and lost than
to never have loved at all.
Bonies; ballies; food; and "go for a walk,"
were the simple things you thrived and excelled for.
You also excelled in love and affection,
and the family and I will be eternally grateful.
You served as our four-legged key;
our bolt of lightening; our sparkle
of sunshine—opening, modelling and nurturing
our ability to love and be loved.

Tozai, you dear creature
You were and always will be
A yellow Lab with a truly
Golden heart.

I love you, dog.
9/5/85

It is crucial that the grieving survivors have an adequate support system of family, friends, or professionals who can lend their shoulders to cry on and be there whenever needed. It is important these supporters do not attempt to discount the grieving person's pain.

One way to find support is at a pet-loss support group. Like Alcoholics Anonymous, being with others who are going through the same thing provides great comfort and support. You see that you are not the only one experiencing these feelings of loss over your pet. You realize that you will get through the most intense part of your pain because you see others in the group making progress and receiving empathy from fellow group members who are not merely paying lip service. There's an atmosphere of caring, feeling, and respect.

You can find a pet-loss support group by contacting your veterinarian, local pet cemetery, county or state psychological association, or nearest veterinary college. The Delta Society in Renton, Washington, also has a listing of pet-loss support groups throughout the country.

Whether it is you or a friend or loved one who is grieving, it is important to understand the different phases of grief. Swiss psychiatrist Elisabeth Kübler-Ross first delineated the various stages of grief people go through following any type of significant loss, including death, divorce, loss of health, and loss of job. It has been through Dr. Kübler-Ross's lectures and books—such as *On Death and Dying: The Final Stage of Growth*—that millions of people began to realize their feelings of depression and anger over a loved one's death were perfectly normal and necessary if they were to successfully integrate their loss as part of their lives and move on.

I was fortunate enough to attend one of Dr. Kübler-Ross's lectures, in which she reviewed her research and the five stages of grief. She stressed a point that bears repeating: Not everyone will go through all five stages; some will skip stages and some will go back and forth between stages. The stages are not set in concrete. Indeed, some other mental health professionals have delineated close to a dozen types of grief reactions people may experience while mourning a loss. So don't think you must go through these stages in order, one by one, in a robot-like sequence. These are general maps of what to expect in the grieving process.

Dr. Kübler-Ross's five stages of grief are:
1. Denial and isolation
2. Anger
3. Bargaining
4. Depression
5. Acceptance

Denial often manifests itself in an owner's refusal to believe the diagnosis and continuing on with one's life as if nothing is wrong, completely ignoring one's illness or one's animal's illness as a way of not having to deal with the impending tragedy. With animals, I sometimes see owners who, upon being told by their veterinarian that their dog or cat has inoperable malignant cancer or severe heart disease, react with, "No, you must be mistaken. He is eating fine and plays well. You probably got the wrong set of tests. Re-do them, doc." Or they go to a dozen different veterinarians hoping to hear what they want to hear: That their animal is really not chronically sick or dying, and that all is well and will remain so.

Anger is normal and expected, although most people initially cannot empathize with angry emotions in a family in which someone is dying. Most people expect only sadness and depression. However, if you were told your life would be cut short, and you have all along paid taxes and not committed crimes, you too, would be angry. Our loving, safe, and fun dog is dying sooner than that jerky pit bull mix down the street who seems in perfect health and has eaten ten mailmen. The unfairness of it all! There is anger at the loss of the future, of hopes and plans, anger that this is being "done to me" or the family.

Bargaining. Sometimes we try to bargain our way out of the terminal illness diagnosis or the realization that our loved one is gone. We promise God, the doctor or our spouses, that we will "be good," stop eating fatty foods, give to charities, and so on, if only He will save us or a loved one.

Depression hits hard when we finally realize that the inevitable is the inevitable and it is pretty much out of our control. We feel hopeless. We feel fatigued. We feel pain. We cry, shake, and have nightmares. We lose our appetite. These are all indicators of depression. We look at the future through emotionally clouded goggles that create a bleak perspective and cause us to grope for adjustment and try to figure out how we will get along without our loved one.

Acceptance begins when we no longer find ourselves bargaining, and our anger and denial have subsided. Then, in our pain and depression, we accept the fact that our beloved dog is no longer with us. We begin to integrate its loss into the larger tapestry of our daily lives and take up our daily routines again. In Jamie Quackenbush's 1985 book, *When Your Pet Dies: How to Cope With Your Feelings*, he states that besides the five stages of grief, animal owners frequently experience a sixth stage: guilt. The pet that has died or is dying often is completely dependent on the owner for its welfare. Therefore, when its health is slipping away, many owners feel they should have or could have done something more to help it. This is a natural reaction. But gradually you will realize that at some point, your dog's health and destiny were taken out of your hands.

To help you in the grief process, actively adjust your routine and do something else during the time you would have been spending with your dog. You can also devote some special time in honor of your pet's memory and respectfully use the time you would have had together in a way that gives testimony to your dog's contributions to your life. For example, one of my pet-loss group members began volunteering her time at a local animal shelter to help other dogs in need of care and love. Others contribute to animal welfare groups.

William Kay, in his book *Pet Loss and Human Bereavement*, discusses how one's health can be adversely affected by the death of the family pet. The pet's death affects the owner's health in two ways: First, it triggers grief and often depression. Nightmares, loss of appetite, loss of sleep, and even minor colds can follow, since the grieving process can impact the body's immune system and make it less able to fight off invading viruses.

Dogs also provide their owners with several health-sustaining behaviors that are abruptly discontinued after the dog dies. The dog demanded exercise. It kept the owner externally focused on having to feed and groom a dependent creature. It provided the owner with social contacts with other dog lovers. And petting the dog lowered the owner's blood pressure and increased touching experiences.

POSTVENTION

I remember quite vividly the story of one member of my early pet bereavement support group. When he told a therapist that his pet died, the therapist rebuffed the man, belittled his feelings and invalidated his pain by chastising the client for calling him early in the morning and being so upset over a dog's death. The therapist told the client that from the way the client was carrying on, the therapist had thought the call was regarding something "more important" than the loss of a pet. Unfortunately, too many mental health professionals are culturally conditioned to look at animals as mere property. If they are not animal owners themselves, they tend to have a hard time empathizing with clients and validating their clients' pain when their clients are grieving over a lost pet.

Health professionals need to recognize that bereaved persons, whether grieving the loss of humans or pets, are many times in need of "postvention." Edwin Schneidman, in his book *Voices of Death*, said he learned from his work with grieving persons that prevention, intervention, and postvention are synonymous with the concepts of immunization, treatment, and rehabilitation. Postvention consists of all those verbal and nonverbal interventions that help reduce the impact and dire aftereffects on the lives of people who have lost a family member. Postvention is not only directed at the initial shock of losing a loved one, but at the longer haul—the day-to-day living with grief for a year or more following the first shock of loss.

Complicating or interfering with postvention is the fact that we live in a culture in which we deal with our fear of death by denying the very fact of death. Dying people are separated from society and placed in hospitals or convalescent homes, far away from the rest of us.

Here are a few survival tips for those of you mourning a loss in your life:

- Recognize that you need time to heal. The greater the loss, the more time it will take.
- Get lots of rest; grieving is tiring.
- It's OK to need comforting. Allow yourself to be "taken care of" for a while.
- Do your mourning now. Don't postpone it or run away from it. The sooner you allow yourself to be with your pain, the sooner it will pass.
- Finally, loss, pain, healing, and understanding all make you expand and grow as a person. As Kübler-Ross wrote, "Death is the key to the door of life. It is through accepting the finiteness of our individual existences that we are enabled to find strength and courage to reject those extrinsic roles and expectations and to devote each day of our lives—however long they may be—to growing as fully as we are able."

ANOTHER PET?

After an individual or family loses a pet, the inevitable question arises: Should I get another pet? Well, it's up to you. You know yourself best. Different people mourn at different rates and in different ways. There are people who vow to never again have another pet, since the loss of their first was too painful and they want to avoid ever experiencing such pain again. Others go right out to a breeder and bring home a new puppy to begin the cycle over.

I strongly suggest waiting at least six months. This allows a grieving owner to come to terms with the death of the first pet and to re-order his or her day-to-day routine. A possible pitfall of rushing out to get a new pet is that grieving people are in weakened emotional—and sometimes physical—states and their stress thresholds are often very low. Usually the dog that just died was an older animal that long ago stopped urinating on the carpet, chewing up slippers, and had mellowed out to an energy level acceptable to its owners. A new puppy will be hyperactive and unhouse-broken and chew everything in sight. In short, it will be very needy.

If the grieving person is still very needy themselves, they probably won't have enough of themselves to give to the new pup. Also, they will be constantly comparing the new animal with the deceased pet, whose behavior was "perfect," and will constantly be disappointed. All of these factors can lead to the stressed owner one day blowing up at a new pup's annoying puppy antics. The owner might feel they do not like this new dog and give it away—then end up grieving over a second animal.

Case Study Postscripts

In the first six months after Tozai's death, I felt emotionally deadened, like being in a fog. Gradually, the fog lifted and both the happy times and sad times my family had with Tozai began to crystallize in my memory. My parents and sister still talk about Tozai, and a painting of him still hangs in my childhood home. It was two years before I was ready to get another dog, which turned out to be Fagan. The sense of loss after Fagan's death was even more intense. First, he was strictly my dog, whereas Tozai had been more of a family dog, and did not go with me when I went away to college. Fagan, however, lived with me for eleven years and was with me through job changes, successful and failing relationships, and the birth of my animal-behavior practice. In addition, with Tozai, there was no viable treatment for his spinal paralysis. With Fagan, however, there was treatment, and for awhile he got better, fostering hope. When the cancer returned, that was shattered and the pain, sadness and realization of what had to be done was front and center.

About a year after Fagan died, I obtained Max, a lively flat-coated retriever. Because I did not wait longer, I found residual feelings of Fagan's loss emerging and found myself repeatedly calling Max by Fagan's name. After a few months, my grieving felt more complete and I began to appreciate Max fully for the dog he is, and not compare him to Fagan. Max has now happily filled the void created when Fagan died. The cycle of life and death continues.

PART II: CHILDREN AND PET LOSS

Jean Piaget, a Swiss naturalist and psychologist, put forth the first formal theory of cognitive development. Beginning in infancy and ending in adolescence, according to Piaget, children pass through four increasingly sophisticated cognitive stages of development.

From birth to two years of age is the sensorimotor stage, during which children learn to coordinate sensory experiences and motor behaviors. They learn to interact with the world by sucking, grasping, crawling, and walking. In just over a year's time, they change from reflexive, passive, helpless, creatures to purposeful, locomoting, language-using individuals.

From two to seven, children go through the preoperational stage, which includes a rapid growth in vocabulary, more sophisticated grammar and the beginnings of the ability to reason and use abstract thinking strategies.

From seven to twelve, children go through the concrete operational stage, in which they learn to reason logically about concrete things and can do moderately successful abstract thinking. From twelve to eighteen, children enter the formal operational stage; they use sophisticated abstract thinking, can test out mental assumptions or hypotheses, and are fluid in engaging in reverse mental processes such as subtracting what was added or dividing what was multiplied.

In addition to these cognitive, or thinking, stages of development, there are social-emotional stages on the road to adulthood. The psychoanalytic theorist Erik Erikson said that each child, as he or she matures physically, must also mature psychologically by successfully working through emotional issues. In the first year of life, a child must develop the ability to trust, followed by the ability to learn, and thus should be somewhat autonomous by age two. By five children are learning to take initiatives and explore the environment. From six through twelve, the child must achieve a feeling of competence versus feelings of inferiority. From twelve through eighteen, the adolescent must form his or her own unique psychological identity.

Both sets of stages are indicators of how a child will react to the loss of a pet and parents need to consider both sets when determining the best way to talk to a child about a loss.

One of the most important things a parent can do in preparing their child for the death of a loved one is to talk with him or her about the life cycle of all living things. Toddlers can see baby birds hatching and leaves falling to the ground. These situations give parents more than enough material from which to launch into discussing birth, life, and death. And most parents do not have a problem talking about birds' eggs or about kittens being born. Both events are the beginning of the life cycle. Many adults do, however, have a hard time talking about the end of the life cycle.

If you are a parent, ask yourself: How comfortable do I feel about the subject of death—my own death, a relative's death, a favorite pet's death? The answer can begin to open your eyes and increase your awareness of your comfort level regarding mortality issues and can serve as a tool when trying to communicate to your child the important issues surrounding death and dying. Your children will take their cues from you. They will sense and observe whether or not you are approachable to discuss death.

Kimberly's father would never talk about death. An unwritten assumption in her home was that if you talked about it, "it" might happen! Even if someone in her family died, she and her family would not talk about it. As a teenager, Kimberly remembers being brave and going against the grain in bringing up the taboo subject. She would often ask, "What do you think happens when you die?" Such queries met with stony silence. Her father would give her the "look," subtly expressing disapproval for her bringing up the subject. Her mother told her later that she never heard Kimberly's father discuss death. The lesson? You as a parent would be prudent to examine your own feelings about death and learn to become comfortable talking about the subject *before* a loved one or a pet dies.

A good metaphor to use with young children when discussing death is the door. Explain that before we were born, we had no idea what our world or life would be like. At birth, we went through a door through which you can pass only one way. That is an easy concept to grasp, since a child can clearly understand that they can never return to their mother's womb. Death, you tell them, is like another one-way door. When a person or animal goes through that door they cannot return. Depending upon your family's religious beliefs, you may want to elaborate at that point on what you believe happens on the other side of the door.

An adult must be careful in using metaphors when explaining death and dying to a young child. A classic mistake is to use the metaphor of sleep. Never tell a child that the family pet "went to sleep" when trying to explain its death. They may always hold out hope that it will wake up. In addition they may fear the same could happen to them upon falling asleep. Be as honest as you can. Tell them the truth.

Tell the child facts—they are more capable than you think of handling the truth. The facts are much better than not knowing what happened to the pet or what led to its demise. If Bruiser was old and suffering from a painful heart condition, then relate the facts: "Bruiser was very sick and Dr. Jones said he was in a lot of pain, so he gave him a certain medicine that would take the pain away and make his heart stop beating." Or if Bruiser was in an accident: "Bruiser was in the street and a car ran over him. We took him to the vet but it was too late. He died." The child may ask, "Was he in pain?" You can answer, "I don't know," or "Yes, he was, but only for an instant," or, "Yes, he was. It was hard for me to see him in so much pain."

Young children might talk about their pet's death over and over. This is merely their need to master the situation emotionally. By going over and over the demise of the family pet, the child integrates the experience into their psyche, achieves understanding and closure. They master the crisis and can move on.

Some children, however, may react to the loss of their pet by clamming up and withdrawing. Kimberly's oldest daughter didn't say anything when one of the family's pets died. When Kimberly would approach her daughter to see if she wanted to talk about it, the child would say that she didn't have anything to say.

Kimberly and her husband reassured their daughter that if she had questions or feelings about the death, they would be glad to listen. A couple of months later, on the way to dance lessons, her daughter blurted out, "I sure miss Bruiser. It makes me sad every time I think about him. I *hate* feeling sad." Kimberly reflected on this and then proceeded to talk to her daughter about experiencing sadness. This opened up the entire subject of death and dying, which led to lots of hugs, kisses, and physical comforting.

Some things Kimberly learned from this experience:
- Think about and be clear on your religious beliefs and values before you have to answer your child's questions.
- Reinforce the message to your child that they were in no way responsible for the pet's death simply because they may have once said they hated their pet, or wished their pet were gone or dead.

- Use the child's own words and slang to phrase your explanations and feed back to them the key words they use when they start revealing their grief to you.
- Answer questions literally. Be concrete, be simple, keep it short and stay in the here and now. Parents tend to read more than they should into children's questions about death and dying.
- Allow yourself to grieve as well.
- Remember, as discussed earlier in this chapter, everyone grieves differently and according to a different schedule. Be patient.
- If your child does not want to talk about how they feel about their pet's death, then you as a parent can share *your* feelings when it is appropriate.
- Provide a rite of passage honoring your deceased pet; do something to help your child and your family say good-bye. This can be a funeral, a song, a poem, a story, whatever, but do it as a family.
- Do not rush out and purchase another pet to replace the dead one. It gives the child the message that it is not OK to feel grief.
- Remember that kids use the defense mechanism of denial just as adults do. "I think Izzy will be home when we get there," a child might say after leaving the vet hospital or animal cemetery. An appropriate answer would be, "You really want him to be there, don't you? It's hard going home and realizing that he died and will not be there."

To further assist you talking to your child about a pet's death, we have prepared an original Parent-Child Dialogue Guide.

PARENT-CHILD DIALOGUE GUIDE ON PET LOSS

AGE: 0–3

GRIEF RESPONSE: Child talking about it all the time or not talking about it at all. They may act it out in play (a doll died) trying to get mastery by repeatedly talking about it.

LANGUAGE SKILLS: Very limited.

SUGGESTIONS: Use terms they know and use. Use illustrations. Talk about the cycle of all things, such as flowers, bugs. "This is a seed. It turns into a flower, then the flower dies. Everything has a beginning, a middle, and an end."

AGE: 4–7

GRIEF RESPONSE: Crying, talking about how much they miss the pet. Anger, outbursts, acting out with friends.

LANGUAGE SKILLS: Can now deal with literal facts. Ready to learn parents' religious beliefs.

SUGGESTIONS: Be honest. Look at your own moral beliefs. Be fairly factual; explain what happened. Use an analogy: bread turns moldy, dust returns to the earth. Or simply say, "His body was so old, it just stopped working, and he died." Answer questions literally, not figuratively.

AGE: 8–12

GRIEF RESPONSE: More extreme reactions similar to the four to seven age group. Aggressive behavior, tantrums, being very emotional, many more tears. More anxiety about death and big spiritual issues. Forming own spiritual beliefs. Will tend to model mom's and dad's grief reactions.

LANGUAGE SKILLS: Can think abstractly. Can see death as final. Begins to fear own death. Sparks existential questions.

SUGGESTIONS: Parents should help child express feelings of grief. They must come to terms with their own mortality issues. Parents should share own reactions to pet's death and provide many opportunities for child to vent grief.

AGE: OVER 12

GRIEF RESPONSE: Withdrawal, depression, adult-like melancholy, rebelliousness. May appear as "having it together," but really doesn't. Engages in denial.

LANGUAGE SKILLS: Adult-like.

SUGGESTIONS: Parents should initiate subtle, directed activities to help teen express pent-up feelings and to express them in an appropriate manner. Make sure that when you talk to the teen you let them know you're also sharing the loss.

CHILDREN'S STORY

THE STORY OF LIZZY AND CHESTER

by Kimberly Whitten Akamine and Larry Lachman

One day, I was playing in a field near my house. I heard a teenie wee-nie voice speaking. So I squatted down to see where it was coming from. I saw a little field mouse talking to a black ant. This is a story about what I heard . . .

"Come on Lizzy! We need to get home," said Chester the mouse to Lizzy the ant. "We're going to be late for dinner. If you're tired, climb on my back and I'll give you a ride." Lizzy the ant crawled on Chester's back and off they went.

While he was trying to hurry home, Chester thought about when they used to spend many hours digging great hideouts, playing hide-and-seek and treasure hunting for treats to eat. Other times, they would lie and watch for clouds that looked like monsters. Lizzy was a good pet and a wonderful friend.

Momma mouse had a wonderful supper of dried sunflower seeds, pine nuts, crumbs from a cracker, and a ripe red strawberry for dessert!

"I wonder where those two are?" Momma thought. "They're never late for dinner."

"Where were you? I was starting to worry. You're late for dinner!," said Momma mouse when Chester and Lizzy finally got home. After dinner, Momma asked Chester, "Is everything OK?"

"No," Chester said. "It's Lizzy. She made me late tonight. She is so-o-o slow! I had to give her a piggy-back ride home or else we would have missed all of our dinner. I don't want her to go with me anymore. She really slows me down. She used to keep up with me . . . but not anymore."

"Well, Lizzy is getting older," said Momma mouse. "One of these days she will not be able to go with you. She will have to stay here with me." Chester was glad Momma said that. He wanted to run races and climb on things again. Yet he felt sad because Lizzy had always been with him and he couldn't imagine having fun without her.

After breakfast the next day, Chester decided to go exploring in the orange grove not far from the mouse hole. "Oranges are starting to fall off the trees. Maybe we can get a sweet one and roll it home," he said to Lizzy. The sun was bright and warm and the wind was blowing so it didn't bother Chester that Lizzy was taking her time getting there.

Chester and Lizzy found their favorite tree near the edge. Oranges were all over the ground. Chester bit into one.

"This is really sweet, take a taste," he said to Lizzy. Sweet orange juice was one of Lizzy's favorite things. "I'm going to find the sweetest one here!," said Chester. "You stay here Lizzy. I'll be back in a flash." And off he went. He began turning oranges over to get a good smell to see which one was the sweetest. There were so many to choose from.

Chester finally chose the sweetest orange and started rolling it towards where he had left Lizzy. "You have to taste this one Lizzy, this one is the sweetest orange you'll taste!" Chester yelled out as he got closer. When he got to the place where he left Lizzy, Chester couldn't find her. "Lizzy, are you playing hide-and-seek?" he yelled. Just then he saw another field mouse who was a friend of his.

"Hi Jake," said Chester. "Have you seen Lizzy?"

"No," said Jake.

"Would you help me look for her, please?"

"Sure," Jake said.

They looked all around the tree but couldn't find Lizzy. Chester was getting mad because he thought she was playing games. Then he became scared.

"Jake, you keep looking while I run home to get Momma." He ran faster than he had ever run before.

"Momma, Momma, come quick! I can't find Lizzy—something has happened to her!" Momma and Chester ran quickly back to the spot. All of a sudden several oranges blew off the tree and almost hit them. Momma thought quickly and said, "Roll around these oranges that are on the ground, maybe one fell on her." All three of them, Momma mouse, Chester, and Chester's friend Jake, scurried about rolling over oranges. Finally, Momma mouse found Lizzy under one of the oranges.

"Here she is," yelled Momma. Lizzy was lying down. She didn't move.

"Lizzy, Lizzy!" yelled Chester. Momma said, "Chester, I think Lizzy is dead."

"She can't be!" yelled Chester. *"She's my pet!"*

Momma held Chester as he stared at Lizzy. He couldn't believe it was true. Lizzy couldn't be dead.

That night Chester kept thinking about Lizzy. *"If only I had taken her with me, this would not have happened,"* he told Momma mouse in an angry voice. *"That stupid orange tree—I hate it!"* Chester was very mad.

Momma said, *"I know you are very angry about what happened. You have lost a wonderful friend and you will really miss her. I want you to know, though, that what happened to Lizzy was an accident. The way the wind was blowing, you could have been hurt yourself. There was nothing you could have done to keep her safe. Accidents happen."*

Chester was mad but most of all he was very, very sad, and he cried. Momma gave Chester lots of cuddles and let him cry.

After many nights, Chester could not sleep. He kept thinking about Lizzy. He remembered all those long days when they would explore and have fun. When Chester would be sad or lonely, Lizzy would crawl up on him and make him laugh because it tickled. Chester missed her. It felt like a great big hole in his tummy, or a heavy, heavy heart.

One night when Chester was in bed he was thinking about Lizzy. He remembered that before their last outing together he told his mom that he didn't want Lizzy to go with him because she slowed him down. When Momma mouse tucked him in bed, he told her, *"Lizzy died because I didn't want her to go with me anymore. It was because I wished I didn't have to take her."*

Momma held Chester close and said, *"Lizzy did not die because of what you wished, thought, or did. Lizzy was getting old and could probably not move out of the way very fast. She probably did not even see the orange falling. It was a terrible accident."*

"I wish she were still here, " said Chester with tears in his eyes.

"You really miss her and feel very sad, don't you Chester?" Momma mouse said.

"Yes," replied Chester. He cried while Momma mouse held him close. It helped to talk to someone who loved him. He fell asleep in his momma's arms and dreamed about Lizzy.

In the days that followed, sometimes Chester felt like being alone and other times he would help his momma do things. He thought about Lizzy a lot.

"Why don't you draw pictures of Lizzy and we will put them on the walls," suggested Momma.

As days passed, and while he drew pictures of Lizzy, Chester would talk to his Momma about his anger, sadness and loneliness and it helped him feel better. As the days became shorter and it started to get colder, Chester didn't feel quite as sad and started to run, jump, and play with Jake and some other new friends he had made. As Chester got bigger, and as he played with all of his new friends, he would many times think of Lizzy and remember her as a true friend he would always love.

14

Cynophobia: The Fear of Dogs

"*I am really getting concerned about my daughter. She's getting worse and worse. Six months ago, she was bitten by our neighbor's dog in our backyard. At first, she was just afraid of their dog, but then she began to be afraid of other dogs. Then it was dogs on television, and even pictures of dogs. Now she won't even go outside to play.*"

"*My husband and my children have been begging me to get a dog for our family for two years. I have always said no. I'm afraid of dogs. When I was five, a neighbor's dog bit me, and ever since then, I am really scared and nervous around dogs; especially big dogs. But my kids really want one.*"

From Larry's Case Files: My Mom

FILE # H-74-00001
PERSON'S NAME: Mrs. Lachman
BREED: Homosapien female
AGE: Adult
PROBLEM: Afraid of dogs

I remember begging for a dog when I was growing up. The answer was always the same: "No!" Mom was afraid of dogs. It seems that when she was a child, she had been frightened by a Great Dane. Ever since then, she had developed fear and avoidance of dogs. From the previous chapter, you know that my family and I eventually got a dog, Tozai. How did we do it? How did mom confront and get over her fear?

Looking back, my father and I accidentally used what psychologists would call systematic desensitization, flooding, and modeling. We systematically desensitized Mom, over a three- to four-month period, encouraging and applauding her when she would approach and interact with Tozai.

We used flooding or implosion by bringing Tozai home *unannounced*! We surprised her.

I vividly recall that Saturday afternoon in 1974 when my dad and I drove up to the house after picking up Tozai. My mother and grandmother were outside on the lawn in some lounge chairs reading. As soon as I opened the door and let Tozai out, Mom screamed and ran in the house. Oooops! We had a problem. For roughly three months, Mom continually threatened to send the dog back to the kennel, me to some far-off military academy, and my dad to divorce court!

In addition to this flooding technique, my dad and I also used the therapeutic principle of modeling, by demonstrating to my mom alternate ways of interacting with a dog by the way we would interact with Tozai.

What is Cynophobia?

Cynophobia is the term used for someone who has a phobia of dogs. Phobias are defined as excessive and inappropriate fears. As such, they fall under the psychological category of anxiety disorders, which are psychological disorders marked by persistent anxiety or fear that disrupts person's everyday functioning (like going to school, work, or being able to play outside). About ten to fifteen percent of Americans suffer from anxiety disorders.

About six to eight percent of patients referred to psychologists have phobias. Around one percent of these phobic patients have animal or dog phobias. Most of the dog phobic patients are female, and many are children. Many are afraid of mainly big dogs and many have never dealt with their excessive fears.

Dog Bites and Children

The roots of the disorder can often be traced to the patient having been bitten by a dog as a child. This is not surprising. Medical, veterinary, and psychology journals estimate there are between three million and five million dog-bite incidents in the United States each year. Most of the victims are children under ten years of age. More boys than girls are bitten, although more girls than boys are referred to mental health practitioners for dog phobias. This may reflect a social stigma: Males are taught it is not OK to verbalize such fears; females do not have the same prohibition.

The fear often begins with the arrival of a puppy in the home. I have a term for the sequence of events. I call it the "child-induced sibling rivalry-nipping syndrome." A child, jealous of the arrival of the puppy as he would be of a new human sibling, intentionally kicks at the puppy, induces the puppy to jump on him or the furniture, and initiates chase-me games throughout the house. This overexcites the puppy, which inevitably leads to the puppy jumping and nipping at the child, which in turn leads to the child crying and screaming and successfully getting the puppy in trouble and punished by the parents.

The child gets further reinforcement for this rivalry dynamic by seeking out mom's hand to hold, or whining or dry-crying whenever the pup merely enters the room, taking on an afraid-of-the-puppy role. This successfully causes the parents to give the child more attention, which can lead to a phobic mind set.

Avoiding Dog Bites in the Home

In some homes, parents fail to notice the sibling rivalry behaviors initiated by their child toward the new puppy. The puppy is relentlessly pursued and annoyed or even harmed by the child until it reaches a point where it defends itself and snaps at the child. This usually causes the child to immediately stop its provocative behavior. The puppy notices the success of its protective-aggressive response. That response is continually reinforced, which often leads, the statistics indicate, to the child being bitten.

In a July 1991 article in the journal *Pediatrics*, Dr. Baker Avner Jr., M.D., wrote that out of 168 children presented at Children's Hospital of Philadelphia for dog-bite evaluations, sixty-one percent of the injuries occurred around the child's home and seventy-seven percent were by a dog the child knew.

There appear to be five factors that determine a dog's tendency to bite:

1. The dog's heredity. It was bred to fight and be aggressive.
2. The dog's early experience. Whether it was socialized adequately

with children, adults, and other dogs as a puppy, and whether it was traumatized or not.

3. Later socialization and training. Whether it was obedience trained and positively socialized with visitors and family members.

4. Health. Whether the dog had an illness or malady that influenced its mood, like an out-of-whack thyroid, or pain due to bad hips, and became pain-defensive-aggressive.

5. The victim's behavior toward the dog.

In an article about children being bitten by dogs, the Missouri Medical Association made several recommendations:

- Practice responsible pet ownership by obedience training your dog and keeping it leashed when in public.
- Do not allow your pet to have unsupervised access to infants.
- Keep children away from the dog's feeding place.
- Teach children how to properly greet and pet the dog—not to try to pet it by reaching over its head.
- Teach children what kind of play is allowable. Teach them what kinds of play (tail-pulling, riding the dog, etc.) cause dogs pain.

However, biting incidents in childhood aren't the only source of cynophobia. One study reported in a behavior-research journal showed that many people who were dog phobic recalled their parents or some adult warning them about dogs. They became afraid of dogs simply because of this, and not because of any actual incident.

In many of the psychological journal articles on cynophobia, one interesting but perplexing finding reappears consistently: Although cynophobic children and adults have usually had an early trauma involving a dog or dog bite, people who are not cynophobic often have experienced a similar trauma with no lasting negative effect. In a couple of studies, the non-cynophobic subjects had even had more of such experiences than the phobic subjects. Clearly then, bad experiences with dogs in childhood are insufficient by themselves to explain why some people become cynophobic and others do not.

One researcher believes there are basically three ways a person acquires a specific phobia like cynophobia:

Conditioning: exposure or repeated exposures to a traumatic situation or object (in this case, a dog).

Vicarious Acquisition: observations of other people displaying fear toward a situation or object.

Information transmission: someone, usually a parent or significant adult, transmits fear-inducing information—such as stories and warnings—to the child, who later becomes phobic.

All three are usually involved in the development of a phobia such as dog phobia. Some researchers believe family modeling and verbal transmissions from parents about fear of dogs might be more important in determining whether a child will become cynophobic than actual traumatic experiences with dogs.

At what age do specific types of phobias have more of a chance of taking hold? Michael Ferrari, in an article in the journal *Child Psychiatry and Human Development*, lists types of phobias and the different ages at which they tend to manifest themselves:

CHILD'S AGE	FEAR TYPES
1st year	loud noises, loss of support, strangers
2nd year	separation from parent, strange situations
3rd year	darkness, separation from parent, being left alone
4th year	**animals**, dark rooms
5th–6th year	wild animals, ghosts, monsters, thunder
6th–8th year	school, supernatural events, physical dangers
9th–11th year	social fears, nuclear war, health, school performance

Treatment for Cynophobia

Behavior therapists who treat people with dog phobias delineate the most common ways therapists treat cynophobic subjects. They are:

Behavior therapy, which attempts to directly reduce a person's fear by modifying his behavior.

Cognitive therapy, which attempts to change a person's fearful thoughts.

Psychoanalytic therapy, which attempts to uncover from the unconscious mind and treat the underlying causes of a person's fear.

BEHAVIOR THERAPY

Behavior therapy is the most widely used and most successful treatment approach to phobias. Within behavior therapy, the most widely used technique is called systematic desensitization. First, the subject is taught to relax on command through breathing and visualization exercises. Then the subject builds a hierarchy of fears, starting with the least fearful presentation of the feared object, working gradually up the hierarchy to the most fearful presentation of the feared object. The subject assigns points reflecting this gradient of fears, ranging from ten points (a minor fear) to one hundred points (overwhelming anxiety and panic.) In the case of cynophobia, seeing a picture of a dog might rate a ten. Visualizing oneself in the same room with a dog might rate a fifty. Visualizing petting a good-sized dog and letting it lick your face might be a one hundred.

Then the therapist has the subject visualize each scene in the hierarchy, beginning with the least fearful (a picture of a dog in a book). When the subject scores ten stress points in discomfort, the therapist has the subject relax until his units of distress go down to about a zero. The procedure is repeated, over and over, until a scene at the bottom of the hierarchy that used to rate ten points in stress elicits a zero, with the subject being able to remain calm and relaxed. Once this scene is mastered, the therapist and subject work their way up the hierarchy, until the subject eventually can visualize the most frightening scene, with a stress rating of a hundred, without experiencing any anxiety and able to remain relaxed with a zero or near-zero rating.

Once the imaginary scenes are conquered, desensitization to real-life circumstances begin, first from a distance, and then closer and closer. Ultimately, the subject should be able to comfortably pet and handle a dog.

It goes without saying that the therapy dog used must be absolutely friendly, mild-mannered, and submissive.

The premise behind systematic desensitization is that a person is incapable of having two incompatible nervous system responses at the same time. A person cannot be relaxed while being scared to death. Gradually, the therapist helps the subject's relaxation response become stronger and their fear response become weaker.

In the last ten years or so, two other behavior therapy techniques have been used to treat phobias like cynophobia: flooding and modeling.

Flooding is when the subject is placed in the situation he fears the most over and over. The subject cannot sustain his state of fear through so many repetitions when no resulting actual trauma is experienced. By being told to "go into his experience" or to "turn on his fear," the subject gradually achieves mastery over his symptoms.

The strategy behind flooding is this: If a person is consistently exposed to the anxiety-producing situation (dogs), and the anxiety response (shaking, stomach aches, crying, and trying to leave) is not reinforced or rewarded by allowing the person to exit the situation, the anxiety-response habit will disappear.

Most phobias are secondarily reinforced by avoidance behavior. Once the subject is phobic of an object or situation, through avoiding the object or situation, the subject avoids feeling their fear reactions, and therefore, their phobic behavior is reinforced. They get to avoid something unpleasant. So they go on avoiding what they are afraid of. By flooding, a person cannot avoid the situation, and thereby reinforce his fear.

In modeling, the therapist actively demonstrates other ways of behaving and acting in the phobic situation. After demonstrating what to do differently, the therapist coaches the subject along in performing these alternate behaviors, which are incompatible with fear or avoidance behaviors.

OTHER METHODS

Behavioral therapists also use the techniques of operant conditioning, positive reinforcement, and cognitive therapy to treat cynophobia.

Positive reinforcement is where something is added to the person's environment in order to increase a desired behavior. With cynophobic individuals, therapists frequently combine systematic desensitization with positively rewarding the subject for making the desired approach attempt through praise, touch, food, and/or monetary rewards.

With older children and adults, one must address their cognitions, or thoughts, in addition to their behavior. A cynophobic individual might constantly tell himself that a dog will attack him, that he cannot handle the situation, and that he will probably collapse and die. These negative cognitions can lead to a negative emotional state, such as fear and panic, which will lead to avoidance or phobic behaviors such as shaking or running away. The therapist must address these negative self-statements and programming and "re-program" the cynophobic subject with positive cognitions, or hopeful and confident thoughts, which lead to a more pleasant emotional state. This will, in turn, lead to a more adaptive behavioral response from the phobic individual. Several cases in psychological literature illustrate the use of these multiple therapies and techniques.

KIM

Dr. Stephen Glassock and his associates described the following case in the *Journal of Clinical Psychology*, Vol. 19, 1990:

Kim was six years old. As the youngest in her family, she was somewhat over-protected by her parents and siblings. One year prior to treatment, Kim was knocked down and attacked by a neighborhood dog she had been playing with. She sustained a scalp wound requiring stitches. After that, she avoided going outside to play and screamed if she saw a dog approaching.

Her therapists developed a list of fearful tasks for Kim to perform in order to cure her cynophobia. Each task was more anxiety provoking than the one before it:

1. Walk outside
2. Walk to a marker fifteen feet from the house
3. Walk to a second marker thirty feet from the house
4. Walk to a third marker ninety feet from the house
5. Call a dog by name from a distance
6. Approach a dog and pet it
7. Pet and talk to a dog for one minute
8. Pet and talk to a dog for two minutes
9. Pet and talk to a dog for three minutes

In addition to the systematic desensitization, the therapist modeled appropriate behavior toward the dog and used physical contact as positive reinforcement to urge Kim on. During the first phase of the program, Kim engaged in these desensitizing behaviors with both her mother and her therapist present. During the second phase, Kim played outside by herself. The family's Labrador retriever was first used. Three other dogs were introduced later in order to have the desensitizing effects generalize, or cover dogs besides her family pet.

Nine months after the treatment, Kim's anxiety was reduced, she played outside by herself, and stopped avoiding contact with dogs.

COLLEEN AND SHARON

In another case, cited by Dr. Uma Sreenivasan and associates in the *Journal of Child Psychology and Psychiatry and Allied Disciplines*, July, 1979, systematic desensitization failed to do the job and the flooding technique was used. Two sisters, Colleen, eleven, and Sharon, ten, had suffered from excessive fear of dogs for five years. They could not recall any specific events that led to their cynophobia. On Sunday evenings, both girls would become apprehensive about running into dogs on the way to school the next morning. Colleen's teacher reported her being on edge and unable to concentrate. She would be ruminating about possibly meeting up with dogs on her way home from school. Sharon made Colleen's anxiety worse by becoming hysterical at the sight of any dog no matter how close or far away. In addition, neighbors began to tease the girls about their fear.

During the clinical interview, Colleen exhibited facial tics and grimaces and extreme anxiety. Their mother previously had been treated for an anxiety condition involving agoraphobia (fear of leaving the house) after the birth of the two girls. Also, a maternal aunt of the girls had been afraid of dogs and cats (possible information transmission and vicarious learning components).

The therapists treating the girls started them on out-patient systematic desensitization. Both girls did fine and there was no problem as long as treatment involved imagined scenes with dogs. Three weeks into the program, the girls' parents obtained a puppy. Sharon approved of the puppy immediately and became less fearful of dogs overall. However, Colleen was unable to progress further and was in constant turmoil at home because of the puppy. Two months later, Colleen was admitted in-patient in a psychiatric unit to reduce her acute anxiety. Since desensitization with the live puppy wasn't working, the therapists decided to try flooding.

The goal was to have Colleen remain in the same room with a live dog. The hospital staff would be present to ensure her safety. Her parents gave their permission. Colleen very reluctantly agreed to this flooding program.

One one-hour flooding session was held each day for ten days. Colleen and her therapist arrived prior to the dog. The staff brought in a two-year-old female cocker spaniel known to be passive and friendly and the dog was taken off its leash. Over the ten days, Colleen's anxiety consistently dropped to acceptable levels. She gradually went from crying and being frozen in the chair, to playing Ping-Pong with a staff member while the dog roamed around, to petting the dog if it didn't face her. At the sixth session, Colleen tolerated the cocker on her lap, and then went on to take the dog for a walk. After this, Colleen was able to interact with her family's puppy and was discharged from the psychiatric hospital seven weeks after admission. Nineteen months after the flooding treatment, the therapists did a home visit and observed Colleen doing very well and no longer being afraid of dogs.

TREATMENT STRATEGIES

Most treatment for cynophobia involves using all three therapy techniques—systematic desensitization, flooding, and modeling—sometimes in unison, sometimes one after another. Family therapy and medication for adults, might also come into play.

If the cynophobic individual improves, but the family still acts and says things to keep his fears going, he may regress and not fully recover. The client, like our dog patients, does not exist in a vacuum. His familial environment needs to be treated also. As psychiatrist Milton Erickson explained in the book *Uncommon Therapy*, "Usually when a child is disturbed, one of the parents is locked with the child in an overindulgent way. The other parent is more peripheral. The treatment usually shifts the more peripheral parent to a more central position to break up the over-intense relationship of the other parent." In other words, the whole family needs to be examined, treated, and involved in changing the cynophobe's behavior.

Antianxiety medication might be used to allow the behavioral techniques to kick in. The medication needs to be gradually reduced and eliminated as the phobic individual becomes less and less phobic and can encounter the object or situation he once feared with little or no anxiety at all.

If you or a family member is cynophobic, contact your state's psychological association, the American Psychological Association in Washington, D.C., the Association of Licensed Clinical Social Workers, or the Association of Marital, Family, Child Counselors. Obtain three referrals for licensed therapists who are experienced in behavior therapy and its techniques and specialize in treating phobias.

Many of the techniques used to solve behavior problems in dogs are the same techniques or approaches used to help children and adults get over their dog phobias—with a little different twist here and there. With this chapter I have come full circle: I am applying what I do for dogs with phobias to people who have phobias about dogs.

Case Study Postscript

By the six-month mark, my mom had accepted Tozai. They grew to love one another and become best friends. She ended up spoiling him the most among everyone in the family. Buttered rolls, sleeping on nice comforters, the works. Even the most severe cynophobics can be helped. By accident and by the seat of our pants, my dad, Tozai, and I proved it.

15

Dangerous Doggy Lifestyles

"I was walking down the street with my dog and this German shepherd came out of nowhere and attacked my dog. I was terrified."

"Our neighbors let their Doberman roam the neighborhood without supervision. It has killed three cats. I've complained to animal control, but nothing has happened."

"I was jogging the other morning and this Australian shepherd walking with its owner bolted and ran up to me and bit me in the leg. I screamed at the owner to get a hold of his dog, but he just ignored me and kept on walking."

Case Studies: Mail Carriers vs. Pit Bulls

PERSON'S NAME: John Doe

OCCUPATION: United States Postal Carrier

AGE: 61

PROBLEM: Victim of a dog attack. Sustained head, neck, and leg injuries. As a result of the attack, developed post-traumatic stress disorder, a generalized anxiety disorder, and a related ulcer.

On June 12, 1984, a mailman we will call John Doe was heading up the front walk of a home on 191st Street in Torrance, California, to deliver the daily mail. As he climbed the stairs to the front porch, three dogs tore through the screen door and charged him, growling and barking. The first dog through the screen was a pit bull, followed by two smaller shepherd mixes.

John tried to shield himself by holding a handful of mail in one hand while shoving a wad of the resident's mail in the mouth of the charging pit bull with his other hand. The pit bull flicked the mail away and kept coming. John retreated, daring not to turn his back on his three attackers. As he was doing this, one of the smaller dogs got behind him and he tripped backwards over it, approximately fifteen feet away from the front porch. As he fell, John hit the back of his head on the pavement. The dogs were on him. He at once felt searing pain.

He tried to reach for his canister of Halt, a pepper spray repellent, but one of the dogs knocked it out of his hand. All three dogs were biting him now. The pit bull, according to John's 102-page legal deposition, was in front and was the most intimidating.

The pit bull went for his face and throat. John fended it off with a wad of mail still in his hand. The dog redirected its attack and bit John hard on the left leg. At this point, a young female resident of the home emerged and stood on the porch steps watching the commotion. After a minute, she went to try and pull the dogs off. In response, the pit bull locked its jaws on John's left leg. John began kicking the dog in the face and flailing the wad of mail at it. He was able to wiggle his leg out of the dog's mouth. As the resident worked to pull off the pit bull, the other two dogs saw their opportunity and began attacking and biting John. Finally, they too were pulled off.

John limped across the street and sought the assistance of another resident. His leg was bleeding badly, and with the help of the resident, he stanched the flow with a towel and ice. John's supervisor came out and took him to a nearby hospital, where an emergency room physician cleaned and dressed his wounds.

Within three days, along with the pain in his badly bitten left leg, John began to feel very sharp pain in his head—in the area that hit the ground during his fall. Over the next several months, due to the stress of the situation, John developed a bleeding ulcer. He also developed a case of cynophobia. In the legal deposition John said:

> Every time I have ever been attacked by a dog before, I was always standing and I always felt like I towered over my opponent. But the tremendous fear that I had when I was on the ground and that dog's face was right there, that pit bull's face was right there, I really thought I was doing to die. That's the first thing that came to me, "My God, I'm going to die." It was absolutely overwhelming. . . .

An investigation following John's attack revealed the pit bull had bitten a mail carrier before. In addition, the occupants of the house had trained the dog to attack anyone in or around their yard.

PERSON'S NAME: Willie Schertzing
OCCUPATION: United States Postal Carrier
PROBLEM: Victim of a dog attack.
    Sustained severe leg injuries.

"When Huntington Beach mail carrier Willie Schertzing thinks about pit bulls, she envisions the snarling machine of teeth and muscle that broke through a screen door, attached its jaws to her right leg and cleaved a hole 'big enough that you could take an egg and put it right in there.'"

That was the lead-in to a 1988 *Orange County Register* story Frank wrote, which talked about the controversy surrounding pit bull attacks. It included the account of Schertzing, who was attacked while delivering mail.

On April 9, 1986, Schertzing was approaching a home on Delaware Street in Huntington Beach, California, when a two-and-a-half-year-old male pit bull named Buster burst through the screen door and attacked her. The owners, who were nearby, acted helpless to stop the attack, but eventually succeeded in freeing Schertzing after cutting away her trousers with scissors around the leg Buster had latched onto.

Schertzing said she fell unconscious three separate times during the attack. "You're in such pain you can't handle it anymore." Months later, when Frank interviewed her, she said that she was still recovering, both physically and emotionally, from the attack. Her leg wounds required eighty stitches to close. She had begun psychotherapy to address the trauma associated with the attack; "I see it in my sleep, I wake up with it and I go to bed with it. It's a part of me now."

Both John and Willie were physically and emotionally scarred as a result of dangerous doggy lifestyles: careless dog-ownership practices by the humans and vicious dogs doing what they do best. Frequently, following a traumatic incident in which great bodily harm or fear of death is present, survivors experience a variety of severe psychological symptoms. This is called post-traumatic stress disorder.

PTSD is characterized by recurrent intrusive recollections of the event, recurrent distressing dreams of the event, and feeling as if the traumatic event were happening all over again. In addition, these thoughts and memories adversely affect the patient's behavior. Someone suffering from PTSD tends to avoid conversations, activities, and places associated with the trauma. The PTSD sufferer might find it hard to sleep or concentrate, will become irritable and hyper-aware, and may experience an exaggerated startle response. These symptoms can permeate the person's entire life and frequently necessitate extensive psychotherapy.

In Chapter 9 I reviewed bite statistics, the different types of aggression exhibited by dogs, and the behavior-therapy programs to treat them. Here I want to touch on the social aspects of aggressive dogs and irresponsible pet ownership—and how people can avoid being bitten.

Taking Responsibility for Your Pet

We have a responsibility to the community and to our animals. We need to protect them, keep them safe, and not harm them. We also need to prevent them from hurting other people or animals.

This means using modern, non-force obedience techniques to teach your dog to sit, lie down, come, stay, heel, and not jump up. When in public, a dog should be leashed (with the other end of the leash firmly attached to the handler's wrist). Allowing a dog to run all over the neighborhood teaches it to be inappropriately and dangerously dominant aggressive. This endangers children and other dogs, since dogs look at small quick-moving children as prey to pursue or hunt, and other same-sex dogs as potential threats. The same applies for letting it loosely roam in an unfenced front yard, or having it unsecured behind a flimsy screen door. There are responsibilities that go along with the right to have a pet.

Pets As "Property"

We often look at our pets as mere "property," to do with what we like. This often leads to irresponsible pet ownership and abuse. Examples include setting a pet astray or asking the veterinarian to "put it to sleep" simply because the owner doesn't want to be bothered with the animal any longer.

This cold, removed view and treatment of our animals frequently stems from our childhood: how we were raised and whether as children we ever learned to experience empathy. Empathy is the ability to see and feel things from another's point of view. Children who are never taught to have empathy and who grow up in severely dysfunctional homes often end up torturing animals. In fact, according to the FBI, people who turn into serial killers often exhibit what is called the Profile Triad. As children, these individuals tortured animals, set fires, and were bed wetters. A severe lack of empathy, taken to the extreme, can lead to disastrous consequences.

If a child is taught and modeled responsibility and compassion for animals or pets in the home, then he will be sensitive to that animal's pain and quality of life. That child grows up to be a person who is more compassionate and kind toward animals and people.

Legal Ramifications of Engaging in Dangerous Doggy Lifestyles

Owning an untrained dog—particularly a large one—or purposely training a dog to be aggressive is about as smart as throwing a children's birthday party and leaving a loaded gun on the coffee table. In most places, if your dog bites someone, even superficially, you will be visited by an animal control or law enforcement officer and the dog will be placed in quarantine for a period of time. The incident will go on record. If it bites someone superficially a second time or kills another animal, the consequences are greater. There might be no quarantine and warning. The dog might be euthanized almost immediately. If your dog attacks a person and inflicts serious injury or kills them, you probably can count on years of legal woes. You probably will be sued; unless you are rich, liens will be placed on your wages or home; and you might be convicted of a crime, pay a fine, or serve jail time. Your dog, of course, will be euthanized.

Is There One Type of Vicious Dog?

There is no one breed of dog that is vicious. Any dog is capable of aggression, attacking, and killing. In my animal-behavior therapy practice, I have seen aggression in Labradors, golden retrievers, Australian shepherds, terriers, poodles, bichon frises, Maltese, you name it. However, when a Chihuahua behaves aggressively or bites, it is inherently less dangerous and lethal than when a pit bull, Rottweiler, or akita behaves aggressively or bites. Not only are these dogs bigger, but they are in the category of dogs intentionally bred for guard work, fighting, or herd protection. These breeds are more likely to be aggressive. If you have young children, stay away from breeds such as the German shepherd, Rottweiler, Doberman pinscher, pit bull, chow chow, shar-pei, akita, and Lhasa apso.

There is no one breed of dog that is inherently aggressive. We are against "breed specific legislation." Any dog of any breed can behave aggressively and bite. In all bite incidents, ultimately the human is at fault. This focus on the human element of dog aggression explains why we entitled this chapter "Dangerous Doggy Lifestyles" and put the onus of responsibility for dog bites on the dog's owner, where it belongs.

In the United States, there are approximately 4–5 million reported dog bite incidents per year. Out of an estimated total dog population of 56–58 million, the dogs who are doing the biting represent only a small percentage of all dogs, most of whom are friendly and safe.

In the United States, most bite victims are children under 10 years of age. Mutts known to the victim or the victim's neighbor are the leading perpetrators.

According to the Centers for Disease Control and the American Medical Association, in 1994 there were an estimated 4.7 million reported dog bites (1.8% of the U.S. population), and out of these, 800,000 people sought medical care. The CDC makes the following recommendations:

- Keep children away from dogs with histories of aggression.
- Be sensitive to cues that a child is fearful of dogs.
- Spend time with the dog before adopting or buying it.
- Spay/neuter the dog.
- Never leave infants or young children alone with ANY dog.
- Properly socialize and train the dog.
- Do not play aggressive games with the dog.
- Immediately seek professional advice if a behavior problem develops.
- Teach children to:

  1. Never approach an unknown dog.
  2. Never run from a dog and scream.

3. Remain motionless when approached by an unknown dog.
4. If knocked over, roll into a ball and lie still.
5. Never play with a dog unless supervised.
6. Avoid direct eye contact with a dog.
7. Do not disturb a dog when it's sleeping, eating, or caring for puppies.
8. Do not pet a dog without allowing it to see and sniff you first.
9. And if bitten, immediately report the bite to an adult.

Finally, the following can help to improve some of these grisly statistics:

- Get a dog not traditionally bred for guarding, sport fighting, or attacking.
- Socialize it in a fun, positive, and safe manner.
- Spay and neuter it.
- Integrate it into the home so it becomes a member of the family.
- Take it to a positive training class (call the Association of Pet Dog Trainers at 1-800-PET-DOGS for a referral).

Bite Avoidance

In 1995, 2,851 United States mail carriers were bitten by dogs. The United States Postal Service suggests five ways customers can be more responsible in the care of their dogs:

1. Don't assume your dog won't bite.
2. Spay or neuter your dog. Un-neutered dogs are three times more likely to bite.
3. Obedience training can teach your dog proper behavior and help you control your pet in any situation.
4. When your letter carrier comes to your home, keep your dog inside, away from the door in another room or on a leash.
5. Don't let your child take mail from the letter carrier in the presence of your dog. Your dog's instinct is to protect the family, and it might misconstrue the handing of mail as a threatening gesture toward the child.

Dog Bite Prevention Week takes place each year in June. During this time, the United States Postal Service and the Humane Society of the United States issue bite-prevention mailers to postal customers. Suggestions for avoiding being bitten by a dog include:

- Don't run past a dog. The dog's natural instinct is to chase and catch prey.
- If a dog threatens you, don't scream. Avoid eye contact, try to remain motionless until the dog leaves, then back away slowly until the dog is out of sight.
- Don't approach a strange dog, especially one that's tied and confined.
- Always let a dog see and sniff you before you pet the animal.

Protecting Yourself and Your Dog

It is frightening to be attacked or menaced by an aggressive dog. I've been seriously attacked once, while conducting an obedience class. I had just finished examining a dog's special collar and turned to walk away. At that moment, Jake, an eighty-pound shepherd-mix, leaped up and bit into my upper left arm. The pain was instant. I felt my body begin to go into a shock/protective mode. Later, I went to the emergency room and had the wound treated and received a tetanus shot in my other arm. What fun.

I have experienced dozens of dog-menacing incidents when walking my own dog. Most of the time, the other dog is trying to attack my dog. The most recent occurred a couple of winters ago. While walking my golden retriever, Fagan, near my home one day, a careless owner allowed her 100-pound great Dane mix to escape her grip and charge Fagan and me from across a parking lot.

I immediately placed himself between Fagan and the great Dane, controlling the leashed Fagan with my left hand while attempting to fend off the attacking unleashed dog with my right hand and leg. The great Dane was growling, showing its teeth, and relentlessly trying to attack Fagan. I tried shouting at the dog first, but to no avail. I then attempted to startle it by stamping my foot. It responded by redirecting its aggression toward me. I kicked it in the face, neck, and chest. No effect. I was now starting to become quite concerned about my ability to avoid injury and protect Fagan. I bopped the dog over the head with a heavy metal police flashlight, which I carry at night for just such situations. That stunned the dog and gave me time to reach for my canister of pepper spray. Dowsed in the face with the repellent, the great Dane finally backed off. All during this the careless owner stood by and watched passively. At no time did she try to call off her dog or help me.

I later filed a complaint with the animal control department and learned the dog had previously attacked other dogs in the neighborhood. Yet the owner, knowing her pet's history, had continued to loosely hold the leash in her hand while out on walks, seemingly oblivious to the danger she was presenting the community.

The Layered Defense

Borrowed from my martial arts buddy Eric Cilley, the layered defense calls for defending oneself with increasing levels, or layers, of lethalness. With a menacing or aggressive dog, here is a suggested defense method:

- Do not look the dog directly in the eyes. That's a direct challenge and can set off the dog, increasing the aggression potential.
- Do not run away. This could trigger its prey-chasing mode.
- Unless it's unavoidable, do not use pain to ward off the dog. Pain frequently increases aggression.
- Move very slowly.
- Do not turn your back on the dog.
- Try to startle the dog without pain. First try:
  1. A loud noise. Frequently, yelling a command like "No!" or "Out!" or "Stay!" will make the dog pause, stand still, or back off.
  2. Always carry a water bottle, umbrella, ultrasonic device, or air horn when venturing into an area known for off-leash menacing dogs. This is the next layer of startle. If the yelling fails, and the dog is still menacing or trying to attack, then blasting it in the face with a water bottle, surprising it with the sudden opening and shield of a large umbrella, or depressing an ultrasonic or other such device should startle the dog and give you time to escape.
- Carry a canister of pepper spray. If the noise devices fail, use it.
- It goes without saying that if these layers of defense fail and someone is in jeopardy of being seriously injured or killed, then you do whatever it takes to stop the attacking dog.

- If the dog is attacking another person or your dog and has its teeth into them, do not go to the attacking dog's head area and try to pry it away. It will only turn on you! The best way is to get behind the attacking dog, grab both of its hind legs firmly and pull it off the victim. If you hang on tight, the attacking dog will not be able to maneuver around to bite you, and it will be disabled.

It's painful to have to write this, because ultimately, it is a human's fault that you might find yourself in the position of having to fend off an attacking or menacing dog. The dog might have been bred to have aggressive traits; or it was never socialized; or it was never obedience trained using non-force, non-pain methods; or it was "trained" using pain and harsh choke-chain corrections (it is worth noting that every dog that ever menaced or attacked me was wearing a choke-chain collar); or it was not neutered or spayed; or the dog was allowed to roam at will—which gives the dog the sense that the entire neighborhood is its territory, which it must defend. While the blame usually rests on the owner's shoulders, it is rare that the owner pays the price. That is borne by the dog's victims—and the dog.

Case Study Postscript

John Doe took medical disability retirement from the Postal Service. John is still afraid of dogs and of leaving his house. Ten years after Frank first interviewed Willie Schertzing, he called her to follow up for this book. Willie was still working for the Postal Service in Orange County, but only inside the office; even a decade after the attack, she is still afraid to deliver mail door-to-door again. "The dog took a bite out of me physically, emotionally, and psychologically," she said. "Right now, if I see a strange dog, I freak out."

Within a few years after the attack, she did find herself able to interact with gentle dogs she had become familiar with, but for a long time, she stayed away from people who had dogs. Ironically, part of her new job at the Postal Service is to deal with the owners of dogs that threaten or attack mail carriers. Frequently, she stops mail delivery at their homes and the owners must get a post office box. She tries to keep her colleagues from having to go through what she did.

16

KNOWING WHEN TO ADOPT OUT

"We initially wanted a family dog—you know, one the whole family could play with. However, our chow is becoming more and more aggressive. It went after one of our daughter's friends last night. And my husband and I are thinking of opening up a day care center in our home."

"My wife and I bought this dog for my mother who lives in a retirement community. It's turned into a nightmare. Here's my mom, who is this frail old woman, with this young German shepherd that is well over 100 pounds and growls and snaps at her if she goes by him when he's eating or chewing on a bone."

"He seems to want to be with the family all the time. He howls if we leave him alone for the weekend. He seems to want all of our attention. He likes to lick and be petted, and barks when he hears someone at the door. We can't have that. He's too demanding."

FROM LARRY'S CASE FILES:
"Carrie" the Ridden-Hard Rottweiler

FILE # 97-000481
DOG'S NAME: Carrie
BREED: Rottweiler
AGE: 5 years
PROBLEM: Dog-child aggression

In 1997, I went out on a consult regarding a five-year-old spayed female Rottweiler named Carrie who had bitten the family's young son on four occasions. In the most recent incident, the child was bitten on the face. A bite to the face of a forty-pound child by a dog weighing close to 100 pounds is a very dangerous situation, and the pediatrician was urging the family to put the dog down. However, looks can be deceiving, and upon investigation some interesting facts came to light.

First, Carrie had gone through my obedience class for older dogs and I knew her to be an exceptionally sweet, well-adjusted, and socialized Rottweiler. She had never displayed aggression in class, either toward me or toward other dogs. In addition, the family also included a nine-year-old girl whom Carrie had never growled at, snapped at, or bitten. Also, neighborhood children could come up to Carrie and pet her with no problem.

When I arrived at the family's home, Carrie proceeded to lie down, roll over on her back, and expose her tummy. This was a vicious dog? Something did not add up.

Upon taking an extensive social, medical, and behavioral history from the family, and in observing each family member's interactions with Carrie, it was clear the only person Carrie shied away from was the son, who was also the only person she had ever bitten. Naturally, I zeroed in on the interaction between Carrie and the boy.

One of the first bite incidents occurred a few years previously. Carrie was chewing on a bone, and the boy, then two, tried to grab it from Carrie's mouth. She growled and bit him in the finger. A pattern of similar, unacceptable behavior from the boy toward Carrie began to reveal itself. Repeatedly, when the dog would be eating or sleeping, the boy would jump up in the air and land on her. The dog would cry, then growl or bite. Then the boy would cry. With the exception of the first bite, the parents were never in the room during these incidents. They would hear the dog cry out and growl, and then their son would cry out that Carrie had bitten him.

I observed that Carrie was most enmeshed with the husband. She was also emotionally attached to the wife and daughter. But she would react fearfully (ears back, head hung low, stump of a tail down) when around the boy, and avoid him or trot away. In addition, the boy's behavior suggested that he was possibly suffering from Attention Deficit Disorder and hyperactivity. He was in constant perpetual motion, unable to focus, and unresponsive to his parents' directions. Indeed, the parents would give up and allow him to do anything he wanted; he was being reinforced for his acting-out behavior.

The picture was becoming clear. Carrie's aggressiveness toward the boy was clearly out of self-protection. In addition, the parents were not able to protect Carrie from their son. The owners were consistently violating one of my child-dog safety rules: *Never leave children under seven years of age alone with any dog at any time!*

While I was interviewing the parents and watching Carrie interact with the family, the boy at one point climbed onto the couch and prepared to take a Superman-like flying leap onto the dog, which was lying on the floor. Knowing the parents would not be able to get to the boy in time to prevent his jump, I blasted the kid in his rear end with my syringe of water and told him "No!" He looked startled and began to cry. Repeatedly during my consult, the boy attempted to kick, hit, leap upon, and throw toys at Carrie. Whenever the parents tried to stop him, he would start a tantrum. In response to his tantrum, the parents threw their arms up and gave in. I eventually asked the mother to place him in a time-out in another room for ten minutes. She looked at me as if I were asking her to hang her son by his fingernails. In this situation, I saw no chance of success and felt the boy's—and the dog's— safety was in jeopardy. *This* dog, with *this* family, was a severe mismatch.

Ooops! Did We Make a Mistake?

A lot of people make a mistake when they get a dog for a pet. Dogs are not birdbaths to be stationed in the backyard and given attention only on sunny days when the owner runs out of things to do. One of my core beliefs, and the foundation of this book, is the concept that the dog must be an integral part of the family. Dogs have feelings. They experience pain and pleasure. They depend on us to be responsible stewards. They truly are family animals.

About ninety-five percent of the dog behavior problems I see when called into someone's home stem from one of two things: the dog's lack of socialization or the dog's isolation from its pack—its human caretakers. The socialization problem arises when the owners of a new puppy do not introduce it in a positive way to a variety of adults, teens, children, safe animals, and geographical locales during the first six months of its life. It takes time and commitment to sufficiently socialize the pup during this critical period. Failure to do so can produce a dog that is aggressive toward or excessively fearful of those outside its pack. Frequently, these dogs end up being adopted out or euthanized.

A little more than half of the behavior problems in dogs are rooted in isolation anxiety—that is, anxiety caused by the dog's prolonged separation from its human pack. Owners mistakenly think they can stick it out in the backyard and throw it some food once in a while and that will suffice. This creates problems. Dogs suffering from isolation-induced anxiety often become compulsive about what are usually considered normal dog behaviors. They dig up backyards when there is no burrowing animal or bone to dig for; they destructively chew (often expensive) objects when there is no nutritional or hunger-satisfying value to them; they nuisance bark when there is nothing to bark at; they mutilate themselves by chewing on forepaws for no apparent reason. The failure of the owner to spend time with the dog is behind these behavior problems. Again, the dog ends up being given away or put down.

You must be committed to training your dog and playing with your dog as part of your "pack's" everyday life. You must be committed to fulfilling whatever the breed's special needs for exercise might be. At a minimum, you need to provide one or two fifteen-minute play or exercise sessions each day.

Financial Considerations

In addition to a time commitment, you need a financial commitment. Purebred dogs sell from $250 to as high as $2,500, although most are under $1,000. Mixed breeds can be found for free, or at humane societies and animal shelters for the cost of shots and licenses. Whatever you pay, realize it's just the beginning. You can easily spend a couple of hundred dollars on a collar, leash, bowl, brush, and bed before you get home with your new pet. Behavior classes with a competent trainer run between $75 and $250 for a six- to twelve-week course. Tack on the monthly expenses of food and occasional veterinary and kenneling fees and you are looking at several hundred dollars a year, minimum. Unexpected injuries or illnesses can result in medical bills ranging from $35 to $3,500. An owner might find himself in way over his head and choose to give up the dog.

"Watchdogs"

Another reason to consider adopting out your dog is if you got it merely so it could guard your property. Most people have a misconception about the dog's role as protector of humans and property. They think a good guard dog should be kept outside day in and day out and attack on sight anything that steps on its turf. We define a good guard dog as one that alerts its owners, through barking, of the presence or approach of a strange person or animal. This allows the human owners to take appropriate action. We want our family dogs to keep watch for us and not to raise a false alarm at every innocuous sound. A dog that indiscriminately barks or attacks is at the very least a nuisance that will make you very unpopular in your neighborhood, and at worst a serious liability that is unpredictable, dangerous, and poses a public menace.

Dogs that are integrated into the family become better bonded to their owners than do dogs that are placed in the cartoon-character watchdog role. This increased bonding promotes better obedience, less hyperactive behavioral displays and naturally increased watchfulness of the owner's home.

Severe Doggy Mismatches

There are safety issues to consider when there are children or elderly people in the home. When a family with young children acquires a dog that is more than six months of age and has no known background of socialization, or selects a dog from a breed traditionally trained for attacking or fighting, the family has set itself up for a severe mismatch. One of the most dangerous mismatches occurs when an elderly person, especially one with a disability, gets a dog whose breed is prone to guard or herd. The dog will have a greater tendency to be dominant aggressive and hyperactive. The dog quickly learns that it has greater physical prowess and can out-muscle its owner. It begins to act dominant toward the owner by growling or biting, especially when the owner tries to remove food or a bone, or tries to get the dog off the furniture. Injury or death can result.

An article in the *Delaware Medical Journal* told the story of a Chesapeake Bay retriever and an elderly owner. The gentleman had just acquired the retriever and was doing yard work. He tied the dog to a tree and placed a pan of dog food in front of it. Soon after that, the man tripped and fell down next to the tethered dog. The retriever attacked the man and mauled him to death in front of his helpless and terrified wife. A severe mismatch.

Another example: In 1989, I went to an in-home consult in Los Angeles involving two four-month-old Labrador mix puppies, a burned-out mother, and two boys under seven years of age. As soon as I entered the home, I was caught up in a whirlwind of activity. The dogs were running, jumping, nipping, and barking. The boys were chasing each other, with the older boy going after his brother with a pair of scissors. Mom, who looked like she hadn't slept in months, was barely able to hold back her tears.

She explained it was her husband's idea to get the puppies. However, he traveled a lot and she was stuck at home with two out-of-control dogs and two young boys who seemed equally out of control. After taking in the whole situation, I looked her straight in the eye and told her it simply was not going to work. It was the wrong time to get two puppies. The kids were too young and needed her undivided attention. And, in spite of his good intentions, the husband was unsupportive in both the child and dog care, and she appeared to be thoroughly overwhelmed.

It was agreed that the best course of action was to adopt out the dogs and wait until her boys were older and her husband was more available before getting another pet.

Inherited Aggression

A case of idiopathic, or biologically inherited, aggression is another situation that calls for the dog to be removed from the household. In such cases, the dog is aggressive, apparently without cause, toward everyone and everything, most of the time. Or the dog, without warning or apparent cause, engages in spurts of aggression toward family members or people it knows. The condition usually appears between one and three years of age and can appear in any breed. In some breeds there is a special label for it. For example, in springers it is referred to as Springer Spaniel Rage Syndrome.

Essentially, the dog is thought to have a biological screw loose, or suffer from some low-level epileptic condition, making it unresponsive to both behavior modification and drug therapy. While idiopathic aggression is rare, the prognosis is poor and the dog usually must be euthanized.

This was the case with Beau, a fifteen-month-old cairn terrier I was called in to observe. In looking at his psycho-social history, he had been socialized adequately with people, neutered at the optimal time, and had not experienced any significant trauma that would lead to his aggressive behavior. Still, at almost a year and half of age, he began to exhibit behavior—which I first classified as dominance aggression—toward the owners. After implementing the anti-dominance-aggression program outlined in Chapter 9, Beau did well for a while. However, at the six-month point, he began lashing out and biting both his owners for no apparent reason. His aggressive behavior escalated quickly. Strengthening the behavior-modification program and initiating psychotropic drug therapy had no effect. The decision was made to euthanize him.

Signs of a Poor Match

These situations are red flags and should help you consider whether you and your dog are a good match.

- You and other family members are busy people who really only see the dog coming and going from work, school, or play. Interaction with the dog is very sporadic.
- You are an elderly or disabled person with a young dog, whose breed was bred for attack or guarding work, and the dog exhibits signs of this.
- You are a member of a family with young children, with a dog that meets most or all of the following criteria:
  1. Was not socialized with children during its first six months of its life.
  2. Was not neutered at six months of age
  3. Was never obedience trained
  4. Is a breed that has been bred for attack and guarding
  5. Is showing aggression toward the children or strangers
  6. Has bitten or has tried to bite a child or an adult.
- You have a dog with no history of trauma that out of nowhere, begins to unpredictably growl, show its teeth, snap, or bite, and:

  1. This behavior is seen to escalate in frequency, intensity, and duration.
  2. This behavior begins to generalize to people and animals outside the home.
  3. Obedience training, behavior modification, and drug therapy have no effect.

Case Study Postscript

Relatives of Carrie's owners loved the dog and agreed to adopt her. At last word, she was doing fine in her new home.

PART FIVE:
CANINE MENTAL
HEALTH

17

HOW TRADITIONAL TRAINING CAN BE HARMFUL TO YOUR DOG

"The trainer told me that if my dog jumps up, I should knee him in the chest. I think I may have done it too hard. He's having a hard time breathing and won't come near me anymore."

"Our dog-obedience class taught us to smack the dog on the nose or under the chin if he misbehaves or nips. All that did was make him more aggressive. He started coming after us."

"For heeling, our trainer told us to hang him off the ground until he submits. First, he's almost too heavy to lift. And what's more, he almost passes out before he gives in. Do we really have to do this?"

FROM LARRY'S CASE FILES:
"Oliver" the Bearded Collie Who Was Hanged!

FILE # 93-151719
DOG'S NAME: Oliver
BREED: Bearded collie
AGE: 5 months
PROBLEM: Trainer-induced head shyness and fear aggression

In 1993, I went out on a behavior therapy consult involving a five-month-old bearded collie that had been abused by a heavy-handed dog trainer. The abuse had led to head-shyness and fear aggression. The trainer, who epitomized the barbarism and abuse in traditional force-method dog training, had conducted a home session during which he squeezed Oliver's lip under and against his canine teeth, severely choke-chained him, hung him, whirled him into the living room furniture, and yelled at him! Oliver howled in pain, urinated, and bled.

Since the incident, Oliver was demonstrating head-shyness and mild to moderate fear aggression by not coming to the owners when they called him, nor allowing them to touch or reach for his head. If they persisted in attempting to handle his face or neck he would snap or gag. The owners had complained to their veterinarian, who referred them to me.

Post traumatic stress disorder in people is defined by the *Diagnostic and Statistical Manual-IV* of the American Psychiatric Association as: "The person has been exposed to a traumatic event in which both of the following were present: 1. The person experienced, witnessed, or was confronted with an event or events that involved actual or threatened death or serious injury, or a threat to the physical integrity of self or others. 2. The person's response involved intense fear, helplessness, or horror." Oliver was indeed suffering from canine PTSD. Prior to being traumatized by the trainer, Oliver had never demonstrated any of these symptoms. The owners had gotten him when he was nine weeks old from a professional breeder in Maryland. Other than a recurring ear infection which necessitated antibiotics and ear drops, he had no previous history of illness or surgery. Prior to the abuse, he was friendly and exuberant with people and cautious but ultimately friendly with other dogs. His owners, prior to the incident with the trainer from hell, had used verbal methods to correct and reward Oliver's behavior. They could approach him while he was eating and could remove chew bones from him with no problem. My mission: To desensitize and counter-condition Oliver to trust his owners and others again. In addition, I needed to demonstrate and outline modern behavior-therapy techniques for the owners, who wanted Oliver to stop jumping up and to heel on the leash.

Among the desensitization procedures I taught Oliver's owners were some face-desensitization techniques in which we paired possibly threatening movements near his face with something intensely positive—like giving treats and praise. I also taught his owners how not to trigger or maintain the fear-based behavior. I instructed them not to use corporal punishment, not look at Oliver directly in the eyes, and not to rush up to him or attempt to pet him. Instead, we induced Oliver to approach us, to sit for treats, and then to increasingly allow us to pet him—initially away from the face and eventually even in this hot zone. I also demonstrated to the owners how to use two humane and non-punitive anti-pull devices to teach Oliver to heel.

Oliver's case clearly illustrates how traditional or standard brute-force dog-training techniques can actually harm your dog.

The Old Way

Picture yourself arriving at your first day of training class with your puppy. It's two months old and has a soft, downy coat. Its bones are still lengthening and thickening, and it seems to be growing bigger every day. It's a little rambunctious but it's basically a good dog. You're very proud of the puppy. What a wonderful addition he has been to your family! At the same time, you realize it is at a very vulnerable stage of its development—both mental and physical. So as you gather with the other dog owners before class, you are excited, happy—and a bit nervous. How will your dog stack up with the other dogs? Will it obey the trainer or will it embarrass you?

The trainer arrives. After a few preliminaries, he asks the dozen or so dog owners to sit their dogs. Most of the dogs sit immediately; their owners had already taught them this easy exercise. But at the sound of your voice, your puppy just stands there and looks up at you. You give the command several more times and try gently pressing your hand against its lower back. But it won't sit down. The trainer notices and walks over. The rest of the class is watching. You're embarrassed. Tension mounts.

The trainer tells you to hold the leash firmly in your left hand—the leash is attached to a choke-chain collar, of course—and to push down hard on the dog's rear with your right hand while giving the sit command. Your dog is trying to turn its head and wiggle out from under your hand. You're pulling ever tighter on the choke chain. Your dog is now resisting your pushing and the trainer is raising his voice, telling you to pull harder on the leash with your left hand and push down harder with your right hand. In your anxiety, you overdo it. Your dog yelps in pain. Your trainer says you did what was necessary. You feel lousy. It wasn't supposed to go like this.

In those kinds of classes, such force "remedies" are the solution to every "problem" that arises.

To get the dog to lie down, you are told to put the dog in the sit position and to pull or yank the leash down, or to pull the dog's forelegs out from under it. Sometimes students are told to put their hands between the dog's shoulder blades and push down or even to put their foot on the top of the dog's neck and force it down.

To get the dog to heel, the old-school trainers give harsh choke-chain corrections every time the dog lunges, with the corrections becoming more violent with each succeeding lunge.

Never mind that your dog may gag, spit up saliva or blood, or can still pull away. Never mind that some breeds have such thick coats around their necks, or build up scar tissue, that they are oblivious to the choke-chain-yank corrections and still go on pulling the owner down the street. Never mind that by doing choke-chain corrections too high under the neck and chin, you can gradually deafen your dog by impinging on the nerves that go to its ears.

The owner's initial instinct was correct; such force is not necessary. But the will of the instructor is dominant.

There's a famous experiment in the annals of psychology called the Milgram Experiment. Dr. Stanley Milgram wanted to learn about the hundreds of Nazi guards who followed orders to execute and mistreat human beings during World War II. Were these guards the subjects of a massive fluke in the history of human behavior, or is it human nature for people to ignore their ethical, moral, and religious values in an effort to please the authority, or to fit in with the demands being made by those in authority.

Dr. Milgram had volunteer subjects come in under false pretenses. They were led to believe they were giving electric shocks to a person located in another room, whom they could hear over a speaker and through the wall. The person who was receiving the shock was actually a hired actor, who pretended he was being shocked. The purpose was to see whether people would cowtow to authority, ignore their morals and ethics, and give what they thought were near-fatal levels of electricity to the recipient merely because the authoritative scientist told them to do it for the "sake of the experiment and science."

Lo and behold, the majority of the subjects, under duress and with the insistence by the scientist, gave what they believed were painful or near fatal shocks to the actor. As Wrightsman writes in his book, *Social Psychology in the Seventies*:

> At a certain point, the person receiving the shocks began screaming and pounding the wall. Milgram's basic research question was what percent of the subjects would continue to obey the experimenter

despite these reactions of the person receiving the shock—that is, what percentage would keep administering shocks of ever-increasing intensity. . . .

Twenty-six of Milgram's forty subjects, or sixty-five percent, administered shocks all the way to the 450-volt maximum. . . . [T]he outcome of Milgram's study is provocative and disturbing evidence of the dominant need to obey and conform to the demands of an authority figure.

What does this tell us? Well, whether it is in a POW camp during wartime, a cult like the Branch Davidians, or a dog training class, most people will go along and carry out what otherwise would be considered cruel or heinous acts merely to please authority or to fit in and not make waves.

You can obtain some results using force methods, but know this: If you continue on the path of meeting all resistance with force, your dog—and your relationship with your dog—ultimately will suffer.

You won't just find these force-method techniques in dog-training class. Dog-training literature (to grossly misuse the word) is littered with them.

One of the training manuals that was a best-seller for decades offers a smorgasbord of brutal solutions for dogs that resist heeling. The dog refuses to move? "Walk. He'll come with you, if only to be near his head," it urges. Dog grabs at the leash? "Lock both hands onto the leash, for maximum traction, and lift straight up. The dog should go up like a rocket and descend like a parachute."

But those techniques are mild compared to those the book recommends for dogs that continue to resist. To cope with the dog that resists to the point of snapping at the owner, the animal should be "jerked from the ground" and the trainer should "hold him suspended until he has neither the strength nor the inclination to renew the fight," the book says. "When [he is] lowered to the ground, he will probably stagger loop-legged for a few steps, vomit once or twice, and roll over on his side."

And if the dog is too big to lift? The professional trainer is urged to "convert" the animal by whacking it across the snout with a sixteen-inch-long rubber hose that has been filled with a wooden dowel.

Other traditional force-method training techniques include plunging a dog's face in its feces if it poops in the house; partially drowning a dog in a hole full of water for digging in the yard, and electrically shocking the dog or cutting its vocal cords for nuisance barking.

Such methods are grounded in military dog-training exercises that go back decades, when the dogs had to be hurriedly trained to meet wartime needs. Civilian trainers—many of them ex-military trainers—simply introduced the methods to the world that didn't wear khaki. Why seek other training methods when these seemed to work?

For years, virtually nobody did. Then, independently, several people schooled in human behavioral sciences started to apply certain human psychological principles to training animals. They quickly discovered that by using techniques based on those principles, they could train dogs without having to hurt them. Slowly, a movement toward non-forced training had emerged.

Still, some dog trainers have resisted. Why? Because they have invested careers in the old methods. And the old methods work—to a point. You know the phrase, "You can't teach an old dog new tricks?" Well, believe us, it is much, much harder to teach an old dog trainer new tricks. And unfortunately, many dog trainers out there are still carrying on the sadistic "might makes right" tradition.

Why? For one thing, it's not as easy to do it the right way. It took me about a decade to combine my psychology and behavior therapy knowledge with animal training to come up with a non-violent, alternative way of training dogs and addressing dog behavior problems. It takes more patience to do it the right way. Traditional trainers figure, "Why bother to learn something that's going to take longer to implement?"

Also, those traditional dog obedience training manuals—and thus the instructors who learned from them—are from the old school of thought in which animals are considered mere property. This is a natural extension of our agrarian roots. As property, the trainers can easily rationalize using the harsh techniques described above.

Enough, you say? I think so. People are unfortunately paying good money for the privilege of wincing at the repeated abusive training techniques used on their dogs by traditional trainers. Frank once interviewed a nationally known leading advocate and practitioner of the traditional training method. He asked the man about using such techniques. The man derided all those who would criticize the sometimes harsh methods he employs as "wincers." Yeah, we do wince—at the very least—when we see an animal mistreated. So do most human beings. We guess we're rather proud, actually, of being wincers.

How I Do It

The truth is, it is not difficult at all to use my techniques—the details of which are set out in Chapter 4. But to use them with confidence, it helps to know what lies behind them.

As we described in the Introduction, there are four basic principles in human behavioral psychology that are as applicable to training animals as they are to raising children or relating to other adults. They are: Positive reinforcement, negative reinforcement, extinction, and punishment.

Punishing a dog might have a short-term result, but, ultimately, it won't pay off. There are several reasons why not:

- It does not offer the animal an alternative behavior; the dog still won't know what you want it to do. By whacking the dog with a rolled-up newspaper or jerking on its choke chain rather than redirecting it to a more appropriate behavior, you have left a void in the dog's mind. The dog is likely to fill it with another bad behavior—or with a more intense version of the same bad behavior.
- Unless the punishment is administered immediately upon the dog's bad act, it will have no idea why you are punishing it. There is a very short period—some behaviorists believe less than three seconds—in which a dog will mentally link its action to a response from you.
- The dog can easily think it is being punished for a behavior you actually want to encourage. Whatever your dog is doing at the moment you punish it, that's the act for which it thinks it is being punished. Let's say your dog greets you at the door wagging its tail. At the same moment, you see it has made a mess on the carpet. You immediately scold the dog and rub its nose in the mess. What you actually accomplish, in the dog's mind, is punishing it for greeting you at the door. Similarly, if your dog has chewed a slipper in the morning and you call the dog over to punish it when you discover the slipper in the afternoon, the dog will think it is being punished for coming when you called it.
- Such harsh treatment can actually create behavior problems that were not present to begin with. It can lead to counter-aggressive responses from the dog, which is only attempting to defend itself from a perceived threat and suffering. A dog can become extremely fearful and

begin to submissively urinate or cower and shake every time the owner or the traditional-method trainer approaches. To correct inappropriate behaviors, the dog must be caught in the act of the crime. And even then, don't punish. Use the Startle-Redirect-Reward method previously discussed.

- Punishment is usually dished out with great anger and emotion and, therefore, is often applied far beyond what would be necessary to make the subject submit. This does more to create fear and counter-anger than it does to achieve conformance. All too often, harsh, physical punishment results in negative side effects. We see this in humans all the time. The abused child becomes resentful. He curses the parent, or runs away from home, or begins to identify with another authority figure and joins a gang or a cult that represents beliefs counter to those of the parents.

- Punishment can destroy your dog's relationship with you. It will stop trusting you. It will discover that learning from its human companion stinks. Heavy-handed punishment can bring two opposite but similarly devastating results: The dog can become afraid of you, or the dog can become aggressive, which can have serious physical and legal ramifications for you and your family.

- Sometimes a dog becomes head shy: When you reach toward its head or collar area, it reacts by snapping at your hand. It will no longer come when you call it. Constantly inducing pain through punishment only increases aggression. By using punishment, you have created new, more serious problems.

These are the practical reasons why resorting to punishment reflects wrong-headed thinking. But there are moral questions I believe one ought to consider as well. What does it say about you and me as humans? Most psychologists say that persons of greater physical strength (parents, spouses, teachers) who use corporal punishment to control another's behavior are often insecure, have a poor self-image, and feel the need to control others' behavior through violence because they cannot control their own lives. These individuals are inadvertently teaching children the might-makes-right model of human behavior and telling them that it is OK to be violent and abusive to smaller and weaker humans and animals.

How to Find the Trainer You Want

It's very easy to determine whether trainers and obedience classes are using harsh and unnecessary techniques. Just look at the dogs themselves and examine their body language.

I remember when I began my search for an animal trainer who used non-violent techniques. When observing traditional trainers, I noticed that many of the dogs had their ears folded back. They also had their tails stuck between their legs and their heads bowed low. These dogs were frightened, anxious, and not enjoying the process. The owners were yelling commands, yanking on the choke collars, and kneeing and hitting their animals. The atmosphere was far from fun. The techniques being used were abusive and were based on punishment and pain.

These techniques are in contrast to the positive reinforcement and behavior modification techniques used by animal behaviorists. How can someone determine whether a trainer is an animal behaviorist? What is the definition of an animal behaviorist?

An animal behaviorist is a person who either has had formal training and earned a degree in psychology or animal behavior, or has apprenticed for several years with an established animal behaviorist or veterinarian who specializes in animal behavior. An animal behaviorist has the knowledge and the hands-on experience to apply positive reinforcement, classical conditioning, and behavior modification techniques in attempting to remedy an animal's misbehavior. A behaviorist is aware of the several different types of aggression displayed by dogs and can implement various schedules of reinforcement to help dogs—and cats, for that matter—get over phobias and reduce anxiety. A behaviorist approaches obedience training and behavior problems in a comprehensive or holistic manner. The behaviorist looks at diet, health, and environment and isn't automatically locked in to the notion that the dog itself is the problem.

Behaviorists focus on positive reinforcement. If it is a complex behavior or trick we are trying to teach the dog, we reward in baby steps, increasing the reward as the dog gets closer and closer to the final product of the behavior we want. This is referred to as "successive approximations" to the goal.

Traditional-method trainers often criticize behaviorists as being too dependent on using food treats to reward desired behavior. What happens when you need a dog to obey and you don't have any treats with you? That's a fair question. There is the risk of the dog becoming food dependent if you always show the food in front of it or have it in noisy, crinkly bags, and you fail to also praise and pet the dog when it obeys. But the dog will not become food dependent if you hide the treats, keep them quiet, and only give them as the last link in a series of events that includes praise and petting. We get into the specifics in detail in Chapter 4 on training.

Training Lasts a Lifetime

Behaviorists also differ from traditionalists in that we don't believe there is one set time to do training. In a sense, the dog's whole life is an exercise in training. Give an obedience command before the dog receives anything it desires or before it receives anything positive. Before you put down its bowl of food, give the sit command. It sits, you give the food. This technique should be used before giving attention, petting, playing, eye contact, letting it in or out, and so on. The dog has to earn a living. Training, as such, becomes a natural part of your lifestyle and will not evolve into being an extra burden made up of contrived and artificial practice sessions.

Behaviorists also see a difference between punishment and discipline. They are two very different things, a concept lost on many traditionalist trainers. Punishment, from our point of view, would be if you were pulled over for speeding by a cop whose idea to cure you of the habit was to shoot you. Punishment is meant to hurt; it is propelled by the need for revenge. Also, it's after-the-fact and is excessive in relation to the misbehavior.

Discipline is when the officer comes up to your car, writes you a ticket, and redirects you to traffic school to learn better driving skills. This is real correction or discipline: It fits the crime; it's a natural consequence for violating a privilege; it is not excessive; it does not stem from wanting to exact revenge.

So don't succumb to the temptation to do things the rushed and dirty way. There's no reason to. In the training chapters you'll learn how to train and discipline your dog in a way that will get results and make both you and your dog happy.

Case Study Postscript

Six weeks following my visit with Oliver and his owners, they reported that he would now come on command, no longer pulled at the leash, and that they could pet him around his head and collar without him gagging or snapping at them.

18

YOUR DOG'S MENTAL
HEALTH NEEDS

"You won't believe this. We came home from work and found a gigantic hole through the drywall leading from the garage into our kitchen. The beast literally chewed his way into the house through the garage wall."

"Our dog has been housebroken since he was a puppy. He's five years old now, and last week out of nowhere he started urinating and defecating in the house for no apparent reason! And he's doing it mostly in our bedroom and the kids' bedroom."

"I've had it! Our boxer tore up the sprinklers in the backyard, chewed the wood siding off of our Jacuzzi deck, and began digging humongous holes in the yard. Not only that, but he's chewing his front legs and feet raw. The vet put him on steroids."

FROM LARRY'S CASE FILES:
"Joey" the Depressed Siberian Husky

FILE # 95-6611014
DOG'S NAME: Joey
BREED: Siberian husky-shepherd mix
AGE: 2 years
PROBLEM: Severe depression and weight loss

In April of 1995, I made an appearance on the Orange County News Channel (OCN) to discuss dog and cat behavior problems. Just before my segment, the station ran a piece describing a Siberian husky named Joey who had been at a local animal shelter for more than six months. Like many dogs—as with people who are imprisoned—Joey was exhibiting signs of being confined in a highly stressful environment. He was not eating, he was withdrawn, he appeared lethargic, and he was losing weight. The veterinarians determined that nothing medically was wrong with Joey. His weight loss was due to depression and his depression was due to his incarceration.

In the field of psychology, symptoms of depression—which include lethargy, sleep disturbances, slowness in intellectual processing, loss of appetite and the like—are referred to as neuro-vegetative symptoms. A human's or dog's physiology can be altered or affected by their depressed mental state. In Joey's case, being in the concrete slab confinement of the shelter, with the absence of a stable home and the stress of dozens of dogs barking, led to his depression. If he were human, Joey would be diagnosed as having a Major Depressive Disorder, characterized by at least five of the following symptoms:

Joey, the formerly depressed Siberian husky-shepherd mix now living in a loving home.

- Depressed mood most of the day, nearly every day
- Markedly diminished interest or pleasure in all or almost all activities
- Significant weight loss when not dieting
- Insomnia or hypersomnia nearly every day
- Psychomotor agitation or retardation nearly every day
- Fatigue or loss of energy
- Diminished ability to concentrate

In addition, when a person is depressed, they frequently hold three perspectives or *cognitions* that feed and maintain their depressive state. These are:

1. A negative view of oneself
2. Interprets ongoing experiences in the environment in a negative way
3. Holds a negative view of the future.

Because dogs don't think abstractly, the first and third cognitions do not apply. The second one, however, clearly applied to Joey.

The video images of Joey broadcast that day on OCN were heart-breaking. He didn't look like a husky anymore. Emaciated, head hung low, walking methodically, the dog looked pitifully depressed. In the studio with me was a photographer who worked for the cable television station and who shared my reaction. Derek Arita and I began talking, and what resulted was a plan to help Joey. Derek agreed to temporarily care for Joey in his home, removing Joey from the noxious elements of confinement that were causing his depression. I would donate my services and come out to his home and work with Derek, his wife, their schnauzer, a cat, and Joey.

A Dog's Emotional Needs

Dogs do experience a psychological identity. They can relate to time and prioritize what is important to them. One of the most important things for canines is their pack—their family! Dogs are pack animals just as their wolf ancestors are. The two most important things pack animals do are eat and sleep together. Isolating a pack animal such as a dog, and insisting it maintain a solitary lifestyle, is akin to taking a human member of your family and placing him in solitary confinement. The human, like the dog, will go nuts! Of course, we're familiar with how people go nuts: They get depressed, have nervous breakdowns, start hearing voices, or go on shooting rampages. Dogs react a bit differently.

When dogs go nuts or experience overwhelming anxiety—especially what we call isolation-induced anxiety—they might exhibit one of a number of troubling behaviors to try and relieve that anxiety: they become aggressive, they hide, they submissively urinate, they shake uncontrollably, they display neurotic repetitive behavior such as obsessive tail chasing, incessant nuisance barking, digging, or destructive chewing. Dogs will, indeed, chew through drywall, patio furniture, and Jacuzzi decking. Some dogs mutilate themselves to relieve anxiety by chewing their front paws raw.

ISOLATION

If your dog is outside and you work all day and you sleep all night, then out of a twenty-four-hour period, that only leaves roughly three to four hours of intermittent contact with your dog. That's not enough for a dog. In my opinion, it is emotionally abusive and cruel to leave a family dog alone day and night with only three hours of intermittent contact a day. Why have a group-dependent animal? Such limited contact is more appropriate for a goldfish or a canary. A group-dependent animal like a dog needs quality and quantity time with its pack.

Failure to properly integrate the dog into the family accounts for about half of my in-home consultations. The various disruptive or destructive behaviors exhibited by the family pet are a direct result of its isolation and loneliness. It's a problem caused by humans.

SOCIALIZATION

The other half of my in-home cases result from inadequate socialization of the dog. If a dog isn't introduced in a positive manner on a repeated basis to other dogs, cats, and people, it will become estranged to these populations and view them as threatening. This can lead to a fearful or angry-aggressive response from the dog. It is the responsibility of the breeder, and then the dog's family, to adequately and positively socialize puppies with a variety of people and with other vaccinated and safe dogs.

Dogs first need to be gently and positively socialized with human beings between the ages of four and seven weeks. Then, after the puppy is purchased or placed in a new home, it is crucial that it be gently and positively introduced to a variety of people of different genders, ages, sizes, and races. (Introductions to small children need to be very closely supervised.) If this is done over the first several months of its life, and the dog is neutered or spayed around six months of age, the developing dog usually assimilates appropriately into its family and the community.

When a person meets your dog, especially for the first time, have the person crouch down (making themselves smaller and less-threatening to the dog), avoid direct eye contact, and extend their hand for your dog to sniff.

Give the person some dog treats to give your dog while they are in this position. If this goes well, the person can progressively pet your dog under its chest area and gradually rise to the full standing position. The person should not reach his hand over the dog's head and try to pet it there.

This approach also applies when you meet any dog for the first time. Running up to a dog you don't know, or reaching quickly or suddenly toward an unfamiliar dog's face, will provoke a defensive response. This defensive response can take the form of either fearfulness or counter-attack, both of which can lead to biting. This will then establish a phobic or traumatic experience for the dog and can adversely affect its mental health. In addition, directly staring into a dog's eyes, especially a dog you do not know, communicates a threat and challenge to that dog and may also provoke an aggressive response.

Teaching young children these safety rules and the appropriate ways of meeting dogs would prevent many dog bites from occurring. Dog bites in this country disproportionately involve children. This can leave severe physical scars, in addition to emotional scars or dog phobias, for a young child.

Proper Training

Of course, one of the chief ways to protect your dog's mental health and make it feel good about itself is by enrolling in a non-violent and non-abusive obedience class. (Contact the Association of Pet Dog Trainers, P. O. Box 385, Davis, CA, 95617, or call 1-800-PET-DOGS.) This cannot be emphasized too much, because abusive force training (as described in Chapter 17) can harm your dog and actually create mental disorders.

Frequently, human owners, unaware of the dog's need to be with its pack or its need to be adequately socialized, seek quick-fix solutions offered by pet shops or force-method trainers. Their "solutions" often focus on the symptoms and not the underlying causes of the behavior problem. Our disposable-society mentality, coupled with the traditional dog trainer's mindset of symptom control, leads people to try to fix their dog's misbehavior through cruel and abusive means. The dog's overall anxiety levels are raised, not lowered, and the symptoms (like barking, chewing, digging, and self-mutilation) worsen—and new ones appear.

Some examples of abusive attempts at symptom control are attempting to stop the dog from barking by using an electric-shock collar; attempting to stop the dog from digging by filling holes with water and practically drowning the dog in them; attempting to stop inappropriate chewing by muzzling the dog, removing its teeth, or drugging it into a stupor. Don't fool yourself for a minute that dogs somehow don't experience pain and sensations as we do. All mammals with nerve endings going up and down the spinal cord feel pain. Being shocked, hit, punched, and drowned hurts and is abusive and cruel for both people and their pets. The end result of such idiotic treatment is that too often, after the dog has had its vocal cords cut out, or is muzzled, or is drowned, or is zonked out on doggy tranquilizers, the family ends up giving the dog away or euthanizing it anyway, because these cruel methods just didn't work. Everyone is upset and depressed. And everyone has lost. A sad ending for both dog and family.

Combating the Underlying Cause

Most canine behavior problems are not terribly mysterious once you know what to look for. With the exception of inherited brain damage or illness, most behavioral problems in dogs have been accidentally induced by owners (by isolation and lack of socialization), or reinforced/rewarded by owners (they look at, speak to, feed, pet, or let their dog in or out when it exhibits the problem behavior). If one looks at the dog's living conditions, the amount of exercise it receives, and the techniques of discipline used in the dog's home, one can quickly ascertain and diagnose why the dog is doing what it is doing and what needs to be done to fix the problem.

As described earlier, fixing it often entails making changes in the dynamics of the entire family system. If the relationship between the dog and its people is estranged, distant, or rigid (the dog is isolated), then, as in human family therapy, the behaviorist needs to increase emotional contact between owners and dogs and create a more permeable emotional boundary. If the relationship between the dog and its people is enmeshed, indulgent, and smothering (the dog growls around food and the owners back off), then the behaviorist is likewise duty-bound to help the owners become more firm in their emotional boundaries. If the dog is being used as an emotional scapegoat, or triangulated, in a relationship conflict between the owners ("He does do that." "Oh no he doesn't!"), then the behaviorist has to bring that out into the open, make appropriate referrals, and/or suggest finding a different home for the dog.

Throughout this book, we outline in detail modern, non-abusive behavior-modification techniques you can use to successfully treat your anxious, aggressive, or depressed dog. By using them, not only will you help your dog recover and maintain its mental health, you will actually help it achieve even higher levels of emotional wellness.

Case Study Postscript

Within three months, Joey was unrecognizable from the wretched cur we had seen on videotape. While living with Derek's family he had gained back his weight, he had become animated, he was wagging his tail, and he had sparkle back in his eyes. Once we implemented a plan to have Joey become accustomed to the Arita's cat, Mac, things turned out quite well. The Aritas reiterated, however, that they were only temporarily fostering Joey.

In February 1996, I made another appearance on OCN and saw Derek. He told me that he and his wife had a change of mind—and heart—and decided to keep Joey permanently. For Joey, it was a dream come true.

19

MATCHING YOUR PERSONALITY TO THE RIGHT DOG

"Do you recommend getting a purebred or a mutt?"

"Should we get a dog from a breeder or a shelter?"

"What do you recommend? A puppy or an older dog?"

FILE # 95-001011
DOG'S NAME: Elvis
BREED: Golden retriever
AGE: 10 weeks, still at breeder
PROBLEM: Pre-selecting the right family dog

In March of 1995, I went out to meet a family of four that wanted help selecting its first dog. The parents had heard the horror stories of dogs mauling kids and, with two young children, had concerns. They were looking for a medium to large dog with a loving disposition that would be easy to train. I spent the hour session with them reviewing which breeds generally have good reputations with children. Among my recommendations were golden retriever, Labrador, collie, beagle, Newfoundland, and airedale.

I stated my bias that families with young children should get a puppy so it can be socialized to children as it grows, thereby avoiding aggressive behavior later on. I also recommended they purchase their puppy from a reputable breeder. They would be able to establish the reputability of the breeder by getting veterinary referrals, going to American Kennel Club–sanctioned dog shows, collecting breeders' business cards, and visiting the breeders announced and unannounced.

I reviewed with them four temperament-testing techniques to carry out when visiting the breeder and interacting with the litter. I also encouraged them to seek out the parents of their prospective puppy, observe their behavior, and interact with them. Genetic predisposition for behavior problems and personality quirks is greater in dogs than in humans. If mommy or daddy dog growls or backs away from them, chances are good that their prospective puppy has inherited these traits, and they would end up with either an aggressive or a fearful puppy.

Armed with these tips and advice on housebreaking and integration, the family began the search. They ended up with a large, very blond, and very loving golden retriever, which they named Elvis.

Elvis, the dream golden retriever, and his owner.

Elvis was sweet, great with the children, non-aggressive and smart. Like most puppies, Elvis had an abundant supply of energy, which would frequently manifest itself in his jumping, puppy nipping, and pulling on the leash. Through my puppy kindergarten and older dog classes, I helped the family address these puppy behaviors, making Elvis an even greater joy to be around.

Puppy or Older Dog? Purebred or Mutt?

If there are children in the family (preferably older than seven), a purebred puppy is the best choice. In this way, the adults can more fully shape and mold the developing dog's personality and can control its early experiences and interactions with children and other novel stimuli. This helps the dog develop a positive attitude toward children (also see Chapters 7 and 11) and greatly increases the chances that the dog will grow up well-adjusted and socialized. In getting a purebred dog that has a reputation for being good with families and young children, you reduce the chance that you'll end up with a dog behaving aggressively toward your children. You also increase the chance that your dog will tolerate friends, neighbors, and other children visiting your home.

For retired individuals or adults living alone, older dogs and mixed breeds can make excellent pets and allow the prospective owner to bypass the housebreaking and teething stages of a pup. Also, the energy level of the dog generally will be lower than that of a younger dog, making the dog easier to handle, especially for an older adult.

Mutts, or mixed breeds, can be great pets. They tend to have a more hardy resistance to diseases that plague many purebreds, because the purebreds are very narrowly and selectively bred. Of course, the intended attributes of a purebred dog will almost certainly emerge as well: the hunters will hunt, the herders will herd, etc. Some folks want these things in a dog. Others, however, don't want to deal with them and the dog is increasingly frustrated as its family constantly tries to redirect behavior that only comes naturally to the dog. It's important to think about the physical and behavioral characteristics you want to have in your new dog—and what you don't want.

Physical and Behavioral Characteristics

How big can the dog be? What should its temperament be? Should it have long hair or short hair? Can you deal with a high-energy dog? Can you handle a dog that sheds and digs and salivates a lot, or do you need a dog that hardly sheds, is content to lie still for hours at a time, and is pretty fastidious about itself?

Here's a chart that lists some of the more popular breeds and their needs and attributes:

Breed	Coat	Energy level	Space needs
Cocker spaniel	medium	medium-high	medium
Saint Bernard	long	low-medium	large
Scottish terrier	medium	high	small
Bichon frise	short	medium	small
Labrador retriever	short	high	large
Golden retriever	medium	medium-high	large
Collie	long	low-medium	large
Poodle	short	medium-high	small
Dalmatian	short	high	medium-large
Doberman pinscher	short	high	large
Rottweiler	short	medium	large
German shepherd	short-medium	medium-high	large

When you narrow down your choice to a few breeds, ask yourself some more questions as you consider each one:
- What is the breed's personality toward kids, other dogs, and strangers?
- Has it been bred for police work, attack work, guarding, or herding? If so, it will be predisposed for high dominance and possible aggressiveness. Do you want this? Can you handle this? Do you want lots of friends and relatives to come over and visit without a hassle?
- What is the average life span of this breed? Do you want a great Dane, which has an average life span of six years? Or do you want a little terrier or dachshund that can live fifteen years?
- What illnesses or conditions are typical to this breed? What is the likelihood that yours will have them? How soon? What will it cost to treat? What's the prognosis?

Here's a chart of some popular breeds and the conditions that they often have or acquire:

Breed	Condition
Boxer	Tumors
Cocker spaniel	Cherry eye, ear infections
Bulldog	Respiratory problems, eye infections
Pug	Respiratory problems
Shar-pei	Skin, respiratory, eye problems
Dalmatian	Skin, inner ear problems, deafness
Labrador retriever	Hip problems
German shepherd	Hip problems
Rottweiler	Hip, elbow problems
Golden retriever	Skin, hips, thyroid, bone cancer
Collie	Eye problems
Bichon frise	Ear problems

Assessing Yourself

To ensure a good person-dog match, it is important to take a thorough inventory of your own personality and temperament characteristics. Are you an outgoing, gregarious, constantly-needing-to-be-in-motion person who is looking for an equally active, high-energy dog? Or are you more of a private, inwardly focused person who enjoys your quiet time and is looking for an equally mellow and sensitive kind of dog? Are you an assertive type of person, or more passive? Can you set firm emotional and disciplinary boundaries? Or are you more easygoing and tend to let whatever happens, happen? These questions are crucial in ensuring a good match with your dog. As shown in Chapter 16, "Knowing When to Adopt Out," in many cases an owner ends up with a dog whose personality clashes with his own. No matter what behavior-therapy techniques we might try, things will not work out. The gulf between owner temperament and dog temperament is just too great. These situations almost always end up with the dog being adopted out, abandoned, or euthanized. So not only is the prospective dog's personality a major factor in selecting the right dog for you, but your own likes and dislikes and fundamental temperament are equally crucial. Merely focusing on the dog will lead to a failed match.

What Temperament Are You?

The Greek philosopher Theophrastus, a pupil of Aristotle, wondered why Greeks differed in personality despite sharing the same culture and geography. Theophrastus concluded it was because of an inborn predisposition for each person to develop into a specific type, which would be reflected by one dominating outstanding characteristic (e.g., melancholic vs. sanguine). Modern theorists, however, think we are who we are because of a combination of characteristics.

One of the most popular modern tests for determining a person's traits, or type, is called the Myers-Briggs Type Indicator. The Myers-Briggs attempts to classify a person in a personality-type category that best fits that person at the time he is taking the test. Among the personality-type classifications are:

- **Extrovert Thinking Type.** This person is captured by ideas and objects, unable to avoid trying to solve problems through intellectual study. "Objective" and "rigid" are adjectives frequently used to describe people with this personality type.
- **Extrovert Feeling Type.** This person is dominated by the feeling function, and is captured by the goal to seek harmony in the external world. "Effervescent" and "sociable" are adjectives frequently used to describe this type.
- **Extrovert Sensation Type.** This person is dominated by the search for new sensations as they relate to concrete objects, such as judging art or fine wines. "Realistic" and "sensual" describe this person.
- **Extrovert Intuitive Type.** This person is dominated by involving himself with one novel idea or event, and then jumping to another, based upon hunches and the feelings of adventure. "Visionary" and "creative" describe this person.
- **Introvert Thinking Type.** This person is dominated by the thinking function, concerned with abstractions and creating theories, often ignoring the practicalities of everyday living. "Theoretical" and

"impractical" are adjectives frequently used to describe this type.

- **Introvert Feeling Type.** This person is dominated by feelings that often remain hidden or unrevealed, making that person appear removed or indifferent to those around him. Common descriptive adjectives are "silent" and "indifferent."
- **Introvert Sensation Type.** This person is dominated by his subjective internal experience of external events that are rapidly changing. He has the ability to be unfazed by such events by psychologically separating himself from what is occurring. "Passive" and "calm" are adjectives frequently used to describe people with this personality type.
- **Introvert Intuitive Type.** This type of person is dominated by the need to shape meaning for his inner self from what he encounters or experiences in the external world. "Mystic" or "dreamer" are adjectives used to describe this person.

In 1978, David Keirsey, a professor of psychology at the California State University at Fullerton, came up with a condensed version of Myers-Briggs. He detailed four basic temperament types:

- **The Dionysian or SP (Sensation/Perceiving) Type.** This person is characterized by the need to be free. He is impulsive and yearns for action.
- **The Epimethean or SJ (Sensation/Judging) Type.** This person is characterized by the need to be useful to society, to feel he belongs, to perform well. He is obligated to work duties.
- **The Promethean or NT (Intuitive/Thinking) Type.** This person is characterized by the need to be competent, and to understand and control nature.
- **The Apollonian or NF (Intuitive/Feeling) Type.** This person has the need to be authentic, to search for self, and to reach his highest potential.

By taking either the Myers-Briggs Type Indicator or the Keirsey Temperament Sorter (the Keirsey test is available in his book, *Please Understand Me*), you will be able to place yourself in one of the four base types: SP, SJ, NT, or NF.

Matching Your Type With
Your Prospective Dog's Personality

If you are an SP (Sensation/Perceiving) type of person, with a yearning for action and impulsiveness, your dog should be one with high energy but appropriately submissive. Because you are impulsive, enjoy high activity, and dislike setting boundaries or rules, dominant breeds are not for you. You'll end up with a dog that is aggressive and running amok. It would be a mistake, for example, to get a breed listed as permissible under the NT category. Consider instead these breeds: boxer, Weimaraner, bichon frise, Labrador retriever, German short-haired pointer, miniature schnauzer, pointer, and old English sheepdog.

If you are an NT (Intuitive/Thinking) and you crave control, order (with no problem setting down boundaries and rules), and being competent, you can consider dogs that require firm boundaries and lots of control. Such breeds are: Australian shepherd, Doberman pinscher, German shepherd, Rottweiler, basset hound, Alaskan malamute, bouvier des Flanders, standard or giant schnauzer, Scottish terrier, Chesapeake Bay retriever, and Rhodesian ridgeback.

If you are an NF (Intuitive/Feeling) with a yearning for authenticity, sensitivity, and genuineness, breeds such as the Brittany, Vizsla, Borzoi, flat-coated retriever, Gordon setter, Italian greyhound, saluki, collie, and whippet might better fit your personality type. With these dogs, merely raising your voice will devastate them.

And finally, if you are an SJ (Sensation/Judging) with a sense of community service and belonging and a desire to do hard work, consider breeds such as the Keeshond, Norwegian elkhound, pug, puli, Newfoundland, poodle, Samoyed, treeing walker coonhound, and Welsh corgi.

Narrowing Your Choice

Once you've really narrowed it to two or three breeds, go to your library's periodical section and find the latest issue of the *AKC Gazette*. Find the listing of dog shows (it's in a supplement called *Events Calendar*) and pick a show you can attend. Contact the show sponsors and find out what time the breed (or breeds) you are interested in is being shown. Go to the show.

Observe the different dogs of the same breed and collect business cards from breeders. Visit the breeders. Check out the facilities. Look for care, cleanliness, and selection. Get client and veterinary references. Be sure the breeder will take back the pup if it doesn't work out. Visit at least three breeders.

Now you should be fairly close to selecting a specific dog. Meet the mom and dad dog of your prospective puppy and interact with them. If the adult dogs won't let you get close enough to pet, they may have passed down this trait to their offspring, setting you up with a potentially unfriendly or aggressive dog.

Ask to observe your potential pup interacting with its siblings. Once you are observing the litter and your potential selection, here is some additional behavioral temperament testing you can do.

- Stay away from the most hyperactive and bossy puppy; that may portend future problems with the dog being excessively dominant or aggressive.
- Stay away from purchasing the most shy, aloof, and scared puppy. That dog may have a higher predisposition for fearfulness or fear-aggression.
- Pursue the puppy that seems to be in the middle of the road in its activity level. With the breeder's permission and supervision—and safely away from momma dog—test your final selections.
- Check its willingness to follow and reach out to you by calling the pup, making some clicking sounds and bending all the way down to the ground.
- Test its ability to be startled (by a loud shout or clapping your hands) and how long it takes to recover after being startled. This also checks for deafness.
- Test how pliable and submissive it is to you by gently rolling it on its back and holding it in that position for a few seconds while petting and talking in soothing tones.

The Decision

The pup you want is the one that readily follows and interacts with you. The pup you want is the one that takes a brief few moments to look around and recover after being startled by the loud hand clap. The pup you want is the one that allows you to roll it over on its back without tremendous struggle, screaming, or biting. These responses indicate the likelihood of a secure and stable personality to build upon through supervised puppy socialization and obedience classes.

Pet Shop and Puppy Mill Warning

Stay away from pet shops that get their dogs from puppy mills. Ask to see documentation on the dog's origin. If it is from Kansas, Missouri, Oklahoma, or Pennsylvania, beware. Some breeders in these states churn out animals without regard for temperament or health. The hygiene conditions are atrocious, with unbathed dogs crammed into cages resembling chicken coops. They generally have been separated from their parents and littermates far too early and have been subjected to harsh weather. When it's time to leave, they are shipped and confined in stress-inducing tight crates and end up in some mall pet shop. There, they are confined in another tight cubicle and forced to do the unnatural for dogs and wolves: eat, defecate, and sleep in the same spot.

These pet shop dogs tend to have higher rates of infections, chronic illnesses and serious behavior problems such as aggressiveness toward humans and other dogs, fearfulness, separation anxiety, and housebreaking difficulties. Do yourself, your family, your dog, your community, and animalkind a favor, and do not patronize such places. Steer yourself toward a professional well-referenced breeder with good references or your local animal shelter.

The Honeymoon Period

See the end of Chapter 12, the subsection titled, "Bringing Home Your New Pack Member," for important tips on introducing your dog to the household. Don't freak out if your dog doesn't immediately act the way it did at the breeder's. All dogs, whether puppies or older dogs, go through an adjustment period in a new home. It usually takes four to six weeks for a dog to adjust, trust, settle down, and begin to show its true personality. Give it time.

Case Study Postscript

Almost three years later, Elvis continues to be a great family dog. He loves his owners, he loves the kids, and he is very social toward their friends and adult strangers.

20

PUPPY PROZAC?
WHEN TO CONSIDER PSYCHIATRIC
MEDICATION

"We got home from doing our Christmas shopping and, to our horror, we found that our dog had chewed up our Christmas tree, shredded all the presents, and dug a hole in the carpet. My husband was ready to kill her."

"We don't understand it. Every morning, our dog begins to frantically chase his tail. We try to stop him, yell at him, and hold him, but it doesn't do any good. He gets so wild that he runs into walls and falls down stairs! He's very aggressive toward strangers. He's tried to bite three people this last week."

FROM LARRY'S CASE FILES:
"Paula" the Petrified Poodle

FILE # 95-000323
DOG'S NAME: Paula
BREED: Toy poodle
AGE: 2 years
PROBLEM: Generalized Anxiety Disorder

In 1995, I went to see a year-old poodle that was exhibiting severe anxiety symptoms. She would urinate, defecate, or secrete anal gland fluids if anyone looked at her or tried to approach her. Paula's owners had two of her siblings, which they adopted when they were puppies. Unfortunately, Paula had not been adopted until she was almost a year old. Many times, if a dog is not adequately socialized during the first six months of its life, or is adopted beyond twelve weeks of age, it becomes phobic toward people and is only comfortable around other dogs.

This was the case with Paula. She was kept in relative isolation from people for the first year of her life by her breeder, who initially contemplated breeding her. Paula's home during this period was a confined cubicle with very little sunlight. She was also subjected to heavy-handed corporal punishment and was de-barked for nuisance barking. Paula was never able to conceive and was eventually taken in by the loving family who had purchased two of Paula's littermates when they were puppies. Because of Paula's isolation from humans, her sensory deprivation and her exposure to abusive discipline, her new family quickly had its hands full with a very petrified creature.

Whenever any family member, especially the husband, approached Paula, she would run away in terror, urinating and defecating along the way. If the owners tried to comfort or restrain her, she would struggle, bite and express her anal glands. Just making eye contact with Paula would trigger a panic response.

Paula initially wouldn't come into the same room with me and the family members. We therefore had to implement a long-term behavior-modification program that centered on systematic desensitization and removal of all verbal and non-verbal actions she could perceive as threatening. Among other things, family members, especially the husband, would not look Paula directly in the eyes nor attempt to pet her. They initially would ignore her, and only reward her when she was not behaving anxiously.

Because Paula had been adequately socialized with dogs, she behaved normally with her siblings. Frequently, she would show curiosity and jealousy when her sisters were getting attention and treats. We used this behavioral predisposition to get her physically and emotionally closer and closer to the family members. Despite these measures, I felt Paula's symptoms were severe enough that the behavior-modification program would have a better chance of working if the dog initially could be helped to relax through medication. I referred Paula and her owners to their veterinarian to be evaluated for an antianxiety drug.

FROM LARRY'S CASE FILES:
"Coffee" the Dachshund Who Wouldn't Come Out of the Closet

FILE # 95-000648
DOG'S NAME: Coffee
BREED: Dachshund
AGE: 11
PROBLEM: Sudden-onset acute stress disorder

In July of 1995, I went out on a truly bizarre case. An eleven-year-old dachshund would not come out of the hall closet. When he did come out, he would look nervously toward the ceiling as if expecting an attack from above.

No environmental trauma could be identified. His upbringing seemed fairly normal. Coffee had been purchased through a breeder and brought home at eight weeks of age.

The owners did relate that when Coffee was two or three years old, he would occasionally seek refuge in the closet when a stranger entered their home. Then, roughly two years before my visit, a new dog moved in next door, and Coffee again sought refuge in the closet. And on one or two occasions, the owners remembered Coffee looking up nervously.

Coffee, the dachshund, out of the closet.

When I visited the home, Coffee was constantly looking up to the ceiling, as if expecting a flock of blue jays to swoop down and attack. To the owners' knowledge, nothing had ever fallen on Coffee, eliminating the probability that such a traumatic incident had induced this behavior. Coffee did not exhibit any other behavior that could be construed as neurological impairment, such as barking at shadows, staring at corners, or charging and running into walls. No seizures were observed and no evidence of epilepsy was included in the veterinary case history.

The only outstanding incident was a severe bacteriological infection that caused Coffee to eat less, consistently pant, and have a substantial fever. In addition, Coffee suffered from hypothyroidism, but was on thyroid medication and his last blood-level tests were within the normal range.

While I was observing Coffee, I noticed that after he looked nervously upward and to the right, he would jump, or grab one of our pants legs and begin tugging compulsively. Coffee's owners responded by lavishly petting and comforting him. Unknowingly, they were reinforcing his phobic behavior.

Although I couldn't definitely rule out some unidentifiable incident to explain Coffee's behavior (like a kid throwing a firecracker over the fence or a car backfiring), I decided to implement a corrective behavior-modification program anyway. The program included continued use of the veterinarian-prescribed tranquilizer Acepromazine. My hypothesis was that Coffee's bizarre behavior was in part due to the bacteriological infection and fever—along with unintentional reinforcement from the owners. Based on the history, the current phobic behavior was merely a chronic and intense exaggeration of previous behavior exhibited sporadically over the dog's eleven-year history. Among many components, the behavior-modification plan included the owners no longer reinforcing the anxious behavior through praise and attention, but instead, noticing non-anxious behavior, and rewarding it verbally and with treats.

Drugs As Treatment

As stated in the Introduction, veterinarians report that the vast majority of the dogs brought into their offices for euthanasia are there solely because of behavior problems! The most serious problems I see in my practice are aggression, separation anxiety (the dog experiences overwhelming anxiety when it is alone and destroys things), and phobias (the dog barks at shadows, compulsively chases its tail, self-mutilates, etc.).

For the past ten years or so, there has been a growing trend in applied veterinary behavioral medicine (reflecting the earlier trend in human psychiatry) to combine the use of behavior modification and drugs to treat severe dog behavior problems such as these. With this trend, behaviorists, psychologists, psychopharmacologists, and veterinarians have come full circle, so to speak. Pharmaceutical manufacturers first tested their drugs on animal subjects, then applied them to humans. However, they were never brought back around to be reapplied to animals with severe behavioral disorders. That is, not until recently.

The *New York Daily News* captured the trend in an October 1997 story that appeared under the headline: "Pup uppers combat depression: Prozac for pooches can ease pet anxiety." The article stated that "an increasing number of owners are turning to Prozac and other antidepressants" to help in cases of separation anxiety; fears of thunder and people; and obsessive-compulsive disorders such as constant licking, spinning, and tail-chasing. The article went on to say that such medications should only be used either in conjunction with behavior-modification techniques, or when they fail. As in humans, the article warned, overuse of antidepressants is a concern. One New York–based animal behavior specialist was quoted as saying, "It's becoming a little too in vogue to medicate animals."

Criteria for Using Psychotropic Medication for Dog-Behavior Problems

Medication may at times be necessary to treat both human and dog behavior problems, but rarely is it sufficient when used alone. With human patients, family dynamics, work environment, support systems, self-concept, nutritional habits, recreational drug and alcohol use, exercise, and other factors must also be considered and addressed to successfully treat the disorder. Negative side effects, possible addiction, and relapse after medication is discontinued are other factors that preclude drugs as the only treatment—for people or dogs.

The animal behaviorist and veterinarian must look at diet, obedience training, environmental triggers, physical health (such as hypothyroidism, which can trigger aggression), and the owner's behavior toward the dog in question. Medication alone, while the animal is being treated cruelly or is isolated from the family, will certainly fail.

In twelve years of practicing animal-behavior therapy and in twenty-two years of human counseling, I have developed very clear criteria for when to recommend that medication be used in treatment. With human patients, it is when I see one of a wide variety of disorders that create real danger to either the patients or the people in their lives. Frequently, these disorders have been linked to biochemical imbalances in the brain, and therefore require drug therapy to help reestablish the chemical balance.

For dog behavior problems, the criteria is clearer. There are three behavior problems for which I recommend drug therapy: moderate to severe phobias, some separation-anxiety cases (addressed behaviorally in Chapter 8), and some aggression cases (addressed behaviorally in Chapter 9).

Mild phobias, most separation-anxiety cases, and most aggression problems can be treated through a combination of changing the family's behavior toward the dog, reconditioning the dog through behavior-therapy techniques, and having the dog participate in a non-violent, non-force method obedience class. These non-medication solutions are also fine for lesser problems such as housebreaking, nuisance barking, jumping and digging.

But sometimes drug therapy is unavoidable. To understand why, let's review basic brain functioning, some common pharmacological agents, some human disorders—and how all this applies to dog behavior problems.

Brain Theory

Since the time of the early Greek philosopher-physician Hippocrates (460–355 BC), man has theorized that imbalances in mood are due to imbalances in brain or body chemistry. In 1949, the Australian psychiatrist John Cade discovered that lithium is effective in treating agitation and psychosis in humans. After World War II, medical researchers concentrated on developing drugs that would reduce complications associated with post-operative shock. In 1951, a compound labeled No. 4560 RP was developed to meet this goal and was successful in relaxing patients, reducing post-operative shock and preventing nausea. Clinical trials in 1952 with this compound saw marked changes in the behavior of manic and schizophrenic patients. In 1954, the drug was approved for use with patients who suffered from such disorders. This drug is called chlorpromazine, or Thorazine.

The 1950s saw the beginning of an era of psychiatric use of drug therapy for severe psychological disorders. Drug therapy for mental disorders may be defined as attempts to modify or correct pathological behaviors, thoughts, or moods by chemical means. As seen here, there are a variety of different drugs for different disorders.

For depression, there are the antidepressants. For mania/anxiety, there are the antianxiety agents, or benzodiazepines. And for psychotic behavior, there are the antipsychotic, or major tranquilizers (also referred to as neuroleptics) dopamine blockade drugs.

The Brain and Chemical Messengers

In order for you and me to experience a thought or feeling, and in order for a dog to perceive, solve problems, and experience sensations (like aggression or fear), there has to be a signal communicated or transmitted in the brain. The cells that do this in the brain are called nerve cells or *neurons*. These neurons have three parts to them: a receiving "antenna" called a *dendrite*, a central processing station called the *cell body* (or *soma*), and a transmitting "antenna" called an *axon*. Between the outgoing antenna of one neuron (the axon) and the receiving or incoming antenna of another neuron (the dendrite), there exists a gap or expanse called the *synapse*. In order for one of your brain cells to transmit a thought or feeling to another brain cell, it needs a "messenger." This messenger crosses the gap, or synapse, to successfully relay the message. These messengers are chemicals in the brain that transmit thoughts or regulate feelings. Hence, they are called *neurotransmitters*.

THE FIVE MOST COMMON NEUROTRANSMITTERS

- **Acetylcholine.** Located in nerve-muscle junctions, the thinking brain (or cortex) and brain structures associated with emotions, alertness and memory.
- **Dopamine.** Contained in many parts of the brain; involved with sensations of pleasure and the regulation of smooth muscle movement.

- **Norepinephrine.** Located in the autonomic nervous system, which regulates functions like breathing and heartbeat. It is affected by fluctuations in its mentor, dopamine.
- **Serotonin.** Located throughout the thinking, emotional, and survival areas of the brain. Serotonin is the master neurotransmitter. Affecting it will affect all of the other transmitters.
- **GABA (Gamma Amino Butyric Acid).** Located in the thinking brain (cortex), the emotional part of the brain (limbic system), and the part of the brain responsible for functions like balance and movement (cerebellum). GABA is an inhibitory neurotransmitter, producing a calming effect on the brain—a lessening of neural activity.

These neurotransmitters are involved in regulating our moods and our ability to think straight. If there are insufficient amounts of some of these neurotransmitters (not enough gasoline), we may have a slowing or inability to think straight and end up in a depressed mood. If there is an overabundance of neurotransmitters (gasoline overflowing our tank and spraying everywhere), we may have an overly accelerated pace to our thinking and end up in a manic or anxious mood. When such imbalances exist, the role of psychiatric drugs (psychotropics) is to regain a balance in brain neurotransmitters.

CAUSES OF NEUROTRANSMITTER IMBALANCE

It is theorized there are three reasons for neurotransmitter imbalances:

1. An insufficient release of neurotransmitters by axons of nerve cells.
2. The receptor sites for the chemical messenger (neurotransmitter) are not functioning properly: not enough; too many; or they show a red light when it should be green, and vice versa.
3. The transmitting neuron is too quickly cleaning up or recycling the neurotransmitter once it's in the synapse, preventing enough "gasoline" from fully conveying the message to the receiving neuron.

Psychiatric medications change the chemical imbalance in our brain by causing an increase or decrease in the release of these chemical messengers. They also influence the activation and deactivation of neurotransmitter receptor sites and can influence the slowing down or speeding up of the cleanup of neurotransmitters in the synapse.

PUTTING IT ALL TOGETHER

When a person suffers from major depression, it is thought the person has insufficient levels of neurotransmitters in their brain. Depression is thought to be caused by overly low levels of the neurotransmitters serotonin and norepinephrine. By prescribing antidepressants such as Elavil or Prozac, the levels are raised. This leads to less-impeded thought and an elevation in mood.

When a person suffers from generalized anxiety disorder or mania, it is thought the person has either too much neurotransmitter in one area of the brain or not enough in another area—or both. Anxiety and mania are thought to be caused by either high levels of the neurotransmitter norepinephrine and/or low levels of the neurotransmitter GABA. By prescribing antianxiety agents like the benzodiazepines or buspirone, it is thought these levels are corrected and the person becomes less anxious.

Finally, when a person suffers from a psychotic disorder like schizophrenia, it is thought the person has excessive levels of neurotransmitter in one part of the brain. Schizophrenia is thought to be caused by overly high levels of the neurotransmitter dopamine. By prescribing antipsychotic or dopamine-blocking drugs, it is thought the high levels of dopamine come down, bringing control or cessation to the related psychotic symptoms such as hallucinations, delusions, bizarre behavior, and so on.

The Dog Parallel

Veterinarians and veterinary behaviorists believe that aggressive and anxiety disorders in dogs are caused by the same imbalances in brain neurotransmitters. So, if the dog has a fear or depression-based behavior problem such as separation anxiety or fear aggression, then antianxiety agents targeting norepinephrine and GABA, or antidepressant agents targeting norepinephrine or serotonin, should have a beneficial effect. Some drugs that might be used in these cases are Valium, BuSpar, or Elavil.

If the dog has an aggressive or bizarre phobic behavior problem, the antipsychotic and antidepressant medications that target dopamine and serotonin should be helpful. Acepromazine or Prozac may be called for.

While veterinarians have found that some antidepressants have been helpful in treating predatory or offensive aggression, cases of defensive aggression (fear aggression) may be better handled by an antianxiety agent such as Buspirone. For fears and phobias, again, Buspirone has been shown to be helpful, along with beta-blockers such as Propranolol and the antidepressant Elavil.

In the following pages, we provide a list of the different antidepressants, antianxiety agents and antipsychotic medications commonly used for humans and, only recently, for dogs.

ANTIDEPRESSANTS

There are three groups of antidepressants:
- **TCAs:** Tricyclic antidepressants
- **SSRIs:** Selective serotonin re-uptake inhibitors
- **MAOIs:** Mono-amine oxidase inhibitors

TCAs

Tricyclic antidepressants have been the mainstay of drug treatment for human depression for years. However, the tricyclics are considered "dirty drugs" because they react with a number of brain-nerve receptors besides the ones mainly responsible for depression. This can lead to a whole panoply of side effects such as dry mouth, dry skin, blurred vision, constipation, sweating, sexual dysfunction, and lightheadedness.

Examples of tricyclic antidepressants:

Generic Name	Brand Names
Amitriptyline	Elavil
Amoxapine	Asendin
Clomipramine	Anafranil
Desipramine	Norpramin, Pertofrane
Doxepin	Sinequan, Adapin
Imipramine	Tofranil
Maprotiline	Ludiomil
Nortriptyline	Pamelor, Aventyl
Protriptyline	Vivactil
Trazodone	Desyrel
Trimipramine	Surmontil

SSRIs

For both humans and animals, the selective serotonin re-uptake inhibitors are a newer, and "cleaner" class of antidepressants with significantly fewer side effects. The SSRIs primarily interact with the neurotransmitter serotonin. They have very little impact on the other two neurotransmitters responsible for the nasty side effects of the tricyclics: acetylcholine and norepinephrine. If there are side effects they are usually nausea, gastrointestinal upset, sweating, anxiety, insomnia, headache, and sexual dysfunction.

Examples of SSRI anti-depressants:

Generic Name	Brand Name
Fluoxetine	Prozac
Sertraline	Zoloft
Paroxetine	Paxil
Nefazadone	Serzone
Fluvoxamine	Luvox

MAOIs

MAOIs, which inhibit the recycling of critical neurotransmitters in the synapses, are a group of antidepressants used mainly when other antidepressants fail. This is because MAOIs can lead to dangerously high blood pressure or hypertensive reaction. This, in turn, can lead to a brain hemorrhage or even death.

Examples of MAOIs:

Generic Name	Brand Name
Phenelzine	Nardil
Tranylcypromine	Parnate
Isocarboxazid	Marplan

Antianxiety Medications

Antianxiety drugs are used to treat anxiety or fear disorders. The type of drugs most commonly used to treat anxiety disorders are a category called benzodiazepines. However, other categories of antianxiety drugs, like beta-blockers and the azapirones (BuSpar/Buspirone) have also been used.

The first benzodiazepine drug to be synthesized was chlordiazepoxide, or Librium, in 1957. Benzodiazepines are used for both sedative purposes (to calm overwhelming anxiety) and hypnotic purposes (to combat insomnia and induce sleep). They have sometimes been used as anesthetics for pain and in the assistance of withdrawal from other drugs. The benzodiazepines work by enhancing the calming effect of the neurotransmitter GABA. However, benzodiazepines can have a variety of unpleasant side effects: slurred speech, lack of coordination, and lessening of behavioral inhibitions. In addition, long-term use of benzodiazepines can lead to addiction and their discontinuation can lead to a rebound-anxiety reaction. It can also lead to liver problems because most of the benzodiazepines are broken down in the liver. Another side effect (in humans) is amnesia—loss of memory—for a short period after the drug has worn off.

Examples of benzodiazepines:

Generic Name	Brand Name
Diazepam	Valium
Chlordiazepoxide	Librium
Flurazepam	Dalmane
Prazepam	Centrax
Clorazepate	Tranxene
Clonazepam	Klonopin
Temazepam	Restoril
Lorazepam	Ativan
Alprazolam	Xanax
Oxazepam	Serax
Triazolam	Halcion
Midazolam	Versed (injectable)
Estazolam	ProSom
Quazepam	Doral
Zolpidem	Ambien

Buspirone is a unique antianxiety agent that targets the neurotransmitter serotonin. Buspirone is classified as an azapirone. Because it primarily targets serotonin and has a delayed time of action, the side effects are minimal compared to the typical benzodiazepine. If there are side effects, they are usually headaches and nausea.

Beta-blockers, also known as antihypertensive medications, have also been used to treat anxiety by targeting the bodily reactions to anxiety without necessarily eliminating the psychological experience of anxiety. The symptoms that may be controlled include increased heart rate, sweating, and muscle tremor. However beta-blockers (with humans) can lead to dizziness, lowered blood pressure, and may cause depression.

Examples of beta blockers:

Generic Name	Brand Name
Atenolol	Tenormin
Metoprolol	Lopressor
Nadolol	Corgard
Propranolol	Inderal

Antipsychotic Agents

Antipsychotic, or dopamine-blocking drugs, are used in the treatment of psychosis and schizophrenia. In humans, psychosis is defined as a severe mental disorder characterized by disorganization of the thought processes, disturbances in emotions, disorientation as to time, space, and person, and the experience of hallucinations and delusions.

Schizophrenia is marked by at least two of the following symptoms:
• Delusions (false beliefs)
• Hallucinations (seeing or hearing things that are not there)
• Disorganized speech
• Negative symptoms: flat emotions, lack of purposeful movement or speech

With schizophrenia, the symptoms must also have caused great disruption in the person's interpersonal, vocational, academic, and recreational life. One theory of psychosis and schizophrenia is that there exists an excessive amount of the neurotransmitter dopamine. By lowering the levels of dopamine through the use of dopamine-blocking drugs, these symptoms should abate.

All of these antipsychotic drugs have been called *neuroleptics* because they can cause neurological side effects such as face and neck tremors and spasms. Antipsychotic drugs also block the neurotransmitter acetylcholine, so, as with the tricyclic antidepressants, the patient who receives these drugs also may experience dry mouth, blurred vision, constipation, difficulty urinating, and poor sexual function. These medications can also cause a dangerous drop in blood pressure.

Two new medications have recently been developed that have few of the negative spasmtic and blood pressure side effects. They are Clozapine and Risperidone.

Examples of antipsychotic drugs:

Generic Name	Brand Name
Chlorpromazine	Thorazine
Thioridazine	Mellaril
Clozapine	Clozaril
Mesoridazine	Serentil
Molindone	Moban
Perphenazine	Trilafon
Loxapine	Loxitane
Trifluoperazine	Stelazine
Fluphenazine	Prolixin
Thiothixene	Navane
Haloperidol	Haldol
Pimozide	Orap
Risperidone	Risperdal

The Right Drugs for Dogs

I have found that in working with severe dog behavior problems, the list of medications that follow were most helpful—when used, of course, in conjunction with behavior therapy for the family and dog, non-violent obedience training, diet change, and proper exercise.

- **Separation anxiety:** Elavil (amitriptyline) and acepromazine
- **Fear aggression:** Elavil (amitriptyline), Anafranil (clomipramine) and BuSpar (buspirone)
- **Sibling dog fighting:** Elavil (amitriptyline) and BuSpar (buspirone)
- **Predatory or dominance aggression:** Prozac (fluoxetine), BuSpar (buspirone), and Elavil (amitriptyline)

Deciding Whether to Use Drugs

The majority of these medications are still experimental in their use with dogs. We know they can cause harmful side effects in humans. They may act differently in dogs. The side affects may not be as severe—or they may be worse. Therefore, the majority of the cases in which I use such medication must not only involve one of the "big three" behavior problems (moderate to severe aggression, separation-anxiety, and phobias), but the use of drugs must also represent a last resort: The dog faces euthanasia or being adopted out.

In addition, many if not most of these drugs cannot be used if the dog has epilepsy, breathing problems, or problems with its adrenal gland, heart, thyroid, liver, or kidneys. Also, the dog cannot be on contraindicated medications for another disease.

Another reality to consider is that many of these drugs are expensive. Veterinarians frequently try Elavil because it is cheaper than Buspirone or Prozac. Elavil, for example, might cost about ten cents per day, or a few dollars per month for an average dog. A dosage of Prozac, on the other hand, might cost five dollars or more *per day*! And the treatment period can been eight to twelve weeks. However, one is then faced with the dilemma that Elavil, being a tricyclic antidepressant, can cause greater side effects.

A dog owner, therefore, must weigh all these factors and consider the risk-to-benefit ratio of using psychiatric drugs to treat a problem dog. If the risk (major side effects) of using such drugs is greater than the benefit (correcting a relatively minor behavior problem that can be fixed through behavior modification alone), then the drugs should not be used. If, however, the benefit of their use (avoiding euthanasia because the behavior problem is severe) outweighs the risks, they should be used.

Suggested Experimental Dosages

What follows is not a prescription, but rather general experimental dosage guidelines taken from veterinary literature. They should be discussed with your veterinarian.

ANXIETY AND FEAR

Serotonin Enhancers:
> *Buspirone (Buspar)   0.5-2 mg/kg bid*
> *Fluoxetine (Prozac)   0.5-1 mg/kg sid*
> *Clomipramine (Anafranil)   1-3 mg/kg sid*
> *Amitryptiline (Elavil)   2-6 mg/kg sid-bid*

GABA Enhancers:
> *Diazepam (Valium)   0.25-1 mg/kg bid*
> *Alprazolam (Xanax)   0.25-2 mg/kg bid*

Beta-Blockers:
> *Propranolol (Inderal)   0.5-2 mg/kg tid*

AGGRESSION

Serotonin Enhancers:
> *Buspirone (BuSpar)   0.5-2 mg/kg bid*
> *Fluoxetine (Prozac)   0.5-1 mg/kg sid*
> *Clomipramine (Anafranil)   1-3 mg/kg sid*

Dopamine Antagonists:
> *Acepromazine   1-2 mg/kid tid*

Progestins:
> *Medroxyprogesterone acetate   5-10 IM single*
> *Megestrol Acetate   2-5 PO sid for one to two weeks, then reduce*

Case Study Postscripts

PAULA

After two months of tedious desensitization and temporary medication, Paula's owners were able to approach her and touch her without her running away or defecating and urinating. She'll never be as calm and easygoing as her two sisters, but she's come a long way.

COFFEE

Two and a half weeks following my visit, Coffee's owner reported that Coffee was practically back to his old pre-anxious self. Even with the acepromazine discontinued, he was no longer running and hiding in the closet. And instead, looking up to the ceiling nervously every few seconds, Coffee was now exhibiting this behavior only twice a week. In addition, after removing the inadvertent reinforcement from his owners, Coffee ceased his attention-getting behavior of grabbing pants legs.

APPENDICES

I
Dog Bytes: Favorite Animal-related Sites on the World Wide Web

LARRY'S WEB SITE

http://www.familyanimal.com

WEB SITES PROMOTING NON-FORCE-METHOD TRAINING AND SIMILAR PHILOSOPHIES

http://www.webtrail.com/petbehavior/index.html
http://www.members.gnn.com/dtortora/stand.htm
http://www.karenpryor.com/
http://www.users.aol.com/jemyers/apdtlist.htm
http://apdtbod@aol.com

GENERAL ANIMAL BEHAVIOR AND WELFARE

http://www.wam.umd.edu/~jaguar

WOLVES

http://www.albany.edu/~knee/wolf.html

PET LOSS

http://www.lavamind.com/pet.html
http://www.primenet.com/~meggie/petloss.htm
http://www.cowpoke.com/~twsean/pet.html
http://ourworld.compuserve.com/homepages/edwilliams

MEDICAL AND PSYCHOLOGICAL INFORMATION SITES

http://www.apa.org
http://netvet.wustl.edu/vet.htm
http://www.avma.org
http://www.73711.555@compuserve.com
http://oncolink.upenn.edu/specialty/vet_one/index.html

11

ANIMAL ORGANIZATIONS
TO KNOW

American Boarding Kennels Association,
4575 Galley Road, Suite 400-A, Colorado Springs, CO, 80915.
Trade association for kennels.

American Humane Association, 63 Inverness Drive East, Englewood, CO,
80112-5117. Phone: (303) 792-9900.
Works to prevent harm to children and animals.

American Kennel Club, 5580 Centerview Drive, Raleigh, NC, 27606.
Principal registry for purebred dogs in the United States.

American Society for the Prevention of Cruelty to Animals (ASPCA),
424 East 92nd St., New York, NY, 10128-6804.
Founded in 1866, it pursues the humane treatment of animals.

Association of Pet Behaviour Counsellors, P.O. Box 46, Worcester, WR8
9YS, England.
Organization of pet behavior therapists.

Association of Pet Dog Trainers, P.O. Box 385, Davis, CA, 95617.
Phone: 1-800-PET-DOGS. Internet: APDTBOD@aol.com.
Association of trainers that promotes non-force methods.

The Greyhound Project, 261 Robbins St., Milton, MA, 02186. (617)
333-4982 or (617) 527-8843.
Promotes adoption of retired racing dogs.

Humane Society of the United States, 2100 L St., Washington, D.C., 20037. Phone: (202) 452-1100.

Largest animal-protection organization in the United States.

BIBLIOGRAPHY

The following books and articles were used in writing this book. In some cases, a partial citation was already given within the chapter; in other cases, the authors referred to a statistic or other fact without attribution within the chapter.

INTRODUCTION

Article on non-force-method dog training: "New Breed of Dog Trainer," Frank Mickadeit, *The Orange County Register*, Oct. 15, 1991.

Opening news report: WPTZ Television, Channel 5 News, Burlington, Vermont, June 17, 1996.

Dog-bite statistics: "Dog-bite-related Fatalities—United States, 1995," *MMWR: Morbidity and Mortality Weekly Report*, Vol. 46, Issue 21, U.S. Centers for Disease Control, May 30, 1997, pp. 463-467; and "Dog Bites Recognized as Public Health Problem," Rebecca Voelker, *Journal of the American Medical Association*, Vol. 277, Jan. 22-29, 1997, pp. 278-280.

Dog euthanasias for behavioral problems: "The Distribution of Canine Behavior Cases at Three Behavior Referral Practices," Gary M. Landsberg, DVM, *Veterinary Medicine*, Oct.1998, p. 1011.

CHAPTER 8

Separation anxiety definition: *Diagnostic and Statistical Manual of Mental Disorders IV*, The American Psychiatric Association, 1994, pp. 110-113.

CHAPTER 9

Insurance and medical statistics on dog bites: Humane Society of the United States, Centers for Disease Control, Insurance Information Institute Inc., and State Farm Insurance.

CHAPTER 13

Coping with loss:
On Death and Dying, Elisabeth Kübler-Ross, Macmillan Publishing, 1969.
Death: The Final Stage of Growth, Elisabeth Kübler-Ross, Prentice-Hall, 1975.
When Your Pet Dies: How to Cope With Your Feelings, Jamie Quackenbush, Simon and Schuster, 1985.
Pet Loss and Human Bereavement, William Kay, Iowa State University Press, 1995.
Voices of Death, Edwin Schneidman, Harper and Row, 1980.
How to Survive the Loss of Love, Melba Cosgrove, Bantam, 1976.

CHAPTER 14

Dog-bite probability: "Canine Aggression Toward People," Wright, *Veterinary Clinics of North America: Small Animal Practice*, March 1991, pp. 299-314.
Dog-bite Statistics in Philadelphia: "Dog Bites in Urban Children," Baker Avner Jr., M.D., *Pediatrics*, July 1991, pp. 55-57.
Cynophobia origins: "Origins of Fears of Dogs in Adults and Children: The Role of the Conditioning Processes and Prior Familiarity With Dogs," Sharon Doogan and associates, *Behavior Research and Therapy*, July 1992, pp. 387-394.
Types of phobias: "The Determinants and Treatment of Simple Phobias," S. Rachman, *Advances in Behavior Research and Therapy*, Volume 13, 1990, pp. 1-30.
Impact of early interactions with dogs: "Dog Bites in Infancy," I. Gislason and associates, *Journal of the American Academy of Child Psychiatry*, March 1982, pp. 203-207.
Ages that fears are established: "Fears and Phobias in Childhood," Michael Ferrari, *Child Psychiatry and Human Development*, Volume 17, 1986, p. 75.

Common treatments for cynophobia: Rachman, Ibid.

Case history of "Kim": "Use of Contact Desensitization and Shaping in the Treatment of Dog Phobia and Generalized Fear of the Outdoors," Stephen E. Glassock and associates, *Journal of Clinical Psychology*, Volume 19, 1990, pp. 169-172.

Case history of "Colleen" and "Sharon": "Treatment of Severe Dog Phobia in Childhood By Flooding: A Case Report," Uma Sreenivasan and associates, *Journal of Child Psychology and Psychiatry and Allied Disciplines*, July 1979, pp. 255-260.

Entire family needing treatment for cynophobia: *Uncommon Therapy*, Jay Haley, W.W. Norton, 1973, p. 278.

CHAPTER 14

Mail carrier Willie Schertzing attacked: "Attack Dog Under Attack: Is Pit Bull Man's Best Friend or Foe?" Frank Mickadeit, *The Orange County Register*, June 28, 1987.

CHAPTER 15

Man attacked by Chesapeake Bay retriever: "A Review of Animal Bites in Delaware," Spence, *Delaware Medical Journal*, December 1990.

CHAPTER 19

Keirsey test: *Please Understand Me*, David Keirsey, Prometheus Nemesis Book Co., 1978.

Background on psychology and development of the field: *Theories of Personality*, Calvin S. Hall and Gardner Lindzey, John Wiley & Sons, 1978; *Beneath the Mask: An Introduction to Theories of Personality*, Christopher F. Monte, Harcourt Brace Jovanovich, 1991; *Psychology*, Lester M. Sdorow, WCB Brown and Benchmark Publishers, 1993.

CHAPTER 20

Trend toward giving psychiatric medication to dogs: "Pup Uppers Combat Depression: Prozac for Pooches Can Ease Pet Anxiety," K. C. Baker, *New York Daily News*, Oct. 4, 1997.

INDEX

ABOUT THE AUTHORS

Larry Lachman

Larry Lachman, M.S., M.A., has been involved in behavior counseling for nearly twenty-one years. While earning his bachelor's degree in psychology, he used behavior-modification techniques in his work with juvenile offenders, troubled couples, and the terminally ill. Similarly, while earning his master's degree in counseling, he used behavior-modification treatments with abused and molested children as a Los Angeles County child-abuse social worker. Now working toward his doctorate in clinical psychology, Lachman is using cognitive-behavioral therapy techniques with the chronically ill, domestic violence offenders, and drug and alcohol abusing patients and their families.

For the last twelve years, Lachman has been a full-time animal behavior consultant, diagnosing and treating dogs and cats for a variety of behavioral disorders. Lachman also teaches training classes for dogs and their owners, stressing non-violent behavior-modification techniques. He founded and runs a special support group for owners grieving over the deaths of their pets. He also publishes a national newsletter on animal behavior. Articles featuring Lachman and his techniques have appeared in publications across the United States, and he has been a guest on television and radio programs. Lachman is at work on a second book dealing with cat behavior. He lives in Laguna Hills, California, with his flat-coated retriever, Max.

Frank Mickadeit

Frank Mickadeit has been an editor and reporter at *The Orange County Register* since 1987. He lives in Rancho Santa Margarita, California, with his wife, Kathy, and their Scottish terrier, Winnie.